Consumer Law

Malcolm Leder
LL B, Solicitor
Head of School of Law, Middlesex Business School,
Middlesex Polytechnic

Peter Shears
BA, LL B, LL M
Head of Law Group, Plymouth Business School,
Polytechnic South West

Third Edition

THE M & E HANDBOOK SERIES

Pitman Publishing
128 Long Acre, London WC2E 9AN

A Division of Longman Group UK Limited

First edition 1980
Second edition 1986
Third edition 1991
Reprinted 1991

© Macdonald & Evans Ltd 1980
© Longman Group UK Ltd 1986, 1991

British Library Cataloguing in Publication Data
Leder, Malcolm J.
 Consumer law. – 3rd ed. – (The M & E handbook series).
 1. Great Britain. Consumer protection. Law
 I. Title II. Shears, Peter
 344.10371

ISBN 0 7121 0841 6

Founding Editor: P. W. D. Redmond

Typeset by FDS Ltd, Penarth
Printed and bound in Singapore

Contents

Preface   vii
Table of cases   ix
Table of statutes   xv
Table of statutory instruments   xxii

Part one: Private law remedies   1
Introductory note

1 **Classification of consumer contracts**   3
   Contracts for the sale of goods; Contracts for the transfer of
   goods; Contracts for the hire of goods; Other contracts
   under which goods pass; Contracts for the supply of services

2 **Ownership and risk**   11
   Transfer of property and risk; Perishing of the goods

3 **Sale by non-owner**   21
   Nemo dat: the basic rule; Principal exceptions; Motor vehicles

4 **Pre-contractual terms**   32
   Trader's puff; Representations; Collateral warranties;
   Contractual terms

5 **Implied terms**   44
   Terms implied by statute in contracts for the sale of goods;
   Terms implied by statute in hire-purchase agreements;
   Terms implied under Part 1 of the Supply of Goods and
   Services Act 1982; Terms implied in contracts for the supply
   of services under Part II of the Supply of Goods and
   Services Act 1982

6 Legal control of exemption clauses   **64**
Control under the common law; Control under the Unfair
Contract Terms Act 1977; Control by the criminal law

7 Performance of consumer contracts for the sale   **82**
of goods
Delivery; Acceptance

8 Remedies   **91**
The trader at fault; The consumer at fault

9 Product liability   **105**
The consumer's contractual rights; The consumer's rights in
tort; Law reform proposals

10 Consumer credit: introductory   **124**
Introduction to the Consumer Credit Act; Basic concepts
and definitions; Hire-purchase, conditional sale and
credit-sale agreements

11 Seeking credit business   **136**
The control of advertising generally; Advertising credit
facilities; Canvassing

12 Formation of credit or hire agreements   **145**
Credit-brokers and credit reference agencies; Entry into
credit or hire agreements; The right of cancellation;
Variation of agreements

13 Consumer credit: Liability for defective goods   **159**
and services
A summary; Persons conducting antecedent negotiations;
Supplier of credit

14 Termination of credit agreement by the debtor   **167**
Rebate on early settlement; Voluntary termination of
hire-purchase or conditional sale agreements; Voluntary
termination of hire agreements

15 Consumer credit: remedies 171
Creditor's remedies; Debtor's protection against snatch
back; Special orders in relation to hire-purchase or
conditional sale agreements; Extortionate credit bargains

Part two: Administrative remedies and criminal law sanctions 183

Introductory note

16 Functions of the Director General of Fair Trading 185
under the Consumer Credit Act
General functions of Director under the Act; Introductory
note on licensing; Licensing functions of Director

17 Fair trading 192
Director General of Fair Trading; Voluntary codes of
practice; Reference of consumer trade practices to Advisory
Committee under Part II of the Fair Trading Act; Action
against persistently unfair traders under Part III of the Fair
Trading Act

18 Consumer safety 207
Introduction; Statutory general safety requirement; Safety
regulations; Prohibition notices, notices to warn and
suspension notices; Enforcement and sanctions; Civil
liability; Towards a European General Safety Duty

19 Trade descriptions 218
The legislation; False trade descriptions as to goods; False
or misleading indications as to price of goods; False or
misleading statements as to services; Defences; Sanctions
and enforcement; Proposals for reform

20 Food 239

21 Compensation orders 244
The discretionary power; Procedure

22 **The settlement of consumer disputes**   248
Sources of advice; Sources of financial assistance; Small
claims

Appendix 1 Examination technique   256
Appendix 2 Recent examination questions   260

Index   273

Preface

This new edition, like its predecessor, aims to deal succinctly with consumer law, gathering all the diverse elements of the subject together within the covers of one book, according to the proven *Handbook* formula.

Consumer transactions may be broadly defined as the business supply of goods or services to the private individual. Clearly there are many different types of consumer transaction. This book does not purport to delineate every byway of consumer law, but concentrates on the legal principles applicable to those areas thought to be of most concern to traders, consumers, and their legal advisers.

The present edition records significant developments in consumer law since the date of the last edition, and indicates some likely future developments. Recent developments considered in the text span the entire spectrum of consumer law, from the Consumer Protection Act 1987 (in all its several Parts) to the Food Safety Act 1990, for instance.

Indeed, one feature of this new edition is the introduction of a short chapter on the law relating to food. Recently there have been a number of 'food scares' and it was thought proper that a book such as this which seeks to be reflective of the many and various elements of consumer law, would benefit from the inclusion of material on food law. As was the case with the treatment of the very complex Consumer Credit Act in the last edition, the treatment of food law does not seek to meet all the fine particulars.

This *Handbook* is intended primarily for the use of undergraduates on both law degree and mixed degree courses, and for prospective solicitors preparing for the Solicitors Final

Examination and for the relevant parts of the examinations set by the Institute of Legal Executives. In addition, business studies and accountancy students who are studying the legal obligations of the business enterprise should find the book helpful, since consumer rights and business obligations are simply the obverse and reverse of the same coin. It is also hoped that anyone whose studies or work involves a consideration of the legal aspects of consumer problems will be able to derive benefit from the book. Some acquaintance with general legal principles is assumed by the text, but where a particular principle is central to an understanding of consumer law the opportunity is taken to review the principle in question.

The author of the first two editions of this book is greatly indebted to Peter Shears for updating and expanding the text for the third edition, and has much pleasure in welcoming him to the title page.

Grateful acknowledgement is made of the several examination bodies which have given their permission for the inclusion of questions in this book.

The law is stated as we believe it to be in the winter of 1990/91, although a number of points of later date are also included.

Malcolm Leder
Peter Shears
November 1990

Table of cases

(Where the facts are noted, the page number is in italics.)

Addis v. Gramophone Co. Ltd [1909] AC 488; [1908–10] All ER Rep 1   93

Adler v. Dickson [1955] 1 QB 158; [1954] 3 All ER 397   66

Ailsa Craig Fishing Co. Ltd v. Malvern Fishing Co. Ltd [1983] 1 WLR 964; [1983] 1 All ER 101   68, 72

Andrews v. Hopkinson [1957] 1 QB 229; [1956] 3 All ER 422   *159*

Anns v. Merton LBC [1977] 2 WLR 1024; [1977] 2 All ER 492   111, 112

Asfar & Co. Ltd v. Blundell [1896] 1 QB 123   17

Aswan Engineering v. Lupdine Ltd [1987] 1 All ER 135   51

Badische Anilin und Soda Fabrik v. Basle Chemical Works [1898] AC 200   15

Barrow, Lane and Ballard Ltd v. Phillip Phillips & Co. Ltd [1929] 1 KB 574   17

Bartlett v. Sidney Marcus Ltd [1965] 1 WLR 1013; [1965] 2 All ER 753   53

Batty v. Metropolitan Property Realisations Ltd [1978] 2 WLR 500; [1978] 2 All ER 445   61

Beale v. Taylor [1967] 1 WLR 1193; [1967] 3 All ER 253   *46*

Beckett v. Cohen [1972] 1 WLR 1593; [1973] 1 All ER 120   *231*

Bentinck Ltd v. Cromwell Engineering Co. Ltd [1971] 1 QB 324; [1971] 1 All ER 33   *177*

Bernstein v. Parsons Motors (Golders Green) Ltd [1987] 2 WLR 220   87

Bishopsgate Motor Finance Corpn v. Transport Brakes Ltd [1949] 1 KB 322; [1949] 1 All ER 37   24

Bolam v. Friern Hospital Management Committee [1957] 1 WLR 582; [1957] 2 All ER 118   59

Bolton v. Mahadeva [1972] 1 WLR 1009; [1972] 2 All ER 1322   *98*

Breed v. Cluett [1970] 2 Q.B. 459; [1970] 2 All ER 662   230, *231*

Bristol Tramways Co. v. Fiat Motors Ltd [1910] 2 KB 831   48

British Airways Board v. Taylor [1976] 1 WLR 13; [1976] 1 All ER 65   *231*

Brown (B. S.) & Sons Ltd v. Craiks Ltd [1970] 1 WLR 752; [1970] 1 All ER 823   50

Bunge Corpn v. Tradax SA [1981] 1 WLR 711; [1981] 2 All ER 513   41

Butterworth v. Kingsway Motors [1954] 1 WLR 1286; [1954] 2 All ER 694   28

Cadbury Ltd v. Halliday [1975] 1 WLR 649; [1975] 2 All ER 226   *221*

Candlewood Navigation Corpn v. Mistui OSK Lines [1985] 2 All ER 935   111

Capital Finance Co. Ltd v. Bray [1964] 1 WLR 323; [1964] 1 All ER 603   177

Car & Universal Finance Co. *v.* Caldwell [1965] 1 QB 198; [1964] 1 All ER 290 *25*

Carlill *v.* Carbolic Smoke Ball Co. [1893] 1 QB 256 *32*, 107

Carr *v.* James Broderick & Co. Ltd [1942] 2 KB 275; [1942] 2 All ER 441 177

Cavendish-Woodhouse Ltd *v.* Manley [1984] Crim LR 239 *79*

Cavendish Woodhouse Ltd *v.* Wright [1985] *The Times*, 8 March 79

Cehave NV *v.* Bremer Handelgesellschaft GmbH [1976] QB 44; [1975] 3 WLR 447; [1975] 3 All ER 739 41, 50, *57*

Central Newbury Car Auctions Ltd *v.* Unity Finance Ltd [1957] 1 QB 371; [1956] 3 All ER 905 *22*

Chapleton *v.* Barry UDC [1940] 1 KB 532; [1940] 1 All ER 356 *66*

Charge Card Services, *Re* [1988] 3 WLR 764 141

Charter *v.* Sullivan [1957] 2 QB 117; [1957] 1 All ER 809 *99*

Chesneau *v.* Interhome Ltd [1983] *The Times*, 9 June 35

Clea Shipping Corpn *v.* Bulk Oil International Ltd [1984] 1 All ER 129 98

Cointat *v.* Myham [1914] 110 LT 749 *67*

Cremdean Properties Ltd *v.* Nash (1977) 244 EG 547 36

Crowther *v.* Shannon Motor Co. [1975] 1 WLR 30; [1975] 1 All ER 139 *53*

Curtis Chemical Cleaning and Dyeing Co. [1951] 1 KB 805; [1951] 1 All ER 631 *67*

Cutter *v.* Powell (1795) 6 TR 320 97

D & F Estates *v.* Church Commissioners [1988] 3 WLR 368 111

Daniels *v.* White and Tarbard [1938] 4 All ER 258 50, *106*, 114

Davies *v.* Sumner [1984] 3 All ER 831 222

Dennant *v.* Skinner and Collom [1948] 2 KB 164; [1948] 2 All ER 29 *14, 222*

Department of the Environment *v.* Bates [1989] 1 All ER 1075 112

Derry *v.* Peek (1889) 14 AC 337; [1886–90] All ER Rep 1 34

Devlin *v.* Hall (1990), RTR 320 222

Dick Bentley Productions Ltd *v.* Harold Smith (Motors) Ltd [1965] 1 WLR 623; [1965] 2 All ER 65 *38*

Dixons Ltd *v.* Roberts [1974] *The Times*, 3 May 229

Donoghue *v.* Stevenson [1932] AC 562 109, 112

Drury *v.* Victor Buckland Ltd [1941] 1 All ER 269 159, 161

Dutton *v.* Bognor Regis UDC [1972] 1 QB 373; [1972] 1 All ER 462 110, 112

Eastern Distributors *v.* Goldring [1953] 2 QB 600 23

Edgington *v.* Fitzmaurice (1885) 29 Ch.D. 459; [1881-85] All ER Rep. 856 34

Elliott *v.* Director General of Trading [1980] 1 WLR 977; [1980] I.C.R. 629 142

Esso Petroleum Co. Ltd *v.* Commissioners of Customs and Excise [1976] 1 WLR 1 6

Esso Petroleum Co. Ltd *v.* Mardon [1976] QB 801; [1976] 2 All ER 5 36, 37

Evans *v.* Triplex Safety Glass Co. Ltd [1936] 1 All ER 283 113

Evans (J.) & Son (Portsmouth) Ltd *v.* Merzario (Andrea) Ltd [1976] 1 WLR 1078; [1976] 2 All ER 930 *68*

Farnworth Finance Facilities Ltd *v.* Attryde [1970] 1 WLR 1053; [1970] 2 All ER 774 87, *88–9*

Financings Ltd *v.* Baldock [1963] 2 QB 104; [1963] 1 All ER 443 174

Fisher *v.* Bell [1961] 1 QB 394; [1960] 3 All ER 731 223

Fisher *v.* Harrods Ltd [1966] 1 Lloyd's Rep. 500 *113*

Fletcher *v.* Budgen [1974] 1 WLR 1056; [1974] 2 All ER 1234 *219*

Frost *v.* Aylesbury Dairy Co. Ltd [1905] 1 KB 608 *56, 116*

Galbraith & Grant Ltd *v.* Block [1922] 2 KB 155 *83*

Geddling *v.* Marsh [1920] 1 KB 668 *48*

Godley *v.* Perry [1960] 1 WLR 9; [1960] 1 All ER 36 *50, 52, 56*, 106

Grant *v.* Australian Knitting Mills Ltd [1936] AC 85 46, *50*, 52, 53, *112*, 114

Greater Manchester Council *v.* Lockwood Foods [1979] Crim LR 593 240

Greaves & Co. (Contractors) Ltd *v.* Baynham Meikle & Partners [1975] 1 WLR 1095; [1975] 3 All ER 99 *59*

Green *v.* Cade [1978] 1 Lloyds Rep 602 72

Greenwood *v.* Bennett [1972] 3 All ER 586 45

Griffiths *v.* Peter Conway Ltd [1939] 1 All ER 685 *53*

Hadley *v.* Baxendale (1854) 9 Ex. 341 91, 95, 96

Harlingdon and Leinster Enterprises Ltd *v.* Christopher Hull Fine Art Ltd [1990] 1 All ER 737 *46*

Havering London Borough Council *v.* Stevenson [1970] 1 WLR 1375; [1970] 3 All ER 609 *222*

Hedley Byrne & Co. Ltd *v.* Heller & Partners Ltd [1964] AC 456; [1963] 2 All ER 575 36, 37, 43, 61

Heil *v.* Hedges [1951] 1 TLR 512 *50*, 53

Helby *v.* Matthews [1895] AC 471 *8*, 27, 88

Heron II, The, Koufos *v.* Czarnikow [1969] 1 AC 350; [1967] 3 All ER 686 92, 115

Heywood *v.* Wellers [1976] 2 WLR 101; [1976] 1 All ER 300 *94*

Hill *v.* James Crowe (Cases) Ltd [1978] 1 All ER 812 114

Hoenig *v.* Isaacs [1952] 2 All ER 176 97

Hoffberger *v.* Ascot International Bloodstock Bureau Ltd [1976] *The Times,* 30 January; (1976) 120 Sol Jo 130 95

Hollier *v.* Rambler Motors (AMC) Ltd [1972] 2 QB 71; [1972] 1 All ER 399 *67*, 68

Holmes *v.* Ashford [1950] 2 All ER 76 *112*

Hong Kong Fir Shipping Co. Ltd Kawasaki Kisen Kaisha Ltd [1962] 2 QB 26; [1962] 2 WLR 474; [1962] 1 All ER 474 41

Horner *v.* Kingsley Clothing Co. Ltd [1989] *The Times,* 6 July *221*

Hughes *v.* Hall (1981) 125 Sol Jo 255 79

Ingram *v.* Little [1961] 1 QB 31; [1960] 3 All ER 332 26, 31

Jackson *v.* Horizon Holidays Ltd [1975] 1 WLR 1468; [1975] 3 All ER 92 *93*

Jackson *v.* Rotax Motor & Cycle Co. [1910] 2 KB 937 *48*

Jarvis *v.* Swans Tours Ltd [1973] 1 QB 233; [1973] 1 All ER 71 *93*

John *v.* Matthews [1970] 2 QB 443; [1970] 2 All ER 643 *218*

Junior Books Ltd *v.* Veitchi Ltd [1982] 3 WLR 477; [1982] 3 All ER 201 *110*

Keeley *v.* Guy McDonald Ltd (1984) 134 NLJ 522 97

Kendall *v.* Cillico [1969] 2 AC 31 67

Kensington and Chelsea (Royal) London Borough Council *v.* Riley [1973] RTR 122 *221*

Ketley Ltd *v.* Scott [1981] 1 CR 241 180

Kinchin *v.* Ashton Park Scooters (1984) 148 JPN 459 *229*

Kolfor Plant Ltd *v.* Tilbury Plant Ltd
[1977] *The Times*, 18 May   86

Lambert *v.* Lewis [1982] AC 225 (CA),
271 (HL); [1980] 1 All ER 978 (CA),
[1981] 1 All ER 1185 (HL)   *33*, 54
Lazenby Garages Ltd *v.* Wright [1976]
1 WLR 459; [1976] 2 All ER 770   *100*
Lee *v.* York Coach and Marine [1977]
RTR 35   96
Leigh and Sullivan *v.* Aliakmon
Shipping [1986] 2 WLR 902   111
L'Estrange *v.* Graucob [1934] 2 KB 394;
[1934] All ER Rep 16   65
Levison *v.* Patent Steam Carpet
Cleaning Co. Ltd [1977] 3 WLR 90;
[1977] 3 All ER 498   *68*
Lewin *v.* Fuell [1990] Crim. LR 658
220

MFI Warehouses Ltd *v.* Nattrass [1973]
1 WLR 307; [1973] 1 All ER 762   *230*
McGuire *v.* Sittingbourne Co-operative
Society [1976] Crim LR 268   233
Mason *v.* Burningham [1949] 2 KB 545;
[1949] 2 All ER 134   *45*
May *v.* Vincent [1990] *The Times* 19th
June   224
Mercantile Credit Co. Ltd *v.* Cross
[1965] 2 QB 205; [1965] 1 All ER 577
177
Midland Bank Trust Co. Ltd *v.* Hett,
Stubbs & Kemp [1978] 3 WLR 167;
[1978] 3 All ER 571   *61*
Millars of Falkirk Ltd *v.* Turpie [1976]
SLT (Notes) 66   *51*
Mitchell (George) (Chesterhall) Ltd *v.*
Finney Lock Seeds Ltd [1983] 3 WLR
163; [1983] 2 All ER 737   *72*
Moorgate Mercantile Co. Ltd *v.*
Twitchings [1977] AC 890; [1976]
2 All ER 641   22, 30
Murphy *v.* Brentwood DC [1990] 2 All
ER 908   112

National Westminster Bank plc *v.*
Morgan [1985] 2 WLR 588; [1985]
1 All ER 821   65

Newell *v.* Hicks [1983] *The Times*,
7 December; (1984) 148 JP 398   *229*
Newtons of Wembley Ltd *v.* Williams
[1965] 1 QB 560; [1964] 2 All ER 135
27
Norman *v.* Bennett [1974] 1 WLR 1229;
[1974] 3 All ER 351   223

Olley *v.* Marlborough Court Ltd [1949]
1 KB 532; [1949] 1 All ER 127
67, 79
Oscar Chess Ltd *v.* Williams [1957]
1 WLR 370; [1957] 1 All ER 325
38, 39
Overbrooke Estates Ltd *v.* Glencombe
Properties Ltd [1974] 1 WLR 1335;
[1974] 3 All ER 511   36
Overstone Ltd *v.* Shipway [1962]
1 WLR 117; [1962] 1 All ER 52   174

Parker *v.* South Eastern Railway Co.
[1877] 2 CPD 416   65
Parsons (Livestock) Ltd *v.* Uttley
Ingham & Co. Ltd [1977] 3 WLR 991;
[1978] 1 All ER 525   *92*
Payzu Ltd *v.* Saunders [1919] 2 KB 581
95
Perry *v.* Sidney Phillips & Son [1982]
1 All ER 1005   *94*, 97
Philip Head & Sons Ltd *v.* Showfronts
Ltd [1970] 1 Lloyd's Rep 140   *16*
Photo Production Ltd *v.* Securicor
Transport Ltd [1980] 2 WLR 283;
[1980] 1 All ER 556   69
Porter *v.* General Guarantee
Corporation Ltd [1982] RTR 384
162
Priest *v.* Last [1903] 2 KB 148   53

R. *v.* Breeze [1973] 1 WLR 994; [1973]
2 All ER 1141   *230*
R. *v.* Ford Motor Co. Ltd [1974] 1 WLR
1220; [1974] 3 All ER 489   223
R. *v.* Hammertons Cars Ltd [1976]
1 WLR 1243; [1976] 3 All ER 758
224

R. *v.* Thompson Holidays Ltd [1974] QB 592; [1974] 1 All ER 823 235, *245*

R & B Customs Bankers Co. Ltd *v.* United Dominions Trust Ltd [1988] 1 WLR 321 77

Rasbora Ltd *v.* J.C.L. Marine Ltd [1977] 1 Lloyd's Rep 645 77

Raynham Farm Co. Ltd *v.* Symbol Motor Corpn Ltd [1987] BTLC 157 *223*

Reardon Smith Line Ltd *v.* Hansen-Tangen [1976] 1 WLR 989; [1976] 3 All ER 570 46

Redgrave *v.* Hurd (1881) 20 ChD 1 34

Reid *v.* Metropolitan Police Commissioner [1973] 1 QB 551; [1973] 2 All ER 97 23

Rickards (Charles) Ltd *v.* Oppenheim [1950] 1 KB 616; [1950] 1 All ER 420 *83*

Robertson *v.* Dicicco [1972] Crim LR 592; [1972] RTR 431 *220*

Rogers *v.* Parish (Scarborough) Ltd [1987] 2 WLR 353 49

Rondel *v.* Worsely [1969] 1 AC 191; [1967] 3 All ER 993 *60*, 61

Rowland *v.* Divall [1923] 2 KB 500; [1923] All ER Rep 270 *45*

Saif Ali *v.* Sydney Mitchell & Co. [1978] 3 WLR 849; [1978] 3 All ER 1033 *60*

Schuler AG *v.* Wickman Machine Tool Sales Ltd [1974] AC 235; [1973] 2 All ER 39 *40*

Shearson Lehman Hutton Inc. Maclaine Watson & Co. Ltd [1989] 140 NLJ 247 *100*

Shine *v.* General Guarantee [1988] 1 All ER 911 49

Simaan General Contracting Pilkington Glass [1988] 2 WLR 761 111

Simmons *v.* Potter [1975] Crim LR 354; [1975] RTR 347 224

Smedleys *v.* Breed [1974] 2 WLR 575 240

Smith *v.* Bush [1989] 2 All ER 514 *73*

Stadium Finance Ltd *v.* Robbins [1962] 2 QB 664; [1962] 2 All ER 633 *25*

Stevenson *v.* Beverley Bentinck Ltd [1976] 1 WLR 483; [1976] 2 All ER 606 *29*

Suisse Atlantique Société *v.* NVR Kolen Centrale [1967] 1 AC 361; [1966] 2 All ER 61 69

Sunair Holidays Ltd *v.* Dodd [1970] 1 WLR 1037; [1970] 2 All ER 410 230

Taylor *v.* Lawrence Fraser (Bristol) Ltd [1978] Crim LR 43 *214*

Tesco Supermarkets Ltd *v.* Nattrass [1972] AC 153; [1971] 2 All ER 127 228, *233*

Thompson (W.L.) Ltd *v.* Robinson (Gunmakers) Ltd [1955] Ch 117; [1955] 1 All ER 154 *99*

Thornett & Fehr *v.* Beers & Sons [1919] 1 KB 486 48

Thorton *v.* Shoe Lane Parking Ltd [1971] 2 QB 163; [1971] 1 All ER 686 65, *66*

United Dominions Trust Ltd *v.* Taylor [1980] SLT 28 *162*

Victoria Laundry (Windsor) Ltd *v.* Newman Industries Ltd [1949] 2 KB 528; [1949] 1 All ER 997 91

Wadham Stringer Finance Ltd *v.* Meaney [1981] 1 WLR 39; [1980] 3 All ER 789 172

Wagon Mound, The, [1961] AC 388; [1961] 1 All ER 404 115

Walker *v.* Boyle [1982] 1 WLR 495; [1982] 1 All ER 634 36

Ward (R.V.) *v.* Bignall [1967] 1 QB 534; [1967] 2 All ER 449 13

Westminster CC *v.* Ray Alan (Manshops) Ltd [1982] 1 WLR 383; [1982] 1 All ER 771 *229*

White & Carter (Councils) Ltd McGregor [1962] AC 413; [1961] 3 All ER 1178 98

Wickens Motors (Gloucester) Ltd *v.*
Hall [1972] 1 WLR 1418; [1972] 3 All
ER 759   *219*, 231
Wills *v.* Wood [1984] *The Times*,
24 March   *180*, 188
Wilson *v.* Rickett Cockerell & Co. Ltd
[1954] 1 QB 598; [1954] 1 All ER 868
48
Wings Ltd *v.* Ellis [1984] 3 WLR 965;
[1984] 3 All ER 577   228, 248
With *v.* O'Flanagan [1936] 1 Ch 575;
[1936] 1 All ER 727   36
Wood *v.* Lectrik Ltd [1932] *The Times*,
13 January   *33*
Woodar Investment Development Ltd
v. Wimpey Construction UK Ltd
[1980] 1 WLR 277; [1980] 1 All ER
571   94

Woodman *v.* Photo-Trade Processing
Ltd, unreported, 7 May, 1981   *72*, 94
Wormell *v.* RHM Agriculture (East) Ltd
[1986] 1 WLR 336   48, *51*
Wren *v.* Holt [1903] 1 KB 610   *50*
Wycombe Marsh Garages Ltd *v.* Fowler
[1972] 1 WLR 1156; [1972] 3 All ER
248   236

Yeoman Credit Ltd *v.* Apps [1962] 2 QB
508; [1961] 2 All ER 281   88, 168
Yeoman Credit Ltd *v.* Waragowski
[1961] 1 WLR 1124; [1961] 3 All ER
145   174

Table of statutes

Administration of Justice Act 1973
  s. 7 253

Broadcasting Act 1981 137
Broadcasting Act 1990 137

Cable and Broadcasting Act 1984 137
Civil Evidence Act 1968 247
Civil Liability (Contribution) Act 1978
  113
Consumer Arbitration Agreements Act
  1988 196
Consumer Credit Act 1974 7, 8, 28,
  124, 136, 149, 185, 187, 190
  Part I 185
  Part III 187
  Part IV 138–40
  Part V 146, 156
  s. 1 185
  s. 1(1) 185
  s. 8(2) 126
  s. 9(1) 126
  s. 9(3) 127
  s. 10(1)(*a*) 130
  s. 10(1)(*b*) 130
  s. 11 130
  ss. 12–13 129
  s. 14 141–2
  s. 15 126
  s. 16 127–8
  s. 16(2) 127, 139
  s. 16(5) 128
  s. 16(6) 128
  s. 17(1) 147
  s. 19 131

s. 19(3) 131
s. 20(1) 127, 134
s. 21 180
s. 21(1) 187
s. 21(2) 187
s. 21(3) 187
s. 22 188
s. 22(5) 189
s. 22(8) 189
s. 23(3) 141, 188
s. 25(1) 188
s. 26 189
s. 28(2) 188
s. 35 189
s. 39 190
s. 40 190
s. 40(4) 190
s. 41 190
s. 42 190
s. 43(1) 138
s. 43(2) 138
s. 43(3) 139
s. 43(4) 139
s. 43(5) 139
s. 44(1) 139
s. 45 140
s. 46(1) 140
s. 46(2) 140
s. 47(1) 140
s. 47(2) 140
s. 48(1) 141
s. 49 141
s. 49(1) 141
s. 49(2) 141
s. 50(1) 141

s. 50(2)   141
s. 51(1)   141–2
s. 51(2)   142
s. 51(3)   142
s. 52   142
s. 53   143
s. 55   147
s. 56   36, 147, 159, 160, 162–4
s. 56(1)   154
s. 56(2)   160, 162
s. 56(3)   160
s. 56(4)   160
s. 57(1)   154
s. 57(2)   154
s. 57(3)   155
s. 58   155
s. 59   155
s. 60   148
s. 60(1)   148
s. 60(2)   148
s. 60(3)   148
ss. 61–3   150
s. 61   148, 155
s. 61(a)   148
s. 61(b)   148
s. 61(c)   148
s. 61(1)   149
s. 61(1)(a)   148
s. 61(4)   149
ss. 62–3   149, 151
s. 63(3)   150
s. 64   150
s. 64(1)   150, 153
s. 64(1)(a)   150
s. 64(1)(b)   150
s. 64(4)   153
s. 64(5)   150
s. 65(1)   151
s. 65(2)   152
s. 66   142
s. 67   152
s. 68   153
s. 69   153
s. 69(1)   131, 153
s. 69(7)   153
s. 70(1)   154
s. 70(2)   154
s. 71   154

s. 71(3)   154
s. 72   154
s. 73   154
s. 74   146
s. 75   30, 160–3
s. 75(1)   161, 162
s. 75(2)   161
s. 75(3)   162
s. 75(4)   162
s. 76(1)   172
ss. 77–9   168
s. 82(2)   155
s. 82(3)   155
s. 84   142
s. 87   173
s. 87(1)   172
s. 88   173
s. 88(4)   173
s. 89   172, 173
s. 90   177
s. 90(1)   176
s. 90(2)   176
s. 90(5)   177
s. 91   177
s. 92(1)   176
s. 92(3)   176
s. 93   170
s. 94   167–169
s. 95   167
s. 97   167
s. 98   173
s. 99   168, 169, 172, 173, 174
s. 99(2)   168
s. 100(1)   168
s. 100(2)   168
s. 100(3)   168
s. 100(4)   168
s. 100(5)   169
s. 101   169
s. 101(7)   169
s. 101(8)   169
s. 102   160
s. 105   151
s. 127   151
s. 127(3)   151
s. 127(4)(a)   151
s. 127(4)(b)   152
s. 129   172, 173, 176

s. 130(2)   172
s. 131   178
s. 132   177, 179
s. 132(2)   178
s. 133   178–179
s. 135   179
ss. 137–40   179
s. 137(2)   179
s. 138   179–180
s. 139(1)   179
s. 139(2)   181
s. 139(4)   180
s. 141   170
s. 145   125, 159, 188
s. 149   190
s. 150   190
s. 155   145
ss. 157–9   145–6
s. 158   146
s. 159   146
s. 161   186
s. 161(2)   186
s. 161(3)   186
s. 166   186
s. 168(1)   140
s. 170(1)   125, 140
s. 170(2)   125
s. 171(7)   180
s. 173(1)   129, 162
s. 173(3)   129, 176–177
s. 180(1)   150
s. 188(3)   126
s. 189   125–7, 132–3, 138
s. 189(2)   188
Sch. 1   125
Sch. 2   125–6, 134–5, 152
Sch. 3   163, 181
Sch. 4   133
Consumer Protection Act 1961
    206, 214
Consumer Protection Act 1987
    206, 214
    Part I   117, 118, 120, 206
    Part II   115, 206, 208, 216
    Part III   193, 224, 225
    s. 1(2)   118
    s. 1(3)   118
    s. 2   118

s. 2(2)   118
s. 2(4)   118
s. 2(5)   118
s. 2(6)   122
s. 3   118, 119
s. 4   119, 185
s. 4(1)(*e*)   119
s. 5   120
s. 6   121
s. 6(4)   121
s. 7   121
s. 8(1)   126
s. 10   118, 208
s. 10(1)   208
s. 10(2)   208
s. 10(3)   208
s. 10(4)   208
s. 10(6)   213
s. 10(7)   208
s. 11(1)   209
s. 11(2)   209
s. 11(4)   209
s. 11(5)   210
s. 11(6)   210
s. 12(5)   213
s. 13(1)(*a*)   210
s. 13(1)(*b*)   211
s. 13(4)   213
s. 14(1)   212
s. 14(4)   212
s. 14(6)   213
s. 14(7)   212
s. 15   212
s. 16   213
s. 16(4)   213
s. 16(5)   213
s. 18(1)   211
s. 18(3)   211
s. 19(1)   208
s. 20   225, 226, 227, 234, 235
s. 20(1)   224, 234
s. 20(2)   225
s. 20(6)   225
s. 21(1)   226
s. 21(2)   226
s. 22   225
s. 23   225
s. 24(3)   234

s. 25(1)   226
s. 25(2)   226
s. 26   227
s. 27(1)   212, 235
s. 27(2)   212
s. 28   212, 235
s. 29   235
s. 29(2)   212
s. 29(4)   213
s. 31   213
s. 32   213, 235
s. 33   213
s. 34   213
s. 35   213
s. 37   213
s. 38(1)   211
s. 39   234
s. 39(1)   214
s. 39(2)   214
s. 39(3)   214
s. 39(4)   214, 215
s. 40(1)   215
s. 40(2)   213
s. 41(1)   215
s. 41(2)   235
s. 41(3)   215
s. 45(1)   212
s. 46   208
s. 46(5)   208
s. 48(2)(*a*)   219
s. 50(7)   117
Sch. 1   121
Sch. 2   211
Consumer Safety Act 1978   206, 244
County Courts Act 1984
s. 15   252
s. 64   253
s. 64(3)   254
Criminal Justice Act 1972   244
Criminal Justice Act 1988   245
ss. 105–6   244

Data Protection Act 1984   187

Emergency Laws (Re-enactments and
   Repeals) Act 1964   133
Estate Agents Act 1979   187, 193
s. 3   187

Factors Act 1889   24
s. 2   24–5
s. 2(2)   24
s. 2(4)   24
s. 9   27
Fair Trading Act 1973   78, 185, 192
Part II   192–193, 196, 199, 200, 205
Part III   192, 196, 202–5
s. 1   192
s. 2   193
s. 2(1)(*a*)   192, 193
s. 2(1)(*b*)   193
s. 3   192
s. 13   197
s. 14   197, 198
s. 14(1)   197
s. 14(3)   197
s. 15   197
s. 16   197
s. 17   198–200
s. 17(4)   199
s. 20   199
s. 21   199
s. 22   199, 200, 201, 205
s. 23   200, 201
s. 24   201
s. 25(1)   201
s. 25(2)   201
s. 25(3)   202
s. 26   201, 244
s. 27   201
s. 28   201
s. 29   201
s. 30   201
s. 34(1)   202, 203
s. 34(2)   202
s. 34(3)   202
s. 35   202
s. 37   203
s. 38   204
s. 39   204
s. 40   204
s. 41   204
s. 42   203
s. 81   198
s. 83   198
s. 124(3)   193, 195
s. 137   197

Sch. 6   198
Food Safety Act 1990   240–3
s. 8   240
s. 10   241
s. 11   241
s. 13   240, 241
s. 15   241
s. 16   241
s. 18   241
s. 19   241
s. 21   242
ss. 29–31   241
s. 35   242

Hire-purchase Act 1964
Part III   22, 28, 29, 30
s. 29(2)   29
Hire-purchase Act 1965   177

Insurance Brokers (Registration) Act
1977   187, 195

Land Charges Act 1925   61
Law Reform (Contributory Negligence)
Act 1943   121
Law Reform (Frustrated Contracts) Act
1943   18
s. 2(5)   18
Legal Aid Act 1974   251
Local Government Act 1972   248

Magistrates Court Act 1980
s. 40   245
Misrepresentation Act 1967   39, 136
s. 2(1)   34, 36, 37, 39, 41
s. 2(2)   35
s. 3   35, 36, 77
Moneylenders Act 1910   179, 180
Moneylenders Act 1927   179, 180

Occupiers' Liability Act 1957
s. 1(1)   71
Occupiers' Liability Act 1984
s. 2   71

Powers of Criminal Courts Act 1973
244
s. 35   244, 245

s. 35(1A)   245
s. 35(2)   245
s. 35(3)   245
s. 35(4)   245
s. 35(4A)   245
s. 37   247
s. 38   247
Prices Act 1974   193

Restriction of Offensive Weapons Act
1959   222

Sale of Goods Act 1893   4, 9
ss. 12–15   44
s. 13(1)   203
s. 14(3)   203
Sale of Goods Act 1979   1, 3, 4, 8, 11,
17, 55, 58, 78, 95, 105, 106, 108
s. 2(1)   4
s. 2(3)   4
s. 2(5)   4
s. 5   4
s. 6   18
s. 7   18
s. 8   5
s. 10   82
s. 11(4)   40, 41, 58, 86, 87, 95, 96
s. 12   21, 45, 57, 75, 81
s. 12(1)   44
s. 12(2)   44
s. 12(3)   45
s. 12(4)   45
s. 13   45–47, 52, 57, 62, 79, 81
s. 13(1)   45
s. 13(3)   46
s. 14   46, 54, 57, 75, 79, 81
s. 14(2)   47, 48, 52, 56, 62
s. 14(2)(*b*)   48
s. 14(3)   52, 53, 56, 62, 116
s. 14(6)   49, 51
s. 15   56, 57, 75, 81
s. 16   12, 18
s. 17   12
s. 18   13, 14, 15, 16, 82
s. 20   11, 12, 13, 17
s. 21(1)   21, 22
s. 22   23
s. 22(1)   23

s. 23   25
s. 24   26
s. 25   26, 27
s. 25(1)   27
s. 25(2)   27
s. 28   100
s. 29(2)   83
s. 29(3)   83
s. 29(5)   83
s. 29(6)   84
s. 30(1)   84
s. 31(1)   84
s. 31(2)   86
s. 32(1)   82
s. 32(2)   82
s. 34   84
s. 35   84, 85
s. 35(1)   84
s. 36   86, 96
s. 37   99
s. 38   100
s. 39(2)   100
s. 41   100
s. 43   100
s. 48(2)   101
s. 48(3)   101
s. 49   98
s. 50(1)   99
s. 50(2)   99, 100
s. 50(3)   99, 100
s. 51   99
s. 51(2)   95
s. 51(3)   95, 96
s. 52   96
s. 53(1)   97
s. 53(3)   97
s. 54   96
s. 55   4
s. 61   4, 40, 82
s. 61(1)   13, 47, 52
s. 61(5)   13
s. 62(2)   4
Supply of Goods (Implied Terms) Act
    1973   3, 8, 44, 49, 58, 75, 161
ss. 8–11   57, 75, 161
s. 14(1)   88
s. 16   8

Supply of Goods and Services Act 1982
    3, 5, 7, 58, 76, 78, 88, 158
Part I   5, 7, 9, 57, 60, 87
Part II   9, 58, 60
s. 1   5
s. 2   57
s. 3   57
s. 4   57
s. 5   57
s. 6   7
s. 7   58
s. 8   58
s. 9   58
s. 10   58
s. 12   9
s. 12(4)   60
s. 13   59, 60
s. 14   59, 83
s. 15   59
s. 18   59

Torts (Interference with Goods) Act
    1977
s. 6   26
s. 6(3)   26
Trade Descriptions Act 1968   47, 136,
    218
s. 1   203, 219, 223, 228, 235
s. 1(1)   219, 221, 222
s. 2   220, 221
s. 2(1)   220, 221
s. 3(1)   220
s. 3(2)   220, 221
s. 3(3)   220
s. 4(1)   222
s. 4(2)   222
s. 4(3)   222, 223
s. 5   222
s. 6   223
s. 8   224
s. 9   224
s. 11   221, 224, 225, 228, 233
s. 11(2)   203, 229
s. 12(1)   224
s. 12(2)   224
s. 14   225, 227, 229, 232, 235, 237
s. 14(1)   228, 230

s. 14(1)(*a*)   228
s. 14(1)(*b*)   228, 230
s. 14(2)(*a*)   228
s. 14(2)(*b*)   230
s. 14(4)   228
s. 21(1)   221
s. 23   221, 232–4
s. 24   228, 232
s. 24(1)   232, 234
s. 24(2)   233
s. 25   234
ss. 26–29   235
s. 35   235, 244
Trade Descriptions Act 1972   219
Trading Stamps Act 1964   8, 78
   s. 4   8
Unfair Contract Terms Act 1977
      4, 60, 64, 65, 68, 69, 70, 75, 80, 81,
      84, 105, 158
   s. 1(3)   70, 71
   s. 2   60, 71, 73, 74, 75, 79
   s. 2(1)   71
   s. 2(2)   71
   s. 3   74
   s. 4   74
   s. 5   74, 75, 108

s. 5(1)   75
s. 5(2)(*a*)   75
s. 5(3)   75
s. 6   21, 44, 74, 75, 76, 78, 161
s. 6(1)   75
s. 6(2)   75
s. 6(3)   76
s. 6(4)   76
s. 7   74, 76, 77, 79
s. 7(4)   76
s. 8   35–6, 77
s. 11   71, 72
s. 11(1)   72, 77
s. 11(3)   72
s. 11(4)   72
s. 11(5)   72
s. 12   72
s. 12(2)   72
s. 12(3)   72
s. 13(1)   74
s. 13(2)   74
s. 14   71
Sch. 1   70
Sch. 2   76
Unsolicited Goods and Services Act
      1971, 1975   15

Table of statutory instruments

Business Advertisements (Disclosure) Order 1977 (SI 1977 No. 1918)   200

Consumer Credit (Agreements to enter Prospective Agreements) (Exemptions) Regulations 1983 (SI 1983 No. 1552)   155

Consumer Credit (Cancellation Notices and Copies of Documents) Regulations 1983 (SI 1983 No. 1557, as amended by SI 1984 No. 1108) and by SI 1989 No. 591   150, 151, 153, 155

Consumer Credit (Conduct of Business) (Credit References) Regulations 1977 (SI 1977 No. 330)   146

Consumer Credit (Credit Reference Agency) Regulations 1977 (SI 1977 No. 329)   146

Consumer Credit (Credit-Token Agreements) Regulations 1983 (SI 1983 No. 1555)   142

Consumer Credit (Enforcement, Default and Termination Notices) Regulations 1983 (SI 1983 No. 1561, as amended by SI 1984 No. 1109)   173, 176

Consumer Credit (Exempt Advertisements) Order 1985 (SI 1985 No. 621)   139

Consumer Credit (Exempt Agreements) Order 1989 (SI 1989 No. 869, as amended by SI 1989 No. 1841)   128, 139

Consumer Credit (Guarantees and Indemnities) Regulations 1983 (SI 1983 No. 1556)   151

Consumer Credit (Increase of Monetary Amounts) Order 1983 (SI 1983 No. 1571)   142, 145, 147, 169

Consumer Credit (Increase of Monetary Limits) Order 1983 (SI 1983 No. 1878)   139

Consumer Credit (Linked Transactions) (Exemptions) Regulations 1983 (SI 1983 No. 1560)   131, 153

Consumer Credit (Notice of Variation of Agreements) Regulations 1977 (SI 1977 No. 328)   155

Consumer Credit (Period of Standard Licence) Regulations 1986 (SI 1986/1016)   188

Consumer Credit (Prescribed Periods for Giving Information) Regulations 1983 (SI 1983 No. 1569)   168

Consumer Credit (Quotations) Regulations 1989 (SI 1989 No. 1126)   142

Consumer Credit (Rebate on Early Settlement) Regulations 1983 (SI 1983 No. 1562)   167

Consumer Credit (Repayment of Credit on Cancellation) Regulations 1983 (SI 1983 No. 1559)   154

Consumer Credit (Running-Account Credit Information) Regulations 1983 (SI 1983 No. 1570)   168

Consumer Credit (Settlement Information) Regulations 1983 (SI 1983 No. 1562)   167

Consumer Credit (Total Charge for

Credit) Regulations 1983 (SI 1983
No. 51)   127

Consumer Protection (Cancellation of
Agreements Concluded away from
Business Premises) Regulations 1987
(SI 1987 No. 2117)   155

Consumer Transactions (Restrictions
on Statements) Order 1976 (SI 1976
No. 1813, as amended by SI 1978 No.
127)   78, 108, 200

County Courts Jurisdiction Order 1981
(SI 1981 No. 1123)   252

County Court Rules 1981 (SI 1981 No.
1687, as amended)   253, 254

Food Labelling Regulations 1984 (SI
1984 No. 1305)   243

Insurance Brokers Registration
Council (Code of Conduct) Approval
Order 1978 (SI 1978 No. 1394)   195

Mail Order Transactions (Information)
Order 1976 (SI 1976 No. 1812)   199

Price Marking Order 1991
(SI 1991 1382)   227

Price Marking (Bargain Offers) Order
1979 (SI 1979 No. 364, as amended
by SI 1979 No. 633 and SI 1979 No.
1124)   193, 224

Trade Descriptions (Sealskin Goods)
(Information) Order 1980 (SI 1980
No. 1150)   224

Part one

Private law remedies

Introductory note

In a sense there is no such creature as 'consumer law'. English law has never developed a fully coherent body of law designed to protect the consumer. The consumer and his advisers have instead been obliged to utilize a hotchpotch of common law concepts and doctrines designed primarily for other purposes. Even the recent statutory consumer protection developments have been piecemeal, and do not amount to a comprehensive code.

The upshot of this characteristically empirical approach of English law is that consumer law is a hybrid creation. The student accordingly needs to study a number of disparate categories of law, but at the same time needs to be constantly aware of their interrelationships from the consumer viewpoint. This book draws attention to the interrelationships in its discussion of the law.

Part One of the text considers the consumer's rights and remedies under private (or civil) law. The text deals not only with the law of sale of goods as it relates to consumers, but also with analogous contracts and with contracts involving the supply of a service. After a review of product liability, attention is directed at the consumer credit dimension.

For various reasons indicated in the text, private law remedies do not by themselves afford adequate consumer protection. Part Two of this book therefore deals with intervention in the consumer interest by administrative remedies, backed by criminal law sanctions. It may well be that administrative remedies and criminal law sanctions now play a more significant role in consumer protection as a whole than does private law. Nevertheless, the individual consumer with a particularised complaint lives, so to speak, in a mixed legal economy; private law is not obsolete and the consumer's adviser must master its details.

1
Classification of consumer contracts

1. Introductory

The law relating to the sale of goods has long been largely regulated by statute. For most practical purposes, so too have hire-purchase agreements. Contracts of hire, on the other hand, and contracts for the transfer of goods analogous to contracts of sale (e.g. exchange, or supply of work and materials — defined below) have until recent times been left to be regulated by the common law.

The enactment of the Supply of Goods and Services Act 1982, which complements the Sale of Goods Act 1979 and the Supply of Goods (Implied Terms) Act 1973, has in considerable measure rationalized the position. That is to say, whatever the type of contract under which goods are supplied, there is a basic package of consumer protection implied into the transaction. In this respect it is really a question of asking 'where do I find the law?', a question which this chapter answers through classification of the various types of contract into which consumers enter.

It must be emphasized that unlike the Sale of Goods Act, the 1982 Act regulates only the implied terms. Other aspects (e.g. formation, performance, remedies) of contracts falling within the scope of the Act remain to be governed by the common law, reference to which will be made where appropriate. Chapter 5 will deal with the implied terms themselves, as imposed under the Sale of Goods Act 1979, the Supply of Goods (Implied Terms) Act 1973, and the 1982 Act respectively.

Contracts for the sale of goods

2.   Sale of Goods Act 1979

The law relating to the sale of goods was codified in the Sale of Goods Act 1893. This Act and the amendments made to it from time to time were consolidated in the Sale of Goods Act 1979 (SGA). The legislation was in its origins more concerned with regulating commercial relations than with protecting consumers, but consumers must nevertheless have regard to its provisions. Common law rules, however, continue to apply save in so far as they are inconsistent with the Act: s. 62(2). Moreover, subject to the Unfair Contract Terms Act 1977 (*see* Chap. 6) both the Act and common law rules may be negatived or varied by usage, or by express agreement or a previous course of dealing between trader and consumer: s. 55.

3.   Definitions

Only contracts for the *sale* (not e.g. hire) of *goods* (not services) are governed by the Sale of Goods Act. The Act defines a contract for the sale of goods as 'a contract by which the seller transfers or agrees to transfer the property in goods to the buyer for a money consideration, called the price': s. 2(1). The contract of sale may be absolute or conditional: s. 2(3). The definition covers both a sale, where the ownership of goods is transferred to the buyer, and an agreement to sell, where the ownership is to be transferred at some future time or subject to some condition yet to be fulfilled: s. 2(5). A sale of 'future goods' (goods to be manufactured, such as a suit, or grown, such as a crop, or acquired by the seller after making the contract of sale) operates as an agreement to sell: s. 5. The interpretation section of the Act (s. 61) throws further light on the definition of a contract for the sale of goods: a seller is a 'person who sells or agrees to sell goods' and likewise a buyer is a 'person who buys or agrees to buy goods'; 'property' means ownership and 'goods' are defined to include 'all personal chattels other than things in action and money'.

4.   The price

This can be either money or goods and money. It cannot, however, be goods alone, which would make the arrangement amount to a contract of exchange (*see* 8). Where the price is not fixed by the contract or by a previous course of dealing between the parties, the buyer has to pay a reasonable price: s. 8. So the consumer who orders (say) 300 kg of coal without inquiring about the price cannot thereafter claim the contract to be void for uncertainty: the price payable will be the current market price.

Contracts for the transfer of goods

5. Contracts for the transfer of property in goods

Part I of the Supply of Goods and Service Act 1982 ('SGSA') regulates 'a contract for the transfer of goods', defined as being 'a contract under which one person transfers or agrees to transfer to another the property in goods': s. 1. A contract may be a contract for the transfer of goods whatever the nature of the consideration for the transfer and whether or not the supply of services is included.

6. The excepted contracts

Certain contracts are excepted from the above definition because statutory implied terms already exist in regard to goods supplied thereunder. The excepted contracts are:

(a) contracts of sale;
(b) hire-purchase agreements (*see* 13);
(c) contracts involving the supply of goods on the redemption of trading stamps (*see* 12).

> NOTE: Also excepted (for reasons of policy) are transfers or agreements to transfer made by deed for which there is no consideration other than the presumed consideration imported by the deed; and contracts intended to operate by way of security.

7. Work and materials

Contracts for the supply of work and materials pre-eminently fall within the definition of a contract for the transfer of goods and consequently are governed by the SGSA and not the SGA. They are analogous to contracts for the sale of goods because ownership in goods is transferred, yet they are distinct. Contracts for *services* alone (e.g. insurance, a package holiday, or cleaning curtains) may be easily recognized and distinguished from the sale of goods. The difficulty of classification arises where there is involved a combination of services and goods. Is this sale of goods or work and materials? The test for classifying the contract is: what is the essence of the transaction, the production of something to be sold (sale of goods) or the expenditure of skill and labour (work and materials)? Painting a portrait, repairing a car, applying a hair dye, roofing a house — all have been held to be contracts for work and materials. Likewise, contracts for the installation of double glazing or central heating would be contracts for work and materials. But a meal in a restaurant is regarded as a contract for the sale of goods.

8. Exchange or barter

It has already been noted that the Sale of Goods Act defines a contract for the sale of goods as a contract for the transfer of property 'for a money consideration, called the price'. It follows that a simple exchange of goods (barter) is not a sale of goods, because no money is payable. The nature of a contract of exchange is not purely a matter of theoretical interest to the consumer. The promotion of products through the distribution of coupons, vouchers, wrappers, labels, etc., may amount to a contract of barter on redemption by the consumer. Likewise barter, perhaps, is the part-exchange transaction whereby used goods are traded in as part-consideration for new. Once it is established that a contract is one of exchange or barter it comes within the definition of a contract for the transfer of goods and is governed by the SGSA. Redemption against trading stamps is governed by another statute (*see* **12**).

9. Free gifts

'Free gifts' agreed to be supplied with products (e.g. 'free cassette with every VCR purchased') are not, it seems, supplied on a contract of sale but on a collateral contract: cf. *Esso Petroleum Ltd* v. *Commissioners of Customs and Excise* (1976), in which judicial opinion in the House of Lords on the status of 'free gifts' (World Cup coins) was divided. If it is correct that a free gift is supplied on a collateral contract, then it will be a contract for the transfer of goods within the SGSA.

On the other hand, if the gift is merely a free sample

distributed as part of the promotion of a product without any connection with a contract of supply so that there is technically no consideration for the gift, then there can be no contract at all and no implied terms will be applicable. (In such a case the consumer might have a remedy in the tort of negligence if the free sample turned out to be a dangerous product: *see* Chap. 9.)

Contracts for the hire of goods

10. The nature of hire

Hire is a contract for the bailment of goods in consideration of a rental whereby the hirer obtains possession of the goods for an agreed time and purpose. Hire is legally quite distinct from sale in that a hirer obtains possession only, not ownership.

> NOTE: An agreement for hire to an individual which is capable of subsisting for more than three months and does not require the hirer to make payments exceeding £15,000 is a 'consumer hire agreement' and is regulated under the Consumer Credit Act 1974 (*see* Chap. 10 *et seq.*).

11. Hire under the Supply of Goods and Services Act

Part I of the SGSA implies similar terms, *mutatis mutandis*, in contracts of hire to those it does in contract for the transfer of goods (*see* Chap. 5). The SGSA s. 6, defines 'a contract for the hire of goods' as being 'a contract under which one person bails or agrees to bail goods to another by way of hire'. Excepted from this definition are hire-purchase agreements (*see* **13**), and contracts involving the bailment of goods on the redemption of trading stamps (*see* **12**). The fact that services may be supplied under a contract will not prevent it from being a contract for the hire of goods; nor is the nature of the consideration relevant.

Other contracts under which goods pass

12. Trading stamps

The supply of goods on the redemption of trading stamps is not a sale of goods (*see* **4**), nor is it a contract within the SGSA (*see*

6, 11). In fact, special legislation protects the consumer. The Trading Stamps Act 1964 regulates the use of trading stamps, by providing that they must be marked with their cash value; that they must be redeemable for cash at the consumer's option; that retailers must display information enabling consumers to calculate the number of stamps they should receive; and prohibiting misleading advertising as to the value of trading stamps. Section 4 of the 1964 Act, as amended by s. 16 of the Supply of Goods (Implied Terms) Act 1973, also imposes implied obligations as to title and merchantable quality 'notwithstanding any terms to the contrary'. These obligations correspond to the Sale of Goods Act provisions as to title and merchantability in contracts of sale (*see* Chap. 5).

13. Hire-purchase

This is a contract of hire which grants the debtor (i.e. the hirer) the option to purchase the goods if the terms of the agreement are complied with by him. But the debtor is not bound to exercise the option to purchase. Accordingly he is not someone who 'agrees to buy' goods, and so the transaction does not fall within the scope of the Sale of Goods Act. However, a consumer who enters into a hire-purchase agreement is in reality, if not in law, acquiring goods, albeit on credit. Since the passing of the Supply of Goods (Implied Terms) Act 1973, the policy of the law has been to assimilate the implied obligations of the supplier in sale and hire-purchase transactions (*see* 5:**13**). As will be seen later, the Consumer Credit Act includes hire-purchase contracts under its umbrella, and, indeed, makes certain special provisions concerning them.

> *Helby* v. *Matthews* (1895): the owner of a piano let it on hire at a rent of 10s. 6d. a month. Under the agreement the hirer could return the piano at any time, the hirer remaining liable for all arrears of hire. It was agreed that the hirer would become owner of the piano on paying all the stipulated instalments, but that meanwhile the piano should continue in the sole ownership of the original owner. HELD: These arrangements amounted to what is now called a hire-purchase agreement. The hirer had not

'agreed to buy' and the contract did not fall within the provisions of the Sale of Goods Act (House of Lords).

Contracts for the supply of services

14. Services under Part II of the Supply of Goods and Services Act

Whilst Part I of the SGSA 1982 regulates contracts for the transfer of goods and contracts of hire, as outlined above, it is Part II which deals with the supply of services. Part II implies certain terms into contracts for the supply of services. Details are given in Chapter 5. For present purposes of classification, however, it is sufficient to note that s. 12 SGSA defines a 'contract for the supply of a service' as being 'a contract under which a person ('the supplier') agrees to carry out a service'. Contracts of service or apprenticeship are expressly excluded from this definition. The fact that a contract also provides for the transfer or hire of goods does not prevent it from being a contract for the supply of a service if otherwise within the definition.

NOTE: It will be observed that the various categories of contract which the consumer (or firms, for that matter) may enter into are capable of overlapping.

Progress test 1

1. To what extent may (*a*) common law principles; and (*b*) special stipulations agreed between the parties, be applied to a contract for the sale of goods? **(2)**

2. Define a contract for the sale of goods and distinguish a sale from an agreement to sell. Is a house 'goods' within the meaning of the Sale of Goods Act? What are 'future goods'? **(3)**

3. D fills up the boot of his car with logs which he has obtained from a timber merchant. Nothing has been said about the price. How much must D pay for the logs? **(4)**

4. Define a contract for the transfer of goods. Give examples. **(5–8)**

5. Consider whether the following are contracts for the sale of goods or for work and materials:

    (a) F eats a meal at E's restaurant.

    (b) G repairs H's car and puts a new engine in it.

    (c) I, a hairdresser, applies a hair-dye to J's hair.

    (d) K buys a fitted carpet, which is fitted by the retailer. **(7)**

6. Does the distribution of 'free gifts' involve the making of any contract? If so, what type? **(9)**

7. L redeems several books of trading stamps for a radio. The radio does not work. Can L sue for breach of contract? **(12)**

8. Define a contract for the hire of goods and distinguish between (*a*) a contract of hire; (*b*) a contract of hire-purchase; and (*c*) a contract for the sale of goods. **(10, 11, 13)**

9. Define a contract for the supply of a service. **(14)**

2
Ownership and risk

Transfer of property and risk

1. Ownership and risk

In this chapter we turn to contracts for the sale of goods, as defined and governed by the Sale of Goods Act (*see* 1:3). The essence of the contract is the transfer of ownership in the goods. The point of making the contract is that the buyer will become the owner of the goods (obtain the property in them) and that the seller will be paid money (a money consideration called the price). In English law the transfer of the risk of loss of the goods from trader to consumer is closely connected with the transfer of ownership. This aspect of the law — the transfer of risk — is the subject of this chapter.

2. Property, ownership, title

The Sale of Goods Act uses the expressions 'transfer of property' or 'property passes', meaning transfer of ownership. 'Title' is another word which can be used synonymously with ownership. The reader should note this use of the word 'property' with particular care. It is very easy to become confused and wrongly interpret 'property' as meaning possession.

3. Risk

Section 20 of the Sale of Goods Act provides that risk passes with property, that is the risk of loss or damage to the goods passes to the consumer when ownership passes to him. There are three exceptions to this rule:

(a) the parties may expressly or impliedly agree otherwise;

(b) where delivery has been delayed through the fault of one party, the party at fault takes the risk of any loss which might not otherwise have occurred;

(c) the party in possession, being a bailee of the goods (i.e. in possession of goods he does not own), is liable at common law if he is negligent.

It follows from s. 20 that the transfer of ownership is frequently crucial to the transfer of risk. The consumer would be unlikely to appreciate the point. He would probably assume that he becomes owner of the goods when delivery is effected and that he bears the risk of loss only after delivery. The time of transfer of ownership and (usually) risk can be very important. The buyer may, for example, wish to insure against the risk he then assumes.

4. Goods must be ascertained

The rules as to the transfer of ownership are highly technical. An important preliminary rule is that where there is a contract for the sale of unascertained goods, no property can pass until the goods are ascertained: s. 16. Unascertained goods are not defined in the Act, but may be defined as comprising either:

(a) purely generic goods (e.g. 'a dozen bottles of champagne', or 'a television set'); *or*

(b) goods forming part of a larger specified whole (e.g. 'one of the television sets presently in stock').

Goods may be said to be ascertained when they have been identified and agreed upon after the making of the contract (e.g. when a particular television set of the agreed screen size and make has been selected out of the dealer's stock and, perhaps, labelled with the buyer's name).

5. Intention

Given that the goods are not unascertained, the fundamental and deceptively simple rule concerning the transfer of property is that property in goods passes when the parties intend it to pass: s. 17.

The contract will generally be silent as to the parties' intention (assuming they have one), and the circumstances surrounding the contract may be equally indecisive. The Sale of Goods Act, s. 18, therefore lays down five rules for ascertaining the parties' intention. It is important to note that these rules only apply in the absence of any apparent contrary intention.

6. Specific goods: Rule 1

In an unconditional contract for the sale of specific goods, in a deliverable state, property passes when the contract is made, even though the time of payment and/or delivery is postponed: s. 18, Rule 1. Note the following points.

(a) The Rule only applies to 'specific goods', defined in s. 61(1) as 'goods identified and agreed upon' at the time the contract is made (e.g. 'this television set', 'that one there').

(b) Similarly the Rule only applies when the goods are in a 'deliverable state', defined in s. 61(5) as meaning that they 'are in such a state that the buyer would under the contract be bound to take delivery of them', so they are not, for example, cemented to the floor.

(c) Postponement of delivery or payment, or both, does *not* make the contract conditional and outside the scope of Rule 1.

Rule 1 is inimical to consumer interests, providing as it does that property (and therefore risk: s. 20) passes when the contract is made. Suppose a consumer were to select a specific piece of consumer hardware from a retailer's, but before delivery of that piece was due it was damaged by a fire in the retailer's showrooms. By virtue of s. 20 and s. 18, Rule 1, the consumer would have to bear the loss, unless the retailer had been negligent in causing the fire, or alternatively as a matter of goodwill he did not stand upon his strict legal rights. In view of the strict legal position, it seems likely that the courts will strive to construe a different intention whenever possible: '. . . . in modern time very little is needed to give rise to the inference that property in specific goods is to pass only on delivery or payment' (Diplock LJ in *R.V. Ward* v. *Bignall* (1967)). Often, of course, Rule 1 will not apply on the facts. Thus, where consumers do not take goods away with them immediately on making the purchase, because they have chosen goods from a showroom model and delivery will be made later from another source, Rule 1 will not apply since the goods are not specific — not identified at the time of sale.

> *Dennant* v. *Skinner and Collom* (1948): a rogue successfully bid for a car at an auction. He tendered a cheque and was allowed to drive the car away on signing a form that no property in the car would pass until the cheque was cleared. The rogue resold that car, which was resold in turn to the defendant. The rogue's cheque was dishonoured and the original owners sought to recover the car from the defendant. HELD: As an auction is complete when the hammer falls, under s. 18 Rule 1 property thereupon passes. The form the rogue had signed had no legal effect because property had already passed. The rogue could accordingly pass good title to subsequent purchasers and the original owners could not recover the car.

7. Specific goods: Rules 2 and 3

By Rule 2, if the retailer is bound to do something to put specific goods into a deliverable state, property passes when the act is done and the consumer has notice. For example, if an antique dealer has undertaken to treat certain furniture he has sold for woodworm before delivery, property will not pass until the treatment has been carried out and the consumer has been so informed.

By Rule 3, in a contract for the sale of specific goods, in a deliverable state, if the retailer is bound to do something to the goods to ascertain the price (e.g. weigh, measure or test them), property passes when the act is done and the consumer has notice.

8. Goods on approval

By Rule 4, when goods are delivered to the consumer on approval or on sale or return or similar terms property passes:

(a) when the consumer approves the transaction either by telling the seller, or by doing any other act adopting the transaction; or
(b) when, without giving notice of rejection, the consumer retains the goods for the agreed time, or if no time has been agreed, for a reasonable time (a question of fact).

An example of the operation of these rules would be where the consumer takes bottles of wine on sale or return terms for a party. Once a bottle is opened, even if the contents are not touched, property in the wine will pass, as an act inconsistent with the retailer's ownership will have been done.

9. Mail order

Property in goods sent on approval by a mail order firm would under Rule 4 (*see* **8**) pass when the consumer adopts the transaction, or pass after the lapse of the time specified by the firm for the return of the goods, or if no time had been specified, after the lapse of a reasonable time.

Rule 4 will govern the majority of mail order transactions since the consumer will generally be allowed a short period in which to return unwanted goods, as provided under the Mail Order Traders' Association's Code of Practice (where the consumer buys from a catalogue) and the British Code of Advertising Practice (where the consumer buys in response to a magazine or newspaper advertisement) respectively. Should there be no approval period, however, then it seems that unless a contrary intention can be construed, property would pass under Rule 5 (*see* **10**) as soon as the goods are posted by the seller (cf. *Badische Anilin* v. *Basle Chemicals* (1898) HL).

Unsolicited goods sent by a mail order firm or other business are dealt with differently by the law. Under the Unsolicited Goods and Services Act 1971 and 1975, the consumer may treat unsolicited goods as an unconditional gift to him if they are not collected by the sender (at the sender's expense) within six months, or thirty days if the consumer has given written notice 'however expressed' that the goods were unsolicited. ('Unsolicited' means that the goods were sent 'without any prior request' made by the consumer.) In the period before the goods pass into the ownership of the consumer, the consumer must not unreasonably refuse to permit the sender to collect them. Criminal law sanctions also have a role to play here, in preventing exploitation of consumer ignorance of civil law rights. Demands or threats for payment made by a trader who does not have reasonable cause to believe that there is a right to payment and who knows that the goods were unsolicited, constitute a criminal offence, triable summarily. On conviction of the trader, a consumer who has paid for the unsolicited goods in response to the demands or threats made might be able to obtain a compensation order at the discretion of the criminal court (*see* Chap. 21).

Confusion sometimes arises here with book and record clubs. If the 'editor's choice' has not been declined it is likely to be delivered, and should be paid for. This is, of course, because here we are discussing the performance of a contract — the consumer agreed at the outset to deal this way — whereas with unsolicited goods we are dealing with the formation (or not) of a contract. Naturally if the 'editor's choice' has been declined in the agreed manner and it is still sent, then it will be unsolicited.

10. Unascertained goods

By s. 18, Rule 5, in a contract for the sale of unascertained or future goods by description, property passes when goods of that description in a deliverable state are unconditionally appropriated to the contract by one party with the consent of the other. Such consent may be express or implied, and may be given either before or after the appropriation is made. On a self-service garage forecourt petrol is pumped by the customer (the buyer) with the consent of the proprietor (the seller). Where the forecourt is attended the unconditional appropriation will be made by the seller with the consent of the buyer.

Another example of the operation of Rule 5 would be where a consumer orders a new freezer from a dealer, who in turn orders the model the consumer has chosen from the manufacturer. The goods will be unascertained future goods at the date of the contract. Probably the freezer would not be regarded as unconditionally appropriated to the contract until actually delivered to the consumer. By Rule 5(2) delivery to an independent carrier without the reservation of the right of disposal amounts to an unconditional appropriation of the goods to the contract.

> *Philip Head & Sons Ltd* v. *Showfronts Ltd* (1970): a buyer ordered carpeting which was to be laid by the house furnishers selling it. The carpets were delivered but were stolen before they could be laid. HELD: The house furnishers must bear the loss because property had not passed to the buyer. The carpeting was not in a 'deliverable

state' until it had been laid, and so goods in a deliverable state had not been unconditionally appropriated to the contract.

Perishing of the goods

11. Meaning of 'perish'

Although the Sale of Goods Act uses this term, as will be seen, it does not define it. It clearly covers goods which are physically destroyed. The meaning also includes goods which disappear through theft (*Barrow, Lane & Ballard Ltd* v. *Phillip Phillips & Co. Ltd* (1929), and goods which cease to exist in a commercial sense (*Asfar & Co. Ltd* v. *Blundell* (1896) CA: contaminated dates had 'perished'). Perished goods are those which are unavailable — for one reason or another!

12. When the consumer bears the cost of perished goods

The rules as to the passing of property and risk have been reviewed in the preceding paragraphs. The position may be summarized thus.

(a) *Specific goods*. If they perish after property, and therefore risk, have passed, the consumer bears the loss. (But remember the three provisos to s. 20: *see* **3**). The contract is at an end.

(b) *Unascertained goods*. If they perish after unconditional appropriation to the contract, the consumer again bears the loss (subject to the s. 20 provisos). The contract is at an end. The retailer does not have to supply further goods conforming to the contractual description.

13. Effects of mistake and frustration

Where the rules so work that the retailer bears the cost of perished goods, there may nevertheless still be outstanding obligations to take into account in unscrambling the legal position. The nature of these obligations will depend upon whether the goods are specific or unascertained.

(a) *Specific goods*. Where there is a contract for the sale of specific goods which, without the knowledge of the seller, have perished at the time when the contract is made, the contract is void for mistake (s. 6) and no further obligations arise, except that the consumer is entitled to recover any money paid as there has been a total failure of consideration. On the other hand, if specific goods perish after the contract has been made but before risk passes (so that the retailer still bears the loss) the contract is frustrated (s. 7) and no further obligations arise, except that again the consumer is entitled to recover any money paid.

> NOTE: The Law Reform (Frustrated Contracts) Act 1943 does not apply to any contract to which s. 7 of the SGA applies, i.e. no apportionment of loss can be made between retailer and consumer s. 2(5) of the 1943 Act (as amended).

(b) *Unascertained goods.* If they are purely generic (*see* **4**), the contract is not affected merely because the retailer's intended source of supply is or becomes unavailable. Since ownership (and therefore risk) cannot be transferred in unascertained goods (s. 16) the retailer must bear the entire loss. He will, moreover, still have to supply goods conforming to the contractual description, for which the consumer for his part will have to pay if he has not already done so. On the other hand, if the retailer's source of supply is specified in the contract but is or becomes unavailable, then common law rules analogous to ss. 6 and 7 of the SGA will apply and the contract will be void for mistake or discharged through frustration according to the facts of the case. Consequently, in this eventuality the retailer will not have to supply other goods conforming to the contractual description, though he will (subject to the following note) have to return any money received from the consumer.

> NOTE: Where the contract is frustrated under common law rules, as above, the 1943 Act will apply, e.g. adjustment is possible, out of any advance payment, for any expense incurred by the retailer.

Progress test 2

1. What is the general rule governing the passing of risk? What are the exceptions to the rule? **(3)**

2. What is the meaning of 'unascertained goods'? **(4)**

3. Define 'specific goods'.   **(6)**

4. Decide whether the goods in each of the following cases are unascertained or specific: (*a*) 'a tape recorder'; (*b*) 'that tape recorder'; (*c*) 'one of those tape recorders'.   **(4, 6)**

5. What is the fundamental rule governing the passing of property in goods?   **(5)**

6. A agrees to buy 'this antique table' from B, an antique dealer, 'payment and delivery to be made next week'. When does property pass? If the table is destroyed by fire (*a*) during the week; or (*b*) ten days later while the table is still in B's possession; or (*c*) in transit to A, who bears the loss?   **(3, 6)**

7. When does property pass in goods which are sold at an auction?   **(6)**

8. C agrees to buy a second-hand car from D, a dealer. D agrees to put new tyres on all the wheels before C takes delivery of the car. When does property in the car pass?   **(7)**

9. Every month E receives stamps on approval from a firm of stamp dealers. E keeps one batch of stamps for three months without either paying for them or returning them. Has property passed?   **(8)**

10. The F Mail Order Co. send a quartz watch to G at G's request. Who bears the risk of the watch being damaged in the post?   **(9)**

11. Although J has not requested it, he is sent a set of encyclopaedias by the K Co. The K Co. demands payment. What are J's rights? Has the K Co. committed any criminal offence? Suppose J had agreed to take the set at one volume each month, but decided, after three months, that he did not want any more of the books. Does this affect your answer?   **(9)**

12. L orders an oven from electrical showrooms. The retailers place an order with the manufacturers. The oven duly arrives at the retailer's stock-rooms and L is informed that delivery will be made the next week. Heavy rain floods the stock-room before delivery is due and the oven is damaged. Who bears the loss? **(10)**

13. What is meant when the Sale of Goods Act speaks of goods having 'perished'? **(11)**

14. M inspects a second-hand car at N's premises. Next day M telephones the sales man to confirm that he will buy the car. He puts a deposit in the post. Unknown to either M or the salesman, the car had been stolen overnight from N's yard where it was kept. What are M's rights? **(13)**

15. O contracts to buy eight dozen bottles of a named vintage wine from what are described as 'the renowned cellars' of P, a wine merchant. After the contract is made but before the wine can be selected from stock and despatched to O. P's cellars are devastated by fire and the contents ruined. Consider (*a*) whether O has to pay for the wine; and (*b*) whether P has to supply O with wine of the vintage ordered. **(13)**

3

Sale by non-owner

Nemo dat: the basic rule

1. *Nemo dat quod non habet*

This maxim may be roughly translated as meaning that no one can transfer ownership when he is not the owner. The *nemo dat* rule, as it may be abbreviated, means in practical terms that a consumer who has bought goods may find himself faced with a claim to ownership by a third party, who turns out to have a better right to possession than the seller from whom he acquired the goods. If this is the case, the consumer will still have a personal right of action against the seller, who will be in breach of the implied condition of good right to sell: s. 12 SGA (*see* Chap. 5). This condition cannot be excluded (s. 6. Unfair Contract Terms Act); nevertheless it may be rather cold comfort to the consumer faced with the trouble of finding the seller and the expense of enforcing the right. But whatever the implications for the consumer, the Sale of Goods Act enshrines the *nemo dat* principle in s. 21(1): 'Subject to this Act, where goods are sold by a person who is not their owner, and who does not sell them under the authority or with the consent of the owner, the buyer acquires no better title to the goods than the seller had . . .' Obviously where this principle applies it favours the original owner, and where any exception applies it will benefit third parties.

Principal exceptions

2. The exceptions

The exceptions to the *nemo dat* rule of primary concern to the consumer may be listed as follows:

(a) estoppel;
(b) sale in market overt;
(c) disposition by a mercantile agent;
(d) sale under a voidable title;
(e) second sale by a seller in possession;
(f) sale by a buyer in possession;
(g) sale under various common law and statutory powers;
(h) disposition of a motor vehicle under Part III of the Hire-Purchase Act 1964.

3. Estoppel

This exception is expressly preserved by s. 21(1) of the SGA which, having stated that the buyer acquires no better title to goods than the seller had, continues: '. . . unless the owner of the goods is by his conduct precluded from denying the seller's authority to sell.' This is the essence of estoppel, namely that a person will be prevented (estopped) from denying the truth of a fact previously represented, expressly or impliedly, by him. In practice, however, it will be very difficult for a consumer to succeed in having an owner estopped from asserting his ownership. As Lord Fraser said in *Moorgate Mercantile Co. Ltd* v. *Twitchings* (1976) HL: 'The owner of property is entitled to be careless with it if he likes, and even extreme carelessness with his own property will not preclude him from recovering it from a person who has bought it from someone who dishonestly purported to sell it'.

> *Central Newbury Car Auctions Ltd* v. *Unity Finance Ltd* (1957): a rogue was allowed by a car dealer to take away a car and its registration book on filling up a proposal form for a hire-purchase agreement with a finance company. The rogue sold the car to a third party. The finance company were dissatisfied with the completed hire-purchase proposal form and declined the proposal. Ownership of the car therefore remained at all times with the dealer. The question arose whether the dealer was estopped by his negligence from denying the rogue's authority to sell. HELD by the Court of Appeal (Lord Denning dissenting): The dealer was not precluded by his conduct from setting up his title against the third party and subsequent purchasers. Delivery of goods of itself did not give rise to an

estoppel, even if the owner was careless. The handing over of the registration book (not a document of title) did not without more invest the rogue with the indicia of property. (But cf. *Eastern Distributors* v. *Goldring* (1957).)

4. Sale in market overt

This exception to the *nemo dat* rule is preserved by s. 22(1) of the SGA. 'Where goods are sold in market overt, according to the usage of the market, the buyer acquires a good title to the goods, provided he buys them in good faith and without notice of any defect or want of title on the part of the seller.' Market overt is an open, public and legally constituted market, or the public parts of shops in the City of London. The following points should be noted.

(a) The sale must be public and open (not, say, in a private room of a shop), and by the shopkeeper or stall-holder and not to him, unless such is the custom of the market. The bulk and not merely a sample must have been exposed for sale.
(b) The sale must be according to the custom of the market, and the goods sold should be those usually sold in the market or shop.
(c) The sale must take place between sunrise and sunset, so late-night shopping is unprotected!
(d) The buyer must buy in good faith.
(e) Market overt does not apply to Wales or Scotland.

It will be seen from the foregoing restrictions that the market overt rule is 'capricious in its application' (Law Reform Committee Report on Transfer of Title, Cmnd 2958, 1966). The Law Reform Committee accordingly recommended that 'section 22 of the Sale of Goods Act should be replaced by a provision that a person who buys goods by retail at trade premises or by public auction acquires a good title provided he buys in good faith and without notice of any defect or want of title on the part of the apparent owner . . .' (Lord Donovan in a minority note of reservation thought that the market overt rule should be abolished rather than extended: the majority proposals would make the disposal of stolen goods easier.)

> *Reid* v. *Metropolitan Police Commissioner* (1973): a pair of Adam candelabra was stolen from the plaintiff and subsequently sold at New Caledonian market in Southwark

(a statutory market) early one morning after the market
had opened at 7.00 a.m. but before sunrise at 8.19 a.m. The
plaintiff traced the candelabra and brought an action to
recover them. HELD: The purchaser was not protected by
the market overt rule, which only applies where the sale
takes place between sunrise and sunset, even though the
market may be open for trading outside the period (Court
of Appeal).

Bishopsgate Motor Finance Corpn v. *Transport Brakes Ltd*
(1949): the hirer of a car under a hire-purchase agreement
sold the vehicle privately at Maidstone market. HELD: The
buyer obtained good title to the car as Maidstone market
(established 1747) was market overt and a private sale was
not contrary to the usage of the market (Court of Appeal).

5. Disposition by a mercantile agent

Under the common law rules of agency, an agent who sells
goods will bind his principal to the transaction and give the
consumer good title to the goods if the agent has express or
implied authority to sell. Note that just as possession of goods (e.g.
a car and its registration document) does not of itself give rise to
an estoppel (*see* 3), neither does it amount to ostensible authority
binding the principal if the agent wrongfully sells the goods. But
special statutory rules apply to dispositions by 'a mercantile agent',
defined by the Factors Act 1889 as a person having in the
customary course of his business authority either to sell or buy or
raise money on goods. By s. 2 of the Factors Act, any sale or other
disposition in the ordinary course of his business by a mercantile
agent in possession of goods or document of title with the owner's
consent confers the owner's title on a buyer who takes in good faith
without notice of the agent's lack of authority.

The Factors Act thus affords considerable protection to the
consumer. But note that the mercantile agent must have
possession of the goods for the purpose of the disposition and not
for some other purpose such as repairs. The owner's consent to
possession is valid even if it was obtained by fraud. The owner's
consent is presumed in the absence of evidence to the contrary:
s. 2(4) of the Factors Act. Termination of consent does not affect
a subsequent sale unless the buyer has notice: s. 2(2). So far as

second-hand cars are concerned, the owner's consent must extend to possession of the registration document and ignition key, otherwise the sale will not be in the ordinary course of business of a mercantile agent.

> *Stadium Finance Ltd* v. *Robbins* (1962): the owner of a Jaguar car left it with a car dealer with a view to a purchaser being found. The owner intended to control the sale of the car himself and he took the ignition key away with him but accidentally left the registration book in the locked glove compartment of the dashboard. Without the owner's consent, the dealer opened the glove compartment, obtained possession of the registration book and sold the car. HELD: Title did not pass to the purchaser under s. 2 of the Factors Act because although the dealer was a mercantile agent within the meaning of the Act and the purchaser had taken in good faith, the sale was not in the ordinary course of business as the dealer did not possess the ignition key and had obtained possession of the registration book unlawfully (Court of Appeal).

6. Sale under a voidable title

'Where the seller of goods has a voidable title to them, but his title has not been avoided at the time of the sale, the buyer acquires a good title to the goods, provided he buys them in good faith and without notice of the seller's defect of title': s. 23 SGA.

> *Car & Universal Finance Co.* v. *Caldwell* (1965): the owner of a car sold it to a rogue, who took the car away, paying for it by cheque. When the cheque was dishonoured the owner notified the police and the Automobile Association. Thereafter the car was sold by the rogue to X, who took in bad faith, who in turn resold to the plaintiff, who took in good faith. HELD: The rogue's title was voidable and had been avoided by the owner notifying the police, even though communication of rescission of the contract (which is normally required) had not been possible. Rescission had been effected before the plaintiff purchased the car, and so the plaintiff did not acquire title under s. 23 of the SGA (Court of Appeal).

NOTE: (1) If X in the above case had bought in *good* faith, then under s. 25 of the SGA the plaintiff would have acquired good title (*see* **9**). (2) The Law Reform Committee Report on Transfer of Title (Cmnd 2958, 1966) recommended that an innocent purchaser should obtain a good title until notice of rescission is actually communicated to the other party.

7. Torts (Interference with Goods) Act 1977, s. 6

Where the activities of a rogue are involved, either the innocent original owner, or the innocent third party consumer, will suffer loss. In *Ingram* v. *Little* (1961) CA, Devlin LJ suggested that in such circumstances the loss should be borne equally between the innocent parties. Yet the law does not normally apportion loss, Lord Devlin's suggestion having been rejected by the Law Reform Committee (*ibid.*) as impracticable. An exception occurs where an innocent third party improves goods which he has bought, only to be deprived of them by the true owner when he duly asserts his rights to the goods. Section 6 of the Torts (Interference with Goods) Act 1977 provides that in proceedings for wrongful interference against a person who has improved goods in the mistaken but honest belief that he had a good title to them, or against a subsequent purchaser in good faith, an allowance shall be made for the value of the goods attributable to the improvement.

Example ————————————————————————————————————

(adapted from that given in s. 6): T steals a car from O and sells it to I, who buys in good faith and improves it by putting in a new engine. I then sells to X, who buys in good faith. O traces the car and sues X in conversion. The damages may be reduced to reflect the improvement. Further, under s. 6(3) if X then sues I for failure of consideration, there will be a comparable reduction in the damages which X will recover from I.

---

8. Second sale by a seller in possession

If a seller having sold goods remains in possession of them, any *delivery* of the goods under a second sale or other disposition, to a person taking in good faith and without notice of the previous sale, confers title on that person: s. 24 SGA (s. 8 of the Factors Act 1889 provides similarly).

9. Sale by a buyer in possession

If a buyer who has bought or agreed to buy goods obtains possession of them with the seller's consent, any *delivery* by the buyer under a subsequent sale or other disposition, to a person taking in good faith and without notice of the seller's rights, confers title on that person: s. 25(1) SGA (s. 9 of the Factors Act 1889 provides similarly).

> NOTE: Section 25 does not apply to hire-purchase — indeed it has been suggested that the notion of hire-purchase was developed to avoid s. 25: *Helby* v. *Matthews* (1895) HL (*see* 1:**13**); nor to conditional sale (*see* 10:**15**) if a consumer credit agreement does s. 25 apply (*see* 10:**4**): s. 25(2) SGA.

> *Newtons of Wembley Ltd* v. *Williams* (1965): the plaintiffs sold a car to a rogue who paid by cheque. The cheque was dishonoured and the plaintiffs rescinded the agreement by taking all reasonable steps to trace the rogue and the car by informing the police. The rogue's title to the car was in the circumstances a voidable one, and title reverted to the plaintiffs on rescission of the contract. The rogue subsequently sold the car to a third party in Warren Street market, an established street market for second-hand cars (but not market overt). HELD: Because of the way in which s. 25 is actually worded, the provision only operates if the disposition made by the buyer was in the ordinary course of business of a mercantile agent, i.e. was made in a way in which a mercantile agent could normally be expected to act. By selling in Warren Street market the rogue had acted in such a way. The third party had taken in good faith, and he therefore acquired good title to the car as against the plaintiffs, whose claim accordingly failed (Court of Appeal).

10. Sale under various common law and statutory powers

Certain sales will operate so as to transfer good title to the buyer despite its lack in the seller. These include sales by pawnbrokers, innkeepers, repairers and so on, and sales under court powers, e.g. to enforce judgment debts. All these are subject to procedures and limitations, but nevertheless they are examples of where the buyer obtains more than the seller had to sell.

Motor vehicles

11. The problem

There remains a final exception to the *nemo dat* rule which must be considered. It will not have escaped the reader's notice in the preceding paragraphs that fraud concerning motor vehicles (by definition, as it were, a highly mobile form of wealth) features frequently. A particular problem arises when a motor vehicle is subject to a hire-purchase (or conditional sale) agreement and is wrongfully sold, possibly through a dealer, to an innocent consumer. It should be understood that the typical hire-purchase transaction comprises negotiations between dealer and consumer, followed by a sale of the agreed vehicle by the dealer to a finance company, who lets the vehicle on hire to the consumer with an option to purchase it after payment of the agreed instalments. Unless and until all the instalments under the agreements are paid, title to the vehicle remains with the finance company. The consumer cannot therefore sell the vehicle in the interim. If he wrongfully purports to do so, title will not in principle pass to the purchaser, however innocent he may be. Section 25 will not avail: see note in preceding paragraph. The third party buying a vehicle subject to a hire-purchase agreement can only acquire title where:

(a) title is 'fed' to him by the outstanding instalments being paid to the finance company (*Butterworth* v. *Kingsway Motors* (1954)); *or*

(b) somewhere along the chain of transactions since the original hire-purchase agreement a sale has been made in market overt to a *bona fide* purchaser, so that the purchaser and all subsequent purchasers acquire title; *or*

(c) Part III of the Hire-Purchase Act 1964 applies.

12. Part III of the Hire-Purchase Act 1964

The relevant provisions will be found in Schedule 4 to the Consumer Credit Act 1974, para. 22. The provisions are complicated but their effect is to give good title to the innocent purchaser who acquires a motor vehicle which is still subject to a hire-purchase or conditional sale agreement. To be protected, the purchaser must take the vehicle in good faith and without notice of the relevant agreement.

13. The scope of the Part III protection

It is essential to appreciate that the protection afforded to the consumer by Part III applies only in respect of motor-vehicles and not other goods which are subject to a hire-purchase or conditional sale agreement. The following points are also important:

(a) Only a 'private purchaser' is protected, defined by s. 29(2) of the HPA 1964 as a purchaser who, at the time of the sale to him, does not carry on the business of a trade or finance purchaser. A 'trade or finance purchaser' is defined as one who, at the time of the sale to him, carries on a business which consists, wholly or partly

(*i*) of purchasing motor vehicles for the purpose of offering or exposing them for sale; *or*

(*ii*) of providing finance by purchasing motor vehicles for the purpose of bailing them under hire-purchase agreements or agreeing to sell them under conditional sale agreements.

(b) The purchaser is protected whether he buys from the original party to the hire-purchase or conditional sale agreement, or from a dealer or finance company to whom the vehicle has been sold. The purchaser is protected even if he himself takes the vehicle on hire-purchase or conditional sale terms. The essential point is that the *first* private purchaser must take in good faith and without notice of the relevant agreement. Then (and only then) do all subsequent purchasers acquire title whether or not they are trade or finance purchasers and irrespective of their knowledge about the original transaction.

> *Stevenson* v. *Beverley Bentinck Ltd* (1976): X, a tool inspector, bought and sold motor vehicles in his spare time. On one particular occasion he bought a second-hand Jaguar car for his own use. Unknown to him it was subject to a hire-purchase agreement and the finance company seized it two months later. HELD: X was not protected by Part III as he had the *status* of a trade purchaser. It was irrelevant that he had bought the vehicle in a private capacity (Court of Appeal).

NOTE: Trade or finance purchasers can protect themselves by becoming members of Hire Purchase Information Ltd ('HPI'). They can then have a search made of the records of HPI to see if a particular vehicle is registered as being the subject of a hire-purchase agreement (about 98 per cent of all hire-purchase agreements relating to cars are registered with HPI). Consumers can search HPI records by applying through one of the motoring organizations or the Citizens' Advice Bureaux, but Part III of the HPA 1964 renders this unnecessary and, indeed, it seems that (apart from Part III) there is no protection for an inquirer if an agreement has not in fact been registered with HPI or is not reported by HPI as having been so registered (*Moorgate Mercantile & Co. Ltd* v. *Twitchings* (1976) HL).

Progress test 3

1.   What does the maxim *nemo dat quod non habet* mean? What are the principal exceptions to the rule?   **(1, 2)**

2.   Will the careless delivery of goods by an owner to another party give rise to an estoppel against the owner if that other party wrongfully sells the goods to a third-party consumer?   **(3)**

3.   What is the market overt rule? Why is it said to be 'capricious in its application'? What proposals for its reform have been advanced?   **(4)**

4.   A takes his car to B, a used car dealer and repairer, for repairs to be carried out. A carelessly leaves the car's registration document lying on the front passenger's seat. B, without A's authority, sells the car to C, who buys in good faith. B absconds with the proceeds. Will C obtain title to the car? **(3, 5)**

5.   D sells his car to E, who pays by cheque. E drives the car away and sells it to F in Warren Street market. After that transaction has occurred, D learns from his bankers that E's cheque has been dishonoured. D informs the police and the Royal Automobile Club, and the car is traced into F's possession. Does F acquire title to the car? Would it make any difference to the legal result if the facts were that D discovered the fraud and notified the police *before* E sold the car to F? **(6, 9)**

6. 'For the doing of justice, the relevant question in this sort of case is . . . which of two innocent parties shall suffer for the fraud of a third. The plain answer is that the loss should be divided between them in such proportion as is just in all the circumstances' (per Devlin LJ in *Ingram* v. *Little* (1961) CA). To what extent has the law adopted this suggestion? **(7)**

7. G, an antique dealer, sells some furniture to H, who pays for it immediately but who desires to have it delivered after his return from holiday in ten days' time. In the interim G inadvertently sells the furniture to J, who takes delivery directly. G is prepared to refund H's money to him, but cannot supply similar furniture, which being antique is irreplaceable. This does not satisfy H. Can H claim the actual furniture from J? **(8)**

8. The K Finance Co. allows L to take a colour television set on hire-purchase terms. L sells the television set to M. Who owns the television? **(9)**

9. Would it make any difference to the question of ownership in question 8 if L had taken a car (and not a television) from the finance company? **(12, 13)**

10. Is it worthwhile for a consumer to request one of the motoring organizations to have a search made of Hire Purchase Information Ltd's records in respect of a vehicle which the consumer is contemplating purchasing? Would the value of a search be any greater if the consumer were a part-time dealer in used cars who was seeking a car for his own private use? **(13)**

4
Pre-contractual statements and contractual terms

1. Introductory

The legal implications of statements made by a trader to the consumer during negotiations differ according to the circumstances in which the statements are made and the parties' intention. Pre-contractual statements may be classified as falling into one or more of the following categories:

(a) trader's 'puff';
(b) representation;
(c) collateral warranty;
(d) express contractual term.

Trader's puff

2. Contractual intention

Certain statements made by a trader are regarded as mere 'puffs' not intended to have any legal consequences. A typical example is the estate agent's 'puff'. But the courts will generally seek to give legal effects to statements which might otherwise be regarded as puffs whenever they can reasonably find, on an objective assessment of the whole circumstances, an intention to create legal consequences.

> *Carlill* v. *Carbolic Smoke Ball Co.* (1893): an advertisement offered to pay £100 to any purchaser of the company's smoke balls who caught influenza after using the product in the prescribed way. HELD by the Court of Appeal: This was not a mere 'puff'. The advertisers intended the statement to

be legally binding since they had stated in the advertisement that £1,000 had been deposited with their bankers 'to show their sincerity'.

Wood v. *Lectrik Ltd* (1932): the manufacturers of an electric comb advertised thus: 'What is your trouble? Is it grey hair? In ten days not a grey hair left. £500 guarantee'. The plaintiff's hair was still grey after ten days' use of the comb, which had, however, scratched his scalp. HELD: The advertisement had a contractual effect so that the plaintiff succeeded in his claim for £500, even though no money had been deposited with bankers.

Lambert v. *Lewis* (1980): The manufacturers of a towing hitch claimed in promotional literature that it was 'foolproof' and 'required no maintenance'. One hitch was supplied through intermediaries to dealers, who in turn sold it to a customer. The hitch proved to have a design defect, causing a serious road accident. One issue in the litigation arising from this incident was whether the manufacturers' claim gave rise to a contract between themselves and the dealers. HELD by the Court of Appeal: The claims in the promotional literature were not intended to be, nor were they in fact, acted on as being express warranties. Therefore they were not binding on the manufacturers. (NOTE: The decision of the Court of Appeal in respect of the proceedings against the manufacturers was affirmed by the House of Lords (1981), but without reference to this particular point.)

Representations

3. Misrepresentation defined

A representation becomes legally significant if it turns out to be false, i.e. a misrepresentation. A misrepresentation may be defined as a false statement of fact which induces the other party to enter into the contract. Apropos this definition, note that:

(a) the statement must purport to be one of fact, not of law, or opinion, or future intention. A statement of opinion, or of future intention, may be held to be one of fact if the maker of the statement at the time of the contract did not hold the opinion or have the intention in question. ('The state of a man's mind is as much a fact as the state of his digestion' — Bowne LJ in *Edgington* v. *Fitzmaurice* (1885).) A half-truth may be a misrepresentation. Silence, where a duty to disclose existed, can be misrepresentation, e.g. on insurance proposal forms;

(b) the statement must *induce* the consumer to contract, though it need not be the sole inducement. If the consumer does not believe the statement or knows it to be false, it clearly cannot induce him to contract, even if he does in fact go ahead with the contract for some reason. There is no duty on the consumer to verify the truth of a representation, however, it is enough if the statement is believed and the fact that it could easily have been verified by the consumer is irrelevant (*Redgrave* v. *Hurd* (1881) CA).

4.   Categories of misrepresentation

A misrepresentation may be either fraudulent, or negligent, or innocent.

(a) *Fraudulent misrepresentation.* A misstatement is made fraudulently if it is made knowingly, or without belief in its truth, or recklessly, careless whether it be true of false (*Derry* v. *Peek* (1889) HL). Fraud is very difficult to prove in practice. A fraudulent misstatement is actionable, in the tort of deceit, whether or not it led to the conclusion of a contract, provided that the consumer suffered loss.

(b) *Negligent misrepresentation.* A false statement of fact will be deemed to have been made negligently unless the party making the statement 'proves that he had reasonable ground to believe and did believe up to the time the contract was made that the facts represented were true': s. 2(1) Misrepresentation Act 1967. Note from s. 2(1) that the burden of proof will be on the trader to disprove negligence, so this course of action is much more attractive for the consumer than an attempt to prove fraud.

(c) *Innocent misrepresentation*, i.e. a false statement honestly made, where the maker of the statement is able to disprove negligence.

5.   Remedies for misrepresentation

The consumer's remedies depend upon the kind of misrepresentation involved although the basic remedy of rescission ('a giving and taking back on both sides') is available, at least at the outset, for any kind of misrepresentation. After all, the least that can be expected if you have been misled into a contract is to be allowed out of it. The problem is that rescission is an equitable remedy and is therefore only available at the discretion of the court. The usual bars to equitable remedies will thus apply, e.g. there must be no undue delay (laches) prejudicial to the defendant; there must be no undue hardship caused to the defendant; there must be no prejudice to innocent third parties; and the consumer must not have affirmed the contract. Restitution must be possible.

(a) *Innocent misrepresentation.* For innocent (non-negligent) misrepresentation, damages will not normally be available to the consumer, but an indemnity for expenses may be available in appropriate cases. Further, by s. 2(2) of the Misrepresentation Act 1967, the court 'if of opinion that it would be equitable to do so, having regard to the nature of the misrepresentation and the loss that would be caused by it if the contract were upheld, as well as the loss that rescission would cause to the other party' may award damages in lieu of rescission. It is essential to understand that damages can only be awarded under s. 2(2) if rescission is available and has not been lost for one of the reasons indicated above. If damages are awarded under s. 2(2), it is in place of, and not as well as, rescission.

(b) *Negligent misrepresentation.* The remedies available here to the consumer are rescission and/or damages: s. 2(1). While rescission is a discretionary remedy, damages are available as of right. It seems that s. 2(1) creates a statutory tort and that damages thereunder will be assessed in tort on the basis of restoring the consumer to the position he would have been in had neither the misrepresentation nor the ensuing contract been made, rather than in contract on the basis of putting the consumer in the position he would have been in had the facts misrepresented been true (*Chesneau* v. *Interhome Ltd* (1983) CA).

(c) *Fraudulent misrepresentation.* Again, the consumer's possible remedies are rescission and/or damages.

6. Exclusion of liability for misrepresentation

By s. 3 of the Misrepresentation Act, as substituted by s. 8 of the Unfair Contract Terms Act 1977, any purported exclusion of liability for misrepresentation is of no effect except in so far as it satisfies a reasonableness test. The onus is on the trader to show that the purported exclusion is fair and reasonable having regard to the circumstances which were, or ought reasonably to have been, known to or in the contemplation of the parties when the contract was made.

> NOTE: Section 3 of the 1967 Act does not prevent a principal from publicly limiting his agent's authority (*Overbrooke Estates Ltd* v. *Glencombe Properties Ltd* (1974); on the other hand a person who makes a representation of fact cannot negative the representation by asserting that the statement is not to be treated as a statement of fact and is not to be relied upon (cf. *Cremdean Properties Ltd* v. *Nash* (1977) CA; *Walker* v. *Boyle* (1982)).

7. *Caveat emptor*
Section 3 of the Misrepresentation Act 1967 (above), together with s. 2(1) (*see* **4**(*b*)), means that the maxim *caveat emptor* (let the buyer beware) has been effectively reversed; it is now the trader who must beware if he commits himself to any statement. The trader can of course always keep silent, for there is no general duty of disclosure (except that a statement true when made but subsequently rendered untrue by changed circumstances before the contract is actually made, must be corrected: *With* v. *O'Flanagan* (1936)).

> NOTE: Section 56 and 75 of the Consumer Credit Act 1974 provide a means where by an action based upon misrepresentation can be brought against a creditor for the wrongdoing of a supplier (*see* **13**).

8. Trade Descriptions Acts
A misrepresentation may also give rise to criminal liability on the part of the trader under the Trade Descriptions Acts (*see* Chap. 19). On the trader's conviction the consumer may, at the criminal court's discretion, obtain a compensation order (*see* Chap. 21).

9. Damages under the rule in *Hedley Byrne* v. *Heller*
In *Esso Petroleum Co. Ltd* v. *Mardon* (1976) CA, it was held that

a negligent misstatement can give rise to damages in tort under the rule laid down by the House of Lords in *Hedley Byrne & Co. Ltd* v. *Heller & Partners Ltd* (1964), even though the statement is a pre-contractual statement amounting to a misrepresentation. In *Mardon*, Lord Denning MR explained the *Hedley Byrne* rule as it operates in this context as follows:

> 'It seems to me that *Hedley Byrne*, properly understood, covers this particular proposition: if a man, who has or professes to have special knowledge or skill, makes a representation by virtue thereof to another — be it advice, information or opinion — with the intention of inducing him to enter into a contract with him, he is under a duty to use reasonable care to see that the representation is correct, and that the advice, information or opinion is reliable. If he negligently gives unsound advice or misleading information or expresses an erroneous opinion, and thereby induces the other side into a contract, he is liable in damages.'

Mardon involved a contract which was formed before the coming into force of the 1967 Act. Generally the consumer would now rely simply on s. 2(1) because *Hedley Byrne* requires the consumer to prove negligence, the reverse of the s. 2(1) position. In *Mardon* Lord Denning said that damages would be the same whether the plaintiff sued in contract or in tort.

Collateral warranties

10. Collateral warranty

It is not always easy to ascertain whether a pre-contractual statement is a mere representation (or misrepresentation, if inaccurate) or whether it is important enough to amount to a binding contractual promise. Such a binding promise or stipulation may be part of the main contract or it may, strictly speaking, be collateral to it, i.e. binding as a separate contract. In the former instance the statement is called a 'warranty' and in the latter it is called a 'collateral warranty', though in practice the expressions are often loosely used interchangeably.

NOTE: This use of the word 'warranty' meaning binding

promise must be carefully distinguished both from the use of the word 'warranty' meaning a guarantee and from the use of the word in a technical sense meaning a subsidiary contractual term as opposed to a major term called a 'condition' (*see* **13, 14**). 'Warranty' is a slippery word. Its meaning is usually derived from its context.

When will a pre-contractual statement amount to more than a mere representation and have the status of a binding contractual stipulation? The answer is that it is a question of intention — not what the parties actually intended, but what the intelligent bystander would infer as to the parties' intention from their words or conduct. The court will readily infer such an intention where the trader states a fact which is or should be within his own knowledge, and of which the consumer is ignorant, or where the trader makes a promise about something which is or should be within his own control. Obviously the courts will normally construe a statement which has been reduced into writing and incorporated into a written contract as a contractual stipulation.

Oscar Chess Ltd v. *Williams* (1957): the consumer acquired a new car on hire-purchase terms through dealers. The consumer traded in his used car in part exchange, describing it in accordance with the registration book as a 1948 Morris. Eight months later the dealers discovered that the true date was 1939 (car models did not then change so frequently in appearance as they do today). It was far too late for the contract to be rescinded for innocent misrepresentation. The dealers claimed damages for breach of warranty. HELD by the Court of Appeal: The consumer had no personal knowledge of the date of manufacture. The dealers on the other hand, as experts, were in a position to check the point. There was accordingly no inference from the facts that a warranty was intended, and the dealers' claim failed.

Dick Bentley Productions Ltd v. *Harold Smith (Motors) Ltd* (1965): the consumer asked a car dealer to find him a 'well-vetted' Bentley car. The dealer found a car which he told the consumer had done only 20,000 miles since it had been fitted with a replacement engine and gearbox;

unknown to either party the car had done 100,000 miles since then. HELD by the Court of Appeal: In contrast to the *Oscar Chess* case, the maker of the statement (the dealer) was in a position to find out the history of the car. The inference had not been rebutted that the representation was intended to be a warranty, i.e. a binding promise. Lord Denning MR explained: 'Looking at the cases once more, as we have done so often, it seems to me that if a representation is made in the course of dealings for a contract for the very purpose of inducing the other to act on it, and it actually induces him to act on it by entering into the contract, that is prima facie ground for inferring that the representation was intended as a warranty.'

NOTE: These two cases show the general policy considerations which are often (not always) applied in circumstances of inequality of bargaining power and expertise. In short, the traders here ought to have known better!

11. Significance of collateral warranty
The significance of the distinction between representation and (collateral) warranty lies in the remedies available to the consumer (damages will be available for breach of warranty). In many circumstances it will not indeed matter into which classification a statement falls, particularly in view of the Misrepresentation Act 1967 which introduced the remedy of damages for negligent misrepresentation. But the distinction could in certain circumstances still have practical consequences. For example, where the trader can prove that he believed on reasonable grounds that his statement was true, he will not be liable in damages under s. 2(1) of the 1967 Act for a misstatement. But if the statement is also a collateral warranty, the trader's honest and reasonably held belief will be no defence to an action for damages for breach of warranty.

Contractual terms

12. Conditions, warranties, intermediate stipulations
Once it has been determined that a statement has the status

of a contractual term, i.e. a binding contractual stipulation, and is not a mere representation, the final analysis which may be required is identification of the kind of term involved. It might be either a condition, or a warranty, or an intermediate stipulation. The point may be important on account of the remedies available on breach of the term, as will be seen. The analysis in the following paragraphs applies to all contractual terms, whether or not they are reduced into writing, and whether express or implied.

13. Conditions

A condition is a vital or major term, breach of which entitles the innocent party to treat the contract as at an end. Additionally, or as an alternative to termination of the contract, the innocent party can claim damages for breach of condition. But in sale of goods cases, the consumer's right to reject the goods and recover his money is subject to s. 11(4) of the SGA, which provides that 'where a contract of sale is not severable and the buyer has accepted the goods or part of them', the buyer can only claim damages for breach of condition by the seller and he cannot reject the goods. (This severe limitation on the consumer's rights will be examined in detail later: *see* 7:**10–13**.)

> NOTE: In *Schuler A.G.* v. *Wickman Machine Tool Sales Ltd* (1974), the House of Lords held that though the use of the word 'condition' in a written contract gave rise to a presumption that the term was in fact technically a condition entitling the innocent party to repudiate the contract, nevertheless if construction of the term as a condition in this sense produced so unreasonable a result that the parties could not have intended it, then the court was free to construe the word 'condition' as an obligation not carrying that technical meaning. In this event, breach of the obligation would not give rise to a right to repudiation of the contract.

14. Warranties

As opposed to a condition, a warranty is a subsidiary or minor term, breach of which entitles the innocent party to damages only. In the context of sale of goods, s. 61 of the SGA defines a warranty as being 'collateral to the main purpose' of the contract.

15. Intermediate stipulations

'An innominate or intermediate term is one the effect of non-performance of which the parties expressly or (as is more usual) impliedly agree will depend on the nature and consequences of breach' (Lord Scarman in *Bunge* v. *Tradax* (1981)).

It used to be thought that contractual terms could only be conditions or warranties. But the House of Lords in *Bunge* v. *Tradax* confirmed a development first affirmed in modern times by the Court of Appeal in the *Hong Kong Fir* case (1961), and it is now clear that a term may, on its true construction, be neither a condition nor a warranty, but an 'intermediate stipulation' or 'innominate term', allowing the innocent party to claim damages on breach, and also to terminate the contract if the consequences of the breach are sufficiently serious (i.e. such as to deprive him of substantially the whole benefit of the contract) — a 'wait and see' approach.

In *Cehave* v. *Bremer* (1975) the Court of Appeal extended this development to contracts for the sale of goods, and held that an express term that goods were to be shipped 'in good condition' was (in effect) an intermediate stipulation, breach of which in the circumstances of the case was not sufficiently serious as to justify rejection of the goods. (*See* also 5:**6**.)

A term is likely to be construed as an intermediate stipulation, in the absence of some express provision or necessary implication to the contrary, where breach of the term might equally well incur either trivial or serious consequences.

16. Significance of contractual terms

Two points may be specially singled out.

(a) Unlike an action for damages under s. 2(1) of the Misrepresentation Act 1967, the trader's honest and reasonably held belief will be no defence to an action for damages for breach of condition or warranty (*see* **11**).

(b) Where breach of condition can be shown, the consumer can repudiate the contract (subject to s. 11(4) of the SGA in sale of goods cases) even though there is no actionable misrepresentation involved.

Progress test 4

1. What is a trader's 'puff'? Are the following statements puffs: (*a*) 'whiter than white'; and (*b*) 'money refunded if not absolutely delighted'? **(2)**

2. Define misrepresentation. **(3)**

3. During negotiations for the sale of a second-hand car. A, the dealer, tells B, the consumer, that the car 'goes like a bomb'. B buys the car. The engine's big end breaks while B is still driving the car home.

(a) Is A's statement a mere 'puff'?
(b) If not, is it an actionable misrepresentation?
(c) If it is, what kind of misrepresentation is it, and what remedy or remedies are available to B in respect thereof? **(2–5)**

4. Can any of the following statements amount to a misrepresentation; (*a*) a statement of law; (*b*) a statement of intention; (*c*) a statement of opinion; and (*d*) a statement by the trader which the consumer does not believe? **(3)**

5. In respect of a misrepresentation, who has the burden of proving (or disproving) (*a*) fraud; and (*b*) negligence? **(4)**

6. When will the equitable remedy of rescission be unavailable to the consumer in respect of a misrepresentation? **(5)**

7. When may the consumer obtain damages as a remedy for a misrepresentation which is (*a*) fraudulent; (*b*) negligent; and (*c*) innocent? **(5)**

8. What does the maxim *caveat emptor* mean? How true is it today so far as misrepresentation is concerned? **(7)**

9. Does the criminal law have any role to play in the sphere of misrepresentation, and if so, is it of any direct help to the consumer? **(8)**

10. Is it worthwhile for the consumer to plead the rule in *Hedley Byrne* v. *Heller* in respect of a misrepresentation?   **(9)**

11. What is a collateral warranty? In what circumstances will the courts construe such a warranty?   **(10)**

12. Is the dealer's statement in question **3** above a collateral warranty? If so, does that fact add to the consumer's remedies in any real way?   **(2, 10, 11)**

13. Distinguish between (*a*) condition; (*b*) warranty; and (*c*) intermediate stipulation, explaining how the different categories of contractual term affect the remedies available to the consumer.   **(13–15)**

14. Does the fact that a written contract describes a term as a 'condition' necessarily mean that the courts will allow the contract to be repudiated by the innocent party, however trivial breach of the term may be in its consequences?   **(13)**

15. Give an example of circumstances in which it will be of value to the consumer to show that a false statement is a contractual condition which a trader has broken, rather than a mere misrepresentation.   **(16)**

5
Implied terms

Terms implied by statute in contracts for the sale of goods

1. The statutory rights

The Sale of Goods Act 1893, ss. 12–15, imposed a series of implied terms which greatly strengthened the position of the consumer. The precise formulation of these terms was revised to the consumer's advantage by the Supply of Goods (Implied Terms) Act 1973. When in this chapter reference is made to any or all of ss. 12–15, it means the Sale of Goods Act 1979.

For the present it may briefly be noted that the provisions of s. 12 of the SGA cannot be excluded from any contract to which the Act applies, nor can the provisions of ss. 13–15 be excluded as against a person dealing as consumer (*see* s. 6 of the Unfair Contract Terms Act 1977, considered in the next chapter). The 'statutory' or 'inalienable' rights contained in ss. 12–15 of the SGA are therefore central planks in the platform of private law rights erected in support of the consumer.

2. Title

In every contract of sale there is 'an implied condition on the part of the seller that in the case of a sale he has a right to sell the goods, and in the case of an agreement to sell he will have such a right at the time when the property is to pass': s. 12(1).

The Act further implies warranties of freedom from undisclosed encumbrances (e.g. a lien) and of the right to quiet possession of the goods: s. 12(2). Normally the condition of right to sell will be all that will concern the consumer, since if there turns out to be an undisclosed encumbrance, or if the consumer's quiet possession of the goods is in the event disturbed, this will generally mean that the seller had no right to sell at the time of the sale.

The condition of right to sell does not apply where it can be inferred from the circumstances of the contract that the seller is only transferring such title as he or a third party may have: s. 12(3). In such cases limited warranties only as to freedom from undisclosed encumbrances and of right to quiet possession will apply: s. 12(4).

> *Rowland* v. *Divall* (1923): the plaintiff bought a car from the defendant and used it for some four months before discovering that the defendant was not the true owner. The plaintiff, who had to return the car to the true owner, claimed for recovery of the full purchase price, as there had been a total failure of consideration. HELD: The plaintiff was entitled to recovery of the full price. There being nothing to accept, no 'acceptance' had taken place limiting the plaintiff to a claim for damages for breach of warranty. Neither was there need for any allowance to be made for the use the plaintiff had enjoyed of the car, because he had paid for ownership and not just the right to use, and he had been exposed, moreover, to an action for conversion of the car.

> *Mason* v. *Burningham* (1949): the buyer of a typewriter had it repaired before learning that it had been stolen. HELD: The buyer could recover the cost of repairs in addition to the purchase price, for breach of the warranty of quiet possession (and *see Greenwood* v. *Bennett* (1972)).

3. Description

In a contract for the sale of goods by description, there is implied a condition that the goods shall correspond with the description; and in a contract for the sale of goods by sample as well as description, a condition that the goods must correspond with both: s. 13(1).

The following points should be noted.

(a) Like s. 12, s. 13 applies to all contracts including purely private sales and not just sales by trader to consumer.

(b) Section 13(3) accords recognition to modern marketing methods: a sale of goods is not to be prevented from being a sale by description by reason only that, being exposed for sale or hire, they are selected by the consumer (as, for instance, in a supermarket).

(c) Crucial to s. 13 is the question of what is covered by the phrase, 'sale by description'. A sale of future or unascertained goods will necessarily be a sale by description, as where goods are ordered from a mail order company. But there may still be a sale by description where the consumer selects goods himself (cf. s. 13(3)) or even carefully examines them himself, so long as there is some measure of reliance on the description. Specific goods may be sold by description 'so long as it is sold not merely as the specific thing, but as a thing corresponding to a description, e.g. woollen undergarments, a hot-water bottle . . .' (Lord Wright in *Grant* v. *Australian Knitting Mills Ltd* (1936)).

> NOTE: In *Harlingdon and Leinster Enterprises Ltd* v. *Christopher Hull Fine Art Ltd* (1990) a painting was wrongly attributed to a German artist when sold between dealers. It was held by the Court of Appeal not to have been a sale by description — because the description was not sufficiently influential in the sale.

(d) Assuming that there is a *sale by description*, which matters are capable of forming part of the *contract description* itself? The 'description' with which the goods must correspond may not necessarily include everything that has been said about the goods. But it will include matters of quantity, packaging and components. It can also include matters of quality, at least in cases where the description characterizes the goods and allows them to be identified (cf. Lord Wilberforce in *Reardon Smith Line Ltd* v. *Hansen-Tangen* (1976) HL: e.g. if a 'waterproof' watch leaks it has been misdescribed in breach of s. 13. This last point could be especially important in a private sale, where s. 14 (*see* **4** and **7**) is not available to the buyer.

> *Beale* v. *Taylor*(1967): a private motorist advertised his car as a 'Herald Convertible, white, 1961, twin carbs'. The rear of the car carried the figures '1200' as an indication of the

Private sale covered criminal law.
ie Trade Descriptions Act
Sale goods Act not opperated then
Today - Just under criminal law

engine's cubic capacity. The car was bought by another private motorist, who later discovered that the vehicle was an amalgam of two vehicles; the back half was a 1200cc model of 1961, whereas the front half was from an earlier model with an inferior engine, welded on to the back. These facts were unknown to the seller. The composite vehicle was unroadworthy. HELD: Although the buyer had examined the vehicle, he had relied (in part) on the description, so that it was a sale by description, and the seller was in breach of s. 13 and the car was not a '1961 Herald' (Court of Appeal).

NOTE: Misdescription under s. 13 will often overlap with misrepresentation (and also with the Trade Descriptions Act 1968: *see* Chaps 19 and 21). If so, an action for breach of s. 13 is likely to prove more fruitful than one for misrepresentation, because the measure of damages under s. 13 will be on the contractual basis, allowing damages for loss of bargain; moreover, the seller's honest and reasonably held belief will be no defence to an action under s. 13 (cf. 4:5(*b*) and **16**(*a*)).

4.   Merchantable quality

This is the cornerstone of English civil consumer law: 'Where the seller sells goods in the course of a business, there is an implied condition that the goods supplied under the contract are of merchantable quality, except that there is no such condition:

(a) as regards defects specifically drawn to the buyer's attention before the contract is made; *or*
(b) if the buyer examines the goods before the contract is made, as regards defects which that examination ought to reveal': s. 14(2).

Section 14(2) is quoted here verbatim because the wording requires noting with particularity. Thus:

(a) 'In the course of a business': The requirement of merchantability applies only to sales in the course of a business. But the sale need not be in the usual course of business of the seller. 'Business' includes a profession and the activities of any government department or local or public authority: s. 61(1) SGA.
(b) 'Goods supplied under the contract' can include packaging,

instructions for use (*see Wormell* v. *RHM Agriculture (East) Ltd* (1986) in 5 below) and even goods supplied unintentionally.

> *Geddling* v. *Marsh* (1920): bottles of mineral water were sold, the bottles remaining the property of the seller and to be returned to him after use. A bottle burst, causing injury. HELD: The 'goods' were unmerchantable.

> *Wilson* v. *Rickett Cockerell & Co. Ltd* (1954): a lady ordered 'coalite' fuel. A detonator was accidentally included amongst the coalite delivered and it exploded causing injury. HELD: The goods supplied were not merchantable because coalite accompanied by a detonator was not fit for burning (Court of Appeal).

(c) Specified defects: Other than for minor blemishes covered by a phrase such as 'shop-soiled', a general disclaimer (e.g. 'damaged') will not do; if the seller wishes to escape liability he must 'specifically' draw the defect to the customer's attention.

(d) Examination of the goods: There is no obligation on the buyer to examine goods before purchase (though it may be prudent to do so). If the goods are examined, however, it seems from the wording of s. 14(2)(*b*) ('that examination') that the test of what ought to be revealed is subjective, i.e. what the *actual* examination should have revealed, and not objective in the sense of what a reasonable examination would reveal. So a buyer would not be required to discover as much on a cursory examination of the goods as he would on a full examination of them (*Bristol Tramways* v. *Fiat Motors* (1910) CA; for an apparently contrary view, cf. *Thornett & Fehr* v. *Beers & Sons* (1919)).

(e) Repairs: Section 14(2) requires that the goods 'are' of merchantable quality, not merely that they can be made to be merchantable. Therefore if goods are unmerchantable, the fact that they can easily be repaired is no defence.

> *Jackson* v. *Rotax Motor Cycle Co.* (1910): a high proportion of motor horns delivered under a contract for the sale of goods was dented and scratched. HELD: The horns were unmerchantable notwithstanding that they could easily have been repaired at small expense.

(f) Minor defects: This is a different issue from ease of repair.

Consumer dissatisfaction with goods which have minor or cosmetic defects has been one of the key factors behind current proposals for redefining merchantable quality.

5. Statutory definition of merchantable quality

Literally translated, 'merchantable' means 'saleable' or 'marketable', an interpretation which by itself does not greatly advance our understanding. In fact, in the past the courts have been much exercised by the meaning of the term. The Supply of Goods (Implied Terms) Act 1973 introduced a definition, now to be found in s. 14(6) of the Sale of Goods Act 1979. It reads: 'Goods of any kind are of merchantable quality ... if they are as fit for the purpose or purposes for which goods of that kind are commonly bought as it is reasonable to expect having regard to any description applied to them, the price (if relevant) and all other relevant circumstances.'

Whilst this definition does give some guidance it also creates, or at least perpetuates, a real difficulty: the definition is firmly anchored to the concept of fitness, i.e. *usability*. According to this notion the test of merchantability is, do the goods work? A test of this nature leaves unclear whether minor or cosmetic defects are covered by the term. An alternative approach which has been suggested is to align the meaning of merchantability with the notion of *acceptability* to the fully informed buyer acting reasonably. Of course one could argue that the usability test does cover minor or cosmetic defects because consumers buy goods not just with the purpose of using them but for the status and enjoyment which they confer — the scratched finish on the new washing machine interferes with this wider purpose even if the clothes are washed whiter than white. Similarly, with new cars, as Mustill LJ said (in *Rogers* v. *Parish (Scarborough) Ltd* (1987): 'Starting with the purpose for which "goods of that kind" are commonly bought, one would include in respect of any passenger vehicle not merely the buyer's purpose of driving the car from one place to another but of doing so with the appropriate degree of comfort, ease of handling reliability and, one may add, of pride in the vehicle's outward and interior appearance.' *See* also *Shine* v. *General Guarantee* (1988).)

But it is unfortunate if the law in its uncertainty should force reliance on somewhat artificial arguments of this kind. That the problem of minor or cosmetic defects is acute can be seen from decided cases (e.g. *Cehave* v. *Bremer*, or the Scottish case of *Millars of Falkirk Ltd* v. *Turpie*, below), none of which, however, is decisive of the point.

> NOTE: It will be appreciated that one factor influencing the courts is that if they do hold a new car (say) to be unmerchantable on the grounds of a minor defect, then the consumer acting promptly can reject it, leaving the dealer with a greatly depreciated asset on his hands; on the other hand if the car is held to be merchantable then the consumer has no remedy at all outside the manufacturer's warranty.

Leaving aside the question of minor or cosmetic defects and turning to the definition of merchantable quality as it stands, it appears that multi-purpose goods must be fit for all their normal purposes. Further, higher price may sometimes imply higher quality (cf. *Brown* v. *Craiks* (1970) HL), but in consumer contracts price will not generally be relevant. 'Sale' goods, for instance, must not be substandard unless the defect is specified (*see* **4(c)**). Equally, the consumer cannot demand higher quality simply on the ground that, failing to 'shop around', he paid a steep price for a standard product.

> *Godley* v. *Perry* (1960): a catapult which broke after three days' use (sadly blinding in one eye the boy who had purchased it), HELD to be unmerchantable.

> *Wren* v. *Holt* (1903): beer with arsenic in it, HELD to be unmerchantable.

> *Daniels* v. *White and Tarbard* (1938): lemonade contaminated by carbolic acid, HELD to be unmerchantable.

> *Grant* v. *Australian Knitting Mills Ltd* (1936): underpants containing excessive sulphite, HELD to be unmerchantable (Privy Council).

> *Heil* v. *Hedges* (1951): pork chops containing parasitic worms, HELD to be merchantable, because had the chops been cooked properly (which they had not been), the worms would have died.

Cehave v. *Bremer* (1975): part of a consignment of citrus pulp pellets, to be used as an ingredient in cattle food, was damaged by over-heating. HELD by the Court of Appeal: The goods were nevertheless merchantable. The fact that they could be resold only at a reduced price was not conclusive; they had in fact ultimately been used to make cattle feed in much the same way as they would have been had they still been sound.

Millars of Falkirk Ltd. v. *Turpie* (1976): a new car was found to have an oil leak in the power-assisted steering system. Although adjusted once by the dealers it leaked again the following day. HELD by the Inner House of the Court of Session: The car was nevertheless merchantable. The defect was minor, creating no real risk and easily repairable by the dealers who were willing to do so; it was common for new cars to have some defects. (Cf. s. 14(6) SGA: '. . . as fit for the purpose . . . as it is reasonable to expect . . . ')

Wormell v. *RHM Agriculture (East) Ltd* (1986): it was held in this case that the 'goods' supplied within the contract included the instructions for use. Here a herbicide spray carried inadequate instructions concerning its efficacy if used late in the season.

Aswan Engineering v. *Cupdine Ltd* (1987): this case shows that goods need only to be reasonably fit for their purpose. Liquid waterproofing compound was packed in heavy duty plastic pails which collapsed under the intense heat on a quayside in Kuwait. The pails were nevertheless of merchantable quality, despite the fact that they collapsed in these extreme conditions.

6. Redefinition of merchantable quality
The Law Commission have concluded that the present statutory definition of merchantable quality is unsatisfactory and should be replaced by a new definition. Two alternative formulations were suggested, namely:

(a) 'the goods should be of such quality as would in all the circumstances of the case be fully acceptable to a reasonable buyer,

who had full knowledge of their condition, quality and characteristics'; *or*
(b) 'the standard of quality in the goods should be tested against some neutral adjective such as "appropriate", "suitable", or "proper".'

These recommendations very nearly saw the legislative light of day (*see* **9**, below).

7.   Fitness for purpose

Where the seller sells goods in the course of a business and the buyer, expressly or by implication, makes known to the seller (or, where the purchase price or part of it is payable by instalments and the goods were previously sold by a credit-broker to the seller, to that credit-broker) any particular purpose for which the goods are being bought, there is an implied condition that the goods supplied under the contract are reasonably fit for that purpose, whether or not that is a purpose for which such goods are commonly supplied, except where the circumstances show that the buyer does not rely, or that it is unreasonable for him to rely, on the skill or judgment of the seller (or credit-broker) s. 14(3) SGA. (A credit-broker is a person acting in the course of a business of effecting introductions of individuals desiring to obtain credit to other persons providing such credit: s. 61(1).)

The following are points to note.

(a) Overlap with s. 14(2): in many cases the consumer will have a cause of action under s. 14(2) and (3) (and possibly under s. 13 too). For example, neither the catapult in *Godley* v. *Perry*, nor the underpants in *Grant* v. *Australian Knitting Mills Ltd*, were fit for their purpose, quite apart from being unmerchantable (*see* **5**). The likelihood of overlap should never be overlooked. Nevertheless there will be occasions when only s. 14(3) will assist the consumer, namely where the consumer has made known to the seller a particular purpose demanding a higher standard of the goods than the standard required of the goods for fitness for normal purposes.
(b) As with the implied condition of merchantability, the fitness for purpose condition applies only where the sale is 'in the course of a business' (*see* **4**).
(c) Where the purpose is obvious, it is made known by implication

(*Priest* v. *Last* (1903) CA, where a hot-water bottle which burst was held to be unfit for its purpose). But if the purchaser requires the goods for an abnormal purpose, that purpose must expressly be made known to the seller (*Griffiths* v. *Peter Conway Ltd* (1939) CA, where the purchaser of a Harris Tweed coat did not disclose the fact of her abnormally sensitive skin to the seller; HELD: That there was no breach of what is now s. 14(3) when the coat caused the purchaser to contract dermatitis).

(d) The onus of proof is on the seller to show that the consumer did not rely, or that it was unreasonable for him to rely, on the seller's skill or judgment. In the case of a purchase from a retailer, 'the reliance will be in general inferred from the fact that a buyer goes to the shop in the confidence that the tradesman has selected his stock with skill and judgment' (Lord Wright in *Grant* v. *Australian Knitting Mills Ltd*).

(e) The goods need only be 'reasonably' fit for their purpose. Thus the pork chops were reasonably fit in *Heil* v. *Hedges* because they would have been harmless had they been cooked properly; on the other hand the underpants in *Grant* v. *Australian Knitting Mills Ltd* were not fit because it is not reasonably to be expected that the consumer will wash such garments before wearing them for the first time.

> *Bartlett* v. *Sidney Marcus Ltd* (1965): the consumer was informed that the clutch of a car he was contemplating purchasing was defective. Offered the choice of having the dealers put the clutch right, or a price reduction instead, he accepted a £25 price reduction. In the event, after 300 miles of motoring the necessary repair to the clutch cost him £45 more than anticipated. HELD by the Court of Appeal: The car was merchantable and fit for its purpose. It was not unfit merely because the defect proved more serious than anticipated. The car was usable even though not perfect. 'A buyer should realize that, when he buys a second-hand car, defects may appear sooner or later; and in the absence of express warranty, he has no redress' (Lord Denning MR).

> *Crowther* v. *Shannon Motor Co.* (1975): the consumer bought a second-hand Jaguar car from dealers. The car had done over 82,000 miles ('hardly run in' for a Jaguar, said the

dealers). Three weeks and 2,300 miles later the engine seized up completely. The previous owner gave evidence that the car was 'clapped out'. HELD by the Court of Appeal: While the buyer of a second-hand car might expect minor repairs to be necessary sooner or later, replacing the engine was not a minor repair. The car was not reasonably fit for its purpose at the time of sale.

8. Durability

There is no express reference in s. 14 SGA to any requirement that goods need be merchantable or fit for their purpose other than at the time of sale (but *see* 9 below). Of course, if goods prove defective shortly after purchase, that is evidence (as in *Crowther v. Shannon Motor Co.* above) that the goods must have been defective at the time of sale. The Law Commission in 1979 recommended in their *Report on Implied Terms in Contracts for the Supply of Goods* (Law Com. No. 95) that there should be introduced into the SGA an express provision that the goods should continue to be of such quality and fitness as can reasonably be expected at any particular time after their supply. But meanwhile it seems that the House of Lords have recognized a concept of reasonable durability — not yet fully worked out — in advance of legislation. In *Lambert* v. *Lewis* (1981) Lord Diplock (with whom all their Lordships agreed) declared, 'The implied warranty of fitness for a particular purpose relates to the goods at the time of delivery under the contract of sale in the state in which they were delivered. I do not doubt that it is a continuing warranty that the goods will be fit for that purpose for a reasonable time after delivery, so long as they remain in the same apparent state as that in which they were delivered, apart from normal wear and tear. What is a reasonable time will depend on the nature of the goods . . .'

9. The Consumer Guarantees Bill 1990 (a close-run thing)

The Law Commission's work in 1979 and their later Report (*Sale and Supply of Goods,* Law Com. 160, Cmnd 137 1987) nearly resulted in legislation. Their recommended redefinition was reworked and inserted into the ill-starred Consumer Guarantee Bill 1990. The Bill was introduced by Martyn Jones MP who had won the Private Members' Ballot in 1989. It was an amalgam of the Law Commission's work and a National Consumer Council

[handwritten: no be Redefine]

Report on a new form of consumer guarantee which would have
been attached (at the manufacturer's option) to a prescribed list of
goods. Had the manufacturer decided not to so 'guarantee' his
products, he would have been obliged to say so. However, after a
deal of Parliamentary wrangling both parts of the Bill were lost.
So we are left where we started. Nevertheless it seems likely that
the Law Commission's redefinition will soon return to the
Parliamentary agenda.

There would be new definition of the quality required of goods
supplied under contracts to which the SGA applies. Goods would
have to be of 'satisfactory' quality. That is, they would be of a
quality which would have to be regarded by a reasonable person
as satisfactory having regard to the description, the price and other
relevant circumstances. This quality would include 'state' and
'condition' and an open list of other features: *[handwritten: submitted few times + failed]*

(a) fitness for all the purposes for which goods of the kind in
question are commonly supplied;
(b) appearance and finish;
(c) freedom from minor defects; *[handwritten: Conserv. committed to putting this top their agenda]*
(d) safety; *and*
(e) durability.

The redefined requirement of quality would not extend to any
matter making the quality of goods unsatisfactory:

(a) which is specifically drawn to the buyer's attention before the
contract is made;
(b) where the buyer examines the goods before the contract is
made, which that examination ought to reveal; *or*
(c) in the case of a contract for sale by sample, which would have
been apparent on a reasonable examination of the sample.

10. Spare parts and facilities for servicing goods

Although many businesses do provide spare parts and
servicing facilities, unless otherwise agreed there is no legal duty
requiring them to do so. Instead, voluntary Codes of Practice
approved by the Office of Fair Trading are seen as being of
increasing value to consumers, e.g. the Codes produced
respectively by the Association of Manufacturers of Domestic

Electrical Appliances (AMDEA), by the Radio, Electrical and Television Retailers' Association (RETRA), and by the Electricity Boards (*see* **4–6**). These Codes were revised in 1984, although the RETRA Code is being redrawn for republication in late 1990.

11. Sale by sample

In a contract for sale by sample there are implied conditions that the bulk shall correspond with the sample in quality, and that the buyer shall have a reasonable opportunity of checking this; and that the goods shall be free from any defect, rendering them unmerchantable, which would not be apparent on reasonable examination of the sample: s. 15 SGA.

> *Godley* v. *Perry* (1960): the retailer who was liable under what is now s. 14(2) and (3) of the SGA to the boy injured by the defective catapult which the boy had purchased from him (*see* **5, 7**) in turn sued the wholesaler. HELD: The latent defect in the catapult was a breach of s. 15.

12. Strict liability

Once breach of an implied term is proved, liability is strict, i.e. the trader has no defence even if he can prove that all reasonable care had been taken. The trader cannot, for instance, escape liability to his customer simply by blaming the manufacturer. This is an important aspect of civil consumer law based in contract rather than tort. In contract the liability is strict, in tort it is based in fault. That is, somebody must be blamed.

> *Frost* v. *Aylesbury Dairy Co. Ltd* (1905): typhoid germs were found in milk. The dairy as seller was held liable under what is now s. 14(3) of the SGA, even though the exercise of all reasonable skill by the dairy could not have detected the defect which caused the germs.

Terms implied by statute in hire-purchase agreements

13. Hire-purchase

In relation to hire-purchase agreements, the statutory rights in ss. 12–15 of the SGA are repeated in substance in ss. 8–11 of the

Supply of Goods (Implied Terms) Act 1973 (as amended). This is why this piece of legislation is entitled the Supply (rather than Sale) of Goods (Implied Terms) Act. The consumer is in exactly the same position so far as the substantive conditions as to title, description, quality, fitness and samples are concerned (and as regards the prohibition on exclusion clauses), whether he buys outright or with the assistance of some form of financial accommodation. In the latter case, however, the consumer's remedies for breach of implied condition may be superior, as in hire-purchase transactions the right to reject goods is not lost on acceptance (*see* **7:13**). Furthermore, the redefinition of 'merchantable' to 'satisfactory' quality within the SGA and noted above (*see* **9**) would extend to contracts of hire-purchase within the 1973 Act.

Terms implied under Part I of the Supply of Goods and Services Act 1982

14. Contracts for the transfer of goods

These contracts were defined in Chapter 1 (*see* **1:5, 6**). They include contracts for the supply of work and materials and contracts of exchange or barter. Part I of the SGSA clarifies the common law position and provides that implied in all contracts for the transfer of goods are obligations as to title (s. 2), correspondence with description (s. 3) and sample (s. 5), merchantable quality and fitness for purpose (s. 4).

Sections 2–5 above, including the definition of merchantable quality, are modelled exactly on the corresponding provisions in the Sale of Goods Act. However, unlike the SGA, the SGSA does not define the words 'condition' and 'warranty'. (Nor, for that matter, does the Supply of Goods (Implied Terms) Act 1973 define them.) Arguably this could give the courts greater flexibility concerning the appropriate remedies for breach of the terms, though it is probable that the courts will not avail themselves of this opportunity but will treat the words as implying the normal consequences for breach of condition or warranty as the case may be (*see* **4:13, 14**).

It may be added that the 1982 Act, like the 1973 Act, does not contain any equivalent to the restrictive s. 11(4) SGA, and accordingly the right to reject goods will only be lost on affirmation of the contract under common law rules (*see* 7:**10–13**). The question of remedies apart, the technical classification of the contract whereby goods are acquired can now make no difference to the customer's legal position as regards description and quality etc., and in practice this will be true too with regard to exclusion clauses (*see* 6:**20**).

15. Hire
    Part I of the SGSA similarly implies terms modelled on the Sale of Goods Act in all contracts for the hire of goods (*see* 1:**11**), i.e. implied conditions as to correspondence with description (s. 8) and sample (s. 10), merchantable quality and fitness for purpose (s. 9). The nature of hire means that the Sale of Goods Act model for the implied terms about *title* cannot be exactly followed. Instead, the SGSA imposes an implied condition as to the right of the bailor to transfer possession of the goods for the period of the hire, and an implied warranty as to the right of the hirer to quiet possession of the goods for this period (s. 7). These implied terms do not affect any contractual right of the bailor to repossess the goods.

    NOTE: The effect of ss. 7–10 is basically to clarify the common law position. For control over exclusion clauses, *see* 6:**20**.

Terms implied in contracts for the supply of services under Part II of the Supply of Goods and Service Act 1982

16. Services
    A contract for the supply of a service was defined in Chapter 1 (*see* 1:**14**). Part II of the SGSA was based upon a report from the National Consumer Council and arguably did nothing more than put existing common law obligations into statutory form in relation to such contracts.

17. Care and skill
    There is an 'implied term' in a contract for the supply of a service that the supplier acting in the course of a business will carry

out the service with 'reasonable care and skill': s. 13. 'Business' includes a profession and the activities of any government department or local or public authority: s. 18.

The use of the words 'implied terms' here and elsewhere in Part II of the Act leaves the door open for the courts to interpret the terms as intermediate stipulations or innominate terms, with the customer's remedies dependent upon the nature and consequences of the breach (*see* 4:**15**).

> NOTE: When things go wrong with a contract for the supply of work and materials, the consumer may need to ascertain whether the fault lies in the work or the materials. The reason for this is that liability for breach of the statutory obligations as to the description, fitness or quality of the goods is strict (cf. **11**), whereas if the fault lies in the performance of the services part of the contract, then under s. 13 lack of reasonable care and skill must be proved.

The professional or skilled person — architect, engineer, accountant, solicitor, doctor, etc. — has to exercise the ordinary skill of an ordinary competent person exercising that particular profession or art: cf. *Bolam v. Friern Hospital Management Committee* (1957). There is no implied warranty that the professional person will achieve the desired result, however. 'The surgeon does not warrant that he will save the patient. Nor does the solicitor warrant that he will win the case' (Lord Denning MR in *Greaves & Co. (Contractors) Ltd* v. *Baynham Meickle & Partners* (1975) CA).

18. Time
There is an 'implied term' in a contract for the supply of a service that the supplier acting in the course of a business will carry out the service within a reasonable time (a question of fact), unless the contract itself fixes the time or leaves it to be fixed in an agreed manner or determined by a previous course of dealing: s. 14.

19. Price
Where the price in a contract for the supply of a service has not been fixed or left to be determined in an agreed manner or previous course of dealing, then there is an 'implied term' that a reasonable charge is payable for the service: s. 15.

20. Exclusion clauses

Exclusion of obligations arising under Part II of the SGSA will normally be covered by the reasonableness test under the Unfair Contract Terms Act 1977. This is an extraordinary mixture of consumer protection. In a contract for work and materials no exclusion is possible in a consumer sale for liability arising from breach of the implied terms relating to the materials (SGSA Part I), whereas for the work element exclusion is possible but limited by the new test of reasonableness. This situation is the result of a political compromise. It has not, as yet, produced bizarre effects in court. However, the business supplier cannot in any circumstances exclude or restrict liability for death or personal injury resulting from negligence (cf. s. 2 of the Unfair Contract Terms Act: *see* 6: **12**).

21. Exclusion orders

The Secretary of State has power under s. 12(4) to provide by order that one or more of ss. 13–15 of the Act shall not apply to services of a description specified in the order. Under this power orders have been made excluding from s. 13 the services of (*inter alia*):

(a) an advocate in court or before any tribunal, inquiry or arbitrator (this exclusion extends to the carrying out of preliminary work directly affecting the conduct of the hearing); *and*

(b) services rendered by an arbitrator in his capacity as such.

Obligations (if any) owed by such persons will accordingly be governed by the common law.

> *Rondel* v. *Worsley* (1969): a client sued the barrister who had conducted his case, for alleged negligence. HELD: On public policy grounds a barrister owes no legal duty of care to the client in the conduct and management of litigation. Were it otherwise the barrister could not properly fulfil his duty to the court and to the administration of justice (House of Lords).

> *Saif Ali* v. *Sydney Mitchell & Co.* (1978): the House of Lords reviewed *Rondel* and held by a majority that a barrister's immunity in respect of pre-trial work existed only where

the particular work was so intimately connected with the conduct of the cause in court that it could fairly be said to be a preliminary decision affecting the way that the cause was to be conducted at the hearing. (Lords Wilberforce, Diplock and Salmon thought that the same immunity attaches to a solicitor acting as an advocate in court as attaches to a barrister.)

22. Dual liability

Where the consumer has a complaint, particularly a complaint in respect of unsatisfactory services, he may have a cause of action against the supplier sounding in both contract and tort. For example, the supplier of services whose negligence causes loss or injury may be liable both in contract for breach of the implied term to exercise reasonable care and skill, and in tort for the tort of negligence. The Court of Appeal have now made it clear that there is no reason why judgment should not be entered on both heads, contract and tort (*Batty* v. *Metropolitan Property Realisations Ltd* (1978)).

> *Midland Bank Trust Co. Ltd* v. *Hett, Stubbs & Kemp* (1978): solicitors negligently omitted to register an option as an estate contract under the Land Charges Act 1925. HELD: The relationship of professional adviser and client imposed a duty of care irrespective of liability in contract (applying *Hedley Byrne & Co. Ltd* v. *Heller & Partners Ltd* (1964)). The solicitors were therefore liable in tort, and also in contract.

Progress test 5

1. What implied terms as to title does the Sale of Goods Act impose? Are they conditions or warranties? Do they apply where it is clear that the seller is transferring only a limited title? (2)

2. What is the meaning of 'merchantable quality' as used in the Sale of Goods Act? Does it cover minor or cosmetic defects? What modifications have been suggested? How would they improve the position of the consumer? (5–9)

3. B, a consumer, buys a car from A, a dealer. The contract describes the car as 'new'. After B has taken delivery of the car, he discovers that it has already done 5,000 miles, that it has a large dent in one wing, and that the gearbox is defective in that the car will not go into reverse. Consider whether A is in breach of:

(a) s. 13 of the SGA (implied undertakings in sale by description);
(b) s. 14(2) of the SGA (implied undertaking as to quality);
(c) s. 14(3) of the SGA (implied undertaking as to fitness).
(3–9)

4. C, a consumer, buys a second-hand car from D, a dealer. The car is sold 'with all faults'. C gives the car a test drive and agrees to buy it for £1,500. Soon after C has taken delivery of the car, the back axle breaks. Consider whether D is in breach of s. 14(2) and /or s. 14(3) of the SGA. (4, 7)

5. How long do goods have to remain fit for their purpose? (8, 9)

6. E buys an expensive new bone china tea-set. The first time E uses the set, a cup is accidentally broken. When E tries to replace the broken cup, the retailer tells E that there are no more cups in stock and that the manufacturer does not make that pattern any longer. Does E have any rights in the matter? (10)

7. F buys a new carpet from a sample examined by F at the retailers. The carpet is duly fitted at F's home, but already in the first month of use it shows clear signs of disintegration. F discovers that the carpet is made of a mixture of wool and synthetic substances, whereas the sample carpet was made of 100 per cent wool. Is the retailer in breach of contract? If so, would the retailer have any defence if he could prove that the fault lay entirely with the manufacturers of the carpet? (11, 12)

8. G is contemplating purchasing a new washing-machine. G has the money to pay cash for the machine, but is wondering whether his rights as a consumer as regards the quality of the machine will be greater in any way if he acquires it on hire-purchase terms. Advise G. **(13)**

9. J, a garage proprietor, services and repairs cars. Consider the legal position of the respective consumers in the following situations:

(a) J fits a new clutch on L's car. The clutch does not work.

(b) J adjusts and relines the brakes on L's car. The brakes fail shortly thereafter and L is injured.

(c) J services M's car. M objects to the amount of the bill and to the fact that the servicing took over a week to complete. **(14, 17, 19)**

10. N, an architect, prepares plans for an extension to O's house. The roof of the extension is unsatisfactory and leaks, partly for design reasons and partly because of the poor materials used by P, the builder. What is the legal position of O? **(14, 17)**

11. R hires a self-drive van to transport furniture. The van breaks down. What right does R have against the owner of the van? **(15)**

12. S, a plumber, fixes a new washer to T's kitchen tap. S claims £50 for the job, saying that there is a call-out charge of £35. Does T have to pay the £50? **(19)**

6
Legal control of exemption clauses

Control under the common law

1. Freedom of contract

In the nineteenth century the prevalent political and economic philosophy of *laissez-faire* found its legal expression in the doctrine of freedom of contract. According to this doctrine, the parties to a contract were free to make whatever bargain they liked, and, subject to certain requirements of public policy, the law would uphold the results of the parties' negotiations. The notion of *consensus ad idem* — was at the conceptual heart of the law of contract. If the contracting parties had freely agreed the terms of the contract, then those terms, including any exemption clause, governed the contractual relationship.

2. Judicial intervention

While the courts have developed no comprehensive theory with which to protect consumer interests, they have developed a number of techniques for moderating the otherwise severe effects of the doctrine of freedom of contract as applied to exemption clauses. These techniques, still relevant (except as noted below) after the passing of the Unfair Contract Terms Act, may be summarized as falling under one of the following headings:

(a) incorporation;
(b) misrepresentation;
(c) the *contra proferentem* rule;
(d) fundamental breach.

NOTE: The doctrine of inequality of bargaining power has already been overshadowed in the field of exemption clauses by the Unfair Contract Terms Act 1977 (*see* **8** *et seq.*) — cf. Lord Scarman's judgment in the House of Lord's case of *National Westminster Bank plc* v. *Morgan* (1985).

3. Incorporation

Generally, where the consumer signs a contract, he will be bound by its terms, and he cannot argue that he did not read the contract or understand it (*L'Estrange* v. *Graucob* (1934) CA). The signed document merely has to be construed and applied. But where the contract is not signed, the question may arise whether printed conditions have been incorporated into the contract at all; if they have not, no application of them can be possible, for they are ineffective.

Where printed conditions are not regarded by the courts as constituting a contractual document, they are not incorporated into the contract and so are ineffective. Receipts and tickets are frequently not regarded as constituting contractual documents, and therefore conditions contained or referred to on them are not binding. It is true that in the nineteenth century there were a number of 'ticket cases' in which conditions contained or referred to on railway tickets were held to be of contractual effect and binding, providing either that the consumer knew that the ticket was issued subject to conditions, or that the other contracting party had taken reasonable steps to draw the consumer's attention to that fact (*Parker* v. *South Eastern Railway Co.* (1877) CA). But exclusion clauses in the context of public transport are now controlled by legislation, and the modern tendency in other contexts is to regard a ticket as a non-contractual document (cf. *Thornton* v. *Shoe Lane Parking Ltd* (1971) CA, below).

Further, even where a set of printed conditions is capable of constituting a contractual document, the document will not be incorporated into the contract, and so the conditions will be ineffective, if the document with its conditions is introduced after offer and acceptance have been concluded. The exception to this occurs where there has been a consistent previous course of dealing between the parties. Here the consumer may be bound by conditions contained in a document which would not otherwise have been incorporated into the contract.

NOTE: Of course even if an exclusion clause is incorporated

into a contract it cannot, by reason of the doctrine of privity (*see* 9:2), benefit a person not a party to the contract. Thus a negligent employee or agent will not normally be protected by an exclusion clause incorporated into a contract between his employer and the consumer, even though the clause purports to cover employees (*Adler* v. *Dickson* (1955) CA).

Chapelton v. *Barry UDC* (1940): the consumer hired two deck-chairs at 2*d*. each. He was given two tickets on the back of which was printed a condition (which he did not read) purporting to exempt the defendant council from liability. The condition was not contained on the notice by the stack of chairs on the beach giving details of the rate of hire. The canvas on one of the chairs was defective and the consumer was injured. HELD: The printed condition was ineffective and the consumer was entitled to damages. The ticket was a mere voucher or receipt for payment. The notice constituted the offer, which the consumer accepted by taking the chairs. The ticket was not a contractual document (Court of Appeal).

Thornton v. *Shoe Lane Parking Ltd* (1971): the consumer parked his car in the defendants' automatic car-park, which he had not previously used. A machine pushed out a ticket for customers to take as they drove into the car-park. The consumer did not read the words which he had seen printed on the ticket. They stated that the ticket was issued subject to the conditions displayed inside the premises. One condition thus displayed purported to exclude liability not only for damage to cars but also for injury to customers, howsoever caused. The consumer was injured, partly through the defendants' negligence. HELD: The exempting condition was ineffective. The defendants had not done what was reasonably sufficient to draw the customer's attention to the particular condition, which was framed in unusually wide terms. The wider the exempting condition, the more that would be necessary to draw attention to it, as (Lord Denning said: 'printed in red ink with a red hand pointing to it, or something equally startling' (Court of Appeal).

Olley v. *Marlborough Court Ltd* (1949): the consumer, a guest at an hotel, had her furs stolen from the hotel bedroom where she had left them having locked the bedroom door. On one of the walls of the bedroom was a notice stating: 'The proprietors will not hold themselves responsible for articles lost or stolen'. HELD: The contract was concluded before the consumer was shown to the bedroom and the notice was not therefore incorporated into the contract.

Hollier v. *Rambler Motors (AMC) Ltd* (1972): the consumer made an oral contract with the defendant garage proprietors for repairs to his car. A fire broke out in the garage through the defendant's negligence causing damage to the car. The defendants had carried out work for the consumer on some three of four occasions during the preceding five years and on at least two occasions the consumer had signed an invoice stating: 'The company is not responsible for damage caused by fire to customers' cars on the premises. Customers' cars are driven by staff at owner's risk'. The consumer sued in respect of the damage caused to his car. HELD: The consumer succeeded in his claim. Three of four dealings over a period of five years could not amount to a course of dealing such as to incorporate the exemption clause. Nor was the clause itself (even supposing it to have been incorporated) apt to exclude liability for negligence (Court of Appeal). (But cf. *Kendall* v. *Cillico* (1969) where a course of dealing involving 100 transactions over three years was sufficient to incorporate an exclusion clause, and consider incorporation by trade usage — whether or not the parties have dealt together before: *Cointat* v. *Myham* (1914).

4. Misrepresentation
If the effect of an exemption clause is misrepresented to the consumer, then the clause will be ineffective. Likewise, an oral warranty or assurance made to the consumer may bind the trader and overrule any exemption clause contained in the written contract.

Curtis v. *Chemical Cleaning and Dyeing Co.* (1951): the consumer took a wedding dress to the cleaners. When asked

to sign a document the consumer was told that it excluded
liability for damage to beads and sequins only. In fact the
document, which the consumer did not read, excluded
liability for 'any damage howsoever arising'. The dress was
stained through the negligence of the cleaners. HELD: The
cleaners were liable for the damage and could not rely on
the exemption clause as the extent of it had been
misrepresented to the consumer (Court of Appeal).

J. Evans & Son (Portsmouth) Ltd v. *Andrea Merzario Ltd*
(1976): an oral assurance was given that goods would be
loaded under deck. In the event certain goods were loaded
on deck and were lost overboard during the voyage. HELD:
An exemption clause in the written contract excluding
liability for loss and giving the carriers complete freedom as
to the means of transportation was overridden by the oral
assurance and was ineffective (Court of Appeal).

5. The *contra proferentem* rule

The courts do not like exemption clauses. An exemption
clause will be construed against the person putting it forward
(*contra proferentem*), i.e. against the person seeking to rely on it. If
there is any ambiguity, the consumer is entitled to take advantage
of it and to escape liability. Limitations on liability are more
generously construed than claims which attempt to exclude
liability entirely (*Ailsa Craig Fishing Co. Ltd* v. *Malvern Fishing Co.
Ltd* (1983) HL).

Hollier v. *Rambler Motors (AMC) Ltd* (*see* **3**): the exemption
clause, even if it had been incorporated into the contract,
was held not widely enough drafted to exclude liability
arising from negligence (Court of Appeal).

NOTE: As a matter of construction the words 'howsoever
caused' added to an exclusion of all liability will be effective in
excluding liability even where the cause of damage or loss is
negligence (subject to the provisions of the Unfair Contract
Terms Act).

Levison v. *Patent Steam Carpet Cleaning Co. Ltd* (1977): a
valuable Chinese carpet disappeared at the cleaners' in

unexplained circumstances. The printed contract stated that
'All merchandise is expressly accepted at the owner's risk;.
The consumers sued in respect of the missing carpet.
HELD: They were entitled to succeed. The exemption
clause was not sufficiently clear to exempt liability for loss
due to the cleaners' fundamental breach of contract (Court
of Appeal).

6. Fundamental breach

The doctrine of fundamental breach asserts that breaches of
contract which are so fundamental as to defeat the central purpose
of the contract cannot normally be excluded. The House of Lords
have held this doctrine to be a rule of construction only (the *Suisse
Atlantique case* (1967), reaffirmed in *Photo Production Ltd* v. *Securicor
Transport Ltd* (1980) HL), i.e. exemption clauses are presumed not
to be intended to cover a fundamental breach of contract. The
significance of the doctrine in consumer contracts was
substantially diminished by the advent of the Unfair Contract
Terms Act in 1977, as it is unlikely that an exemption clause which
is construed so as to survive fundamental breach will be held to
satisfy the reasonableness test (*see* **14**). Indeed it could be argued
that the doctrine has been so adversely affected by the *Photo
Productions* case and UCTA that it no longer exists for any practical
purpose.

7. The common law after the Unfair Contract Terms Act

The above mentioned judicial techniques for moderating the
effects of exemption clauses remain of value to the consumer after
the coming into force of the Unfair Contract Terms Act 1977.
Where the Act makes an exemption clause totally void, the Act is
all that the consumer need rely on; but where the Act subjects an
exemption clause to the reasonableness test, the consumer might
be better placed under the common law where the common law
strikes down the clause altogether, for otherwise the trader might
succeed in satisfying the reasonableness test. Better to find that a
clause has not been incorporated into the contract, than to find it
incorporated and to run the risk of it then being shown to be
reasonable.

Control under the Unfair Contract Terms Act 1977

8. Unfair Contract Terms Act: no new duties

It should be appreciated at the outset that the title of the Unfair Contract Terms Act (in this chapter referred to as 'the Act' or 'UCTA') is somewhat misleading. The Act does not deal with unfair contracts as such, but merely with one source of unfairness, namely exemption clauses. (On the other hand the Act controls certain non-contractual as well as contractual exemption clauses.) The original title given to the Bill — the Avoidance of Liability Bill — was perhaps more appropriate, for that is what the legislation actually controls. Let it be stressed that the Act does not create new duties: it only controls or prevents the exclusion of liability which would otherwise have arisen under existing rules.

9. Consumer protection

Notwithstanding the point made in the preceding paragraph, the UCTA is of the greatest significance as a measure of consumer protection. But its scope goes beyond this. Often both business and consumers are protected, though not always to an equal extent, as will become apparent.

10. Scope of the Unfair Contract Terms Act

Schedule 1 of the Act gives the exceptions were the Act does not apply. The list given includes:

(a) any contract of insurance;

(b) any contract so far as it relates to the creation, transfer or termination of an interest in land.

(The other exceptions are not of primary concern to the consumer.)

11. Business liability

The control by the Act of exemption clauses applies (subject to the exceptions noted below: *see* **19, 22**) only to business liability. This is an important point to remember, and references to liability in the rest of this chapter mean (unless otherwise stated) liability arising in the course of a business. 'Business liability' is defined in s. 1(3) as 'liability for breach of obligations or duties arising:

(a) from things done or to be done by a person in the course of a business (whether his own business or another's); or
(b) from the occupation of premises used for business purposes of the occupier' (but liability of an occupier for breach of duty towards visitors using premises for recreational or educational purposes is not a business liability unless granting the access falls within the business purposes of the occupier: s. 1(3) UCTA as modified by s. 2 of the Occupiers' Liability Act 1984).

'Business' includes a profession and the activities of any government department or local or public authority: s. 14.

12. Avoidance of liability for negligence
'A person cannot by reference to any contract term or to a notice given to persons generally or to particular persons exclude or restrict his liability for death or personal injury resulting from negligence': s. 2(1).

But while liability for negligence causing personal injury or death cannot be excluded, the position is different in the case of financial loss or damage to property. In this case, continues the Act, 'a person cannot so exclude or restrict his liability for negligence except in so far as the term or notice satisfies the requirement of reasonableness': s. 2(2).

13. Meaning of 'negligence'
Here and elsewhere in the Act (*see* **17. 18**) 'negligence' means 'the breach:

(a) of any obligation, arising from the express or implied terms of a contract, to take reasonable care or exercise reasonable skill in the performance of the contract;
(b) of any common law duty to take reasonable care or exercise reasonable skill (but not any stricter duty);
(c) of the common duty of care imposed by the Occupiers' Liability Act 1957 . . . ': s. 1(1).

14. The reasonableness test
The requirement of reasonableness referred to in s. 2 and elsewhere in the Act is defined only broadly, in s. 11.

(a) In relation to a contract term, the requirement of reasonableness is that the term shall have been a 'fair and reasonable one to be included having regard to the circumstances which were, or ought reasonably to have been, known to or in the contemplation of the parties when the contract was made': s. 11(1).

(b) In relation to a non-contractual notice, the requirement of reasonableness is that it should be 'fair and reasonable to allow reliance on it, having regard to all the circumstances obtaining when the liability arose or (but for the notice) would have arisen': s. 11(3).

(c) Small businesses: with these in mind, s. 11(4) provides that where a contract term or notice seeks to restrict liability to a specified sum of money, and the question arises whether the term or notice satisfies the requirement of reasonableness, regard shall be had in particular to

    (*i*) the resources of the defendant, *and*

    (*ii*) how far it was open to him to cover himself by insurance.

(d) The burden of proving that the requirement of reasonableness has been satisfied is on the party seeking to rely on the exemption clause: s. 11(5).

> *George Mitchell Ltd* v. *Finney Lock Seeds Ltd* (1983): seed merchants supplied farmers with cabbage seed of the wrong variety and inferior quality. There was an exemption clause limiting the merchants' liability to the contract price (some £200), whereas the loss suffered by the farmers on failure of the crop was nearly £62,000. HELD: On its true construction the clause was effective to limit the sellers' liability (applying the *Ailsa Craig* case (*see* 5)); but the clause failed to satisfy the reasonableness test (now in s. 11 UCTA) because: (*a*) the normal practice of the merchants was to negotiate settlements of justified claims without relying on the clause; (*b*) the defective seed was supplied through the negligence of the merchants' associate company; (*c*) the merchants could have insured against claims without materially increasing prices (House of Lords) cf. *Green* v. *Cade* (1978) which involved the sale of seed potatoes on the standard terms of the trade association.

> *Woodman* v. *Photo-Trade Processing Ltd* (1981): photographic processors lost the plaintiff's photographs which he had

taken of a friend's wedding. A clause limited liability to replacement of the missing films with new ones. HELD: the clause was unreasonable because: (*a*) it excluded liability for negligence as well as accident; (*b*) the plaintiff had been given no choice but to accept the clause imposed by the processors in a monopoly situation — in particular a two-tier pricing system should have been available with a higher degree of liability being accepted if the consumer chose to pay the higher price; (*c*) no insurance facility was offered. Damages to include disappointment and distress were awarded in the sum of £75 (Exeter County Court).

Smith v. *Bush* (1989): it was held here that the valuers of the house for mortgage purposes owed a duty of care to the purchasers. This they had purported to exclude. This exclusion was subjected to the test of reasonableness. It failed — in the light of the imbalance of bargaining power between the parties, the unlikelihood of further and independent advice and the practical consequences of the inadequacy of the survey.

15. Meaning of exemption clause
The definition of exemption clause may be usefully considered at this point, although the definition is applicable not only to s. 2, already considered, but generally to the various controls in the Act. The meaning of exemption clause is extremely wide, because to the extent that the Act prevents the exclusion or restriction of any liability it also prevents:

(a) making a liability or its enforcement subject to restrictive or onerous conditions (e.g. by limiting liability to a specified sum or specifying a time limit within which the liability must arise);
(b) excluding or restricting any right or remedy (e.g. by disallowing rescission of a contract and allowing only damages as a remedy), or subjecting a person to any prejudice in consequence of his pursuing any such right or remedy (e.g. by requiring him to indemnify a third party as the 'price' of the remedy);
(c) excluding or restricting rules of evidence or procedure (e.g. by using clauses like 'the customer's signature on this form shall be conclusive evidence that . . .'): s. 13.

NOTE: For the purposes of ss. 2 and 5–7 (*see* **18–20**), terms and notices which prevent a 'relevant obligation of duty' from arising will also be treated as exemption clauses: s. 13(1). (A 'relevant obligation or duty' is presumably one which but for the term or notice in question would otherwise have arisen.) On the other hand note that a written agreement to submit disputes to arbitration is not to be treated under the Act as an exemption clause: s. 13(2) (and *see* the Consumer Arbitration Agreements Act 1989 which prohibits preclusions from courts).

16. Liability arising in contract

Section 3 of the Act restricts the exclusion of liability arising in contract. Where one party to a contract deals as consumer *or* on the other's written standard terms of business, then, as against that party, the other cannot, unless the reasonableness test is satisfied, rely on a contract term which:

(a) excludes or restricts any liability in respect of breach of contract; *or*

(b) purports to entitle him to render a contractual performance substantially different from that which was reasonably expected of him, or to render no performance at all: s. 3.

NOTE: The reasonableness test was considered above (*see* **14**); the meaning of the phrase 'deals as consumer' is more conveniently considered later (*see* **21**).

17. Unreasonable indemnity clauses

A person dealing as consumer cannot, unless the requirement of reasonableness is satisfied, by required by any contract term to indemnify another person in respect of liability for negligence or breach of contract: s. 4.

The example of a case governed by s. 4 given during the progress of the Bill through Parliament was of indemnity clauses found on the back of cross-Channel car ferry tickets. These clauses often required passengers to indemnify the shipowner against damage to third parties caused by negligent handling of the car by the ship's crew. Such clauses must now satisfy the reasonableness test.

18. Manufacturers' guarantees

'In the case of goods of a type ordinarily supplied for private use or consumption, where loss or damage:

(a) arises from the goods proving defective while in consumer use; *and*
(b) results from the negligence of a person concerned in the manufacture or distribution of the goods,

liability for the loss or damage cannot be excluded or restricted by any contract term or notice contained in or operating by reference to a guarantee of the goods': s. 5(1). Goods 'are to be regarded as "in consumer use" when a person is using them, or has them in his possession for use, otherwise than exclusively for the purposes of a business': s. 5(2)(*a*).

Section 5 applies to manufacturers' guarantees, and not 'as between the parties to a contract under or in pursuance of which possession or ownership of the goods passed': s. 5(3). So retailers' guarantees are not covered by s. 5. In such cases the consumer must look to s. 2 (*see* **12**) or s. 6 (*see* **19**) for protection. Note that where s. 5 does apply, it makes the exemption clause void; there is no question of applying a reasonableness test.

19. Sale and hire-purchase

The UCTA 1977 replaces with minor modifications the controls first contained in the Supply of Goods (Implied Terms) Act 1973. By s. 6(1) of the UCTA, liability for breach of s. 12 of the SGA 1979 (implied undertakings as to title) or s. 8 of the 1973 Act (the corresponding provisions for hire-purchase), cannot be excluded or restricted by reference to any contract term. Further, as against a person dealing as consumer, liability for breach of ss. 13, 14 or 15 of the SGA 1979 (implied undertakings as to conformity of goods with description or sample, or as to their quality or fitness for a particular purpose), or ss. 9, 10 or 11 of the 1973 Act (the corresponding provisions for hire-purchase), likewise cannot be excluded or restricted by reference to any contract term: s. 6(2) UCTA.

NOTE: (1) As against a person dealing otherwise than as consumer, a clause excluding liability under ss. 13, 14 or 15 of the SGA or the corresponding hire-purchase provisions, may be allowed in so far as it satisfies the reasonableness test: s. 6(3). Guidelines as to the application of the reasonableness test in these non-consumer cases are given in Schedule 2 to the UCTA. Factors to be taken into account include the relative bargaining position of the parties. (The reader should note carefully that the Schedule 2 guidelines only apply to the attempted exclusion of the statutory rights.) (2) The controls in s. 6 of the UCTA extend not only to business liability, but to liability arising under any contract of sale of goods or hire-purchase: s. 6(4) (contrast s. 7, *see* **20**).

20. Contracts for the transfer of goods and contracts of hire

Section 7 of the UCTA applies to contracts, other than sale or hire-purchase, for the passing of possession or ownership of goods. In other words s. 7 relates to contracts which are regulated by Part I of the Supply of Goods and Service Act 1982. Section 7 (as amended by the 1982 Act) applies only to the business supplier, but otherwise reflects the s. 6 controls (*see* **19**). Thus the implied terms as to title cannot be excluded; and the implied terms as to conformity of goods with description or sample, or as to their quality or fitness for a particular purpose, cannot be excluded against a person dealing as consumer (and as against others cannot be excluded except in so far as is reasonable).

NOTE: The exclusion of business liability for breach of the implied terms about the right to transfer possession etc. in contracts of *hire* (*see* **5:14**) is subject to the reasonableness test irrespective of the status of the hirer: s. 7(4) UCTA (as amended).

21. Dealing as consumer

It is now necessary to examine the exact meaning of the phrase 'deals as consumer' (*see* **16, 17, 19, 20**). Section 12(1) gives the definition: 'A party to a contract 'deals as consumer' in relation to another party if:

(a) he neither makes the contract in the course of a business nor holds himself out as doing so; *and*

(b) the other party does make the contract in the course of a business; and

(c) in the case of a contract governed by the law of sale of goods or hire-purchase, or by section 7 of this Act, the goods passing under or in pursuance of the contract are of a type ordinarily supplied for private use or consumption'.

Note that:

(*i*) the buyer on a sale by auction is not in any circumstances to be regarded as dealing as consumer: s. 12(2);

(*ii*) 'it is for those claiming that a party does not deal as consumer to show that he does not': s. 12(3), i.e. the burden of proof is on the trader.

> *R&B Customs Bankers Co. Ltd* v. *United Dominions Trust Ltd* (1988): here a shipping company (shipping brokers) bought a car for its directors to use. The company was only five years old, but it had bought two or three cars before. Nevertheless, it was held for the purposes of invalidating an exemption clause covering quality that the purchase had been made other than 'in the course of business'. That is, the company had 'dealt as a consumer' within s. 12 of UCTA. (*See* also *Rasbora Ltd* v. *J.C.L. Marine Ltd* (1977) for a similar decision taken on earlier legislation.)

22. Misrepresentation

Section 8 of the UCTA modifies s. 3 of the Misrepresentation Act 1967. Section 3, as modified, subjects to the reasonableness test contained in s. 11(1) of the UCTA (*see* **14**) any contract term which would 'exclude or restrict:

(a) any liability to which a party to a contract may be subject by reason of any misrepresentation made by him before the contract was made; *or*

(b) any remedy available to another party to the contract by reason of such misrepresentation'.

Note that:

(*i*) the burden of proof that the exemption clause satisfies the reasonableness test is on the party seeking to rely on the clause;

(*ii*) s. 3 of the Misrepresentation Act is *not* confined to the exclusion of business liability for misrepresentation. Section 3 is of general application to all contracts.

Control by the criminal law

23. Use of void exemption clauses

While the consumer's statutory rights under the SGA and the Supply of Goods (Implied Terms) Act are made inalienable by s. 6 of the UCTA, there is nothing in these Acts to prevent a trader purporting to exclude liability for breach of the statutory rights in the expectation that some at least of his customers will be taken in by the clause and on that account fail to assert their rights (e.g. by using phrases such as 'bought as seen'). Accordingly, an Order (*see* **24**) under the Fair Trading Act 1973 has been made, invoking the sanctions of the criminal law (*see* 17:**7–14**).

24. Consumer Transactions (Restrictions on Statements) Order 1976

This Order, as amended by the Consumer Transactions (Restrictions on Statements) (Amendment) Order 1978, makes it a criminal offence for persons who, in the course of a business, sell goods to consumers or supply them under hire-purchase or trading stamp agreements:

(a) to purport by notices (Art. 3(*a*)), advertisements (Art. 3(*b*)), or statements on or with goods (Art. 3(*c*) and (*d*)), to apply terms which are void by virtue of s. 6 of the UCTA or inconsistent with a warranty implied by the Trading Stamps Act 1964; *or*
(b) to supply statements about the consumer's rights against the supplier or about the obligations accepted by the supplier in respect of goods which are defective or not fit for a purpose or do not correspond with a description, unless there is in close proximity to any such statement a clear and conspicuous statement to the effect that the statutory rights of the consumer are not affected (Art. 4).

> NOTE: Rules similar to those contained in Art. 4 are applied to manufacturers and wholesalers (Art. 5) *see* 9:**5**.

By way of illustrating the effect of the Order, consider the once common practice of displaying a notice at a sales counter stating something like: 'No cash refunds'. This practice would constitute a criminal offence under Art. 3(*a*). because it purports to restrict the consumer's statutory rights. If the goods were (say) unmerchantable, the consumer would be entitled to have his money back on rejection of the goods for breach of condition. The consumer cannot be obliged to accept less than this entitlement (assuming always that the right of rejection has not been lost through 'acceptance' of the goods). He does not have to accept a credit note, or repairs or replacements, and any notice etc. which asserts the contrary will constitute an offence.

Hughes v. *Hall* (1981): second-hand cars were sold 'as seen and inspected'. HELD: This phrase prima facie purported to exclude the implied term of correspondence with description under s. 13 SGA (because the words meant that the sale would not be a sale by description) and therefore was capable of contravening the Order (Divisional Court).

Cavendish-Woodhouse Ltd v. *Manley* (1984): a suite of furniture was sold in a sale. The words, 'bought as seen' were written on the cash sale invoice. HELD: The Order was not thereby contravened. The sale (it was common ground) was not a sale by description anyway, since the purchaser had chosen specific goods which he had inspected. The words merely confirmed that the purchaser had seen beforehand the goods which he had purchased. The words were not intended to exclude liability for hidden defects or other breach of s. 14 SGA (Divisional Court) (and *see Cavendish Woodhouse Ltd* v. *Wright* (1985)).

NOTE: Somewhat anomalously, the Order does not prohibit exemption clauses void by virtue of s. 7 UCTA (*see* **20**). The use of all sorts of void exemption clauses (e.g. void under s. 2 UCTA (*see* **12**)) is a widespread practice and is not generally prohibited by the criminal law.

Progress test 6

1. In what circumstances would conditions printed on a receipt or ticket be binding on a consumer? **(3)**

2. If the consumer in *Olley* v. *Marlborough Court Ltd* had been an habitual visitor to the hotel, would the exempting condition have been binding on her? **(3)**

3. Summarize the techniques which the courts have developed for dealing with objectionable exemption clauses. Do these techniques continue to be relevant in consumer protection in view of the provisions of the UCTA? **(2, 7)**

4. A notice prominently displayed at the counter of a firm of dry cleaners states: 'Customers are advised that curtaining materials may shrink during cleaning. No responsibility can be accepted for any shrinkage which does occur.' Would the condition bind the consumer in either of the following alternative situations?

(a) The consumer asked the counter assistant whether particular curtains would be likely to shrink, and was told: 'Definitely not.'
(b) The shrinkage occurred solely through the negligence of the cleaners. Would it make any difference to your answer in this second situation if the facts were that the words 'howsoever caused' had been added at the end of the printed condition? **(4, 5, 12)**

5. Give the meaning of 'business liability' as defined in the UCTA, and indicate the provisions of the Act which may also be applicable to the purported exclusion of liability other than business liability. **(11, 19, 22)**

6. In what circumstances can liability for negligence be excluded? What does 'negligence' mean in the context of the UCTA? **(12, 13)**

7. (a) What is the requirement of reasonableness for the purposes of the UCTA (*i*) in relation to a contract term, and (*ii*) in relation to a non-contractual notice? Is it for the consumer to prove that the requirement of reasonableness has not been satisfied?
(b) How does the requirement of reasonableness take special account of the needs of small businesses? **(14)**

8. Consider whether the following printed condition would be an exemption clause within the meaning of the UCTA: 'This film will be accepted by the Company for processing and printing only on the basis that its value does not exceed that of the film itself. In any event the Company's liability is limited to replacement of the film itself'. **(15)**

9. How does the UCTA seek to protect the consumer against the attempted exclusion of liability for misfeasance or nonfeasance of a contract? Is this same protection available in any circumstances when one business contracts with another business? **(16)**

10. How does the UCTA afford the consumer protection in respect of (*a*) manufacturers' guarantees; (*b*) retailers' guarantees? **(18)**

11. Are the rights contained in ss. 12–15 of the SGA (and the corresponding provisions for hire-purchase) 'inalienable'? Can the same be said of the similar terms implied in contracts of hire or contracts for work and materials? **(19, 20)**

12. (a) What does the UCTA mean by the expression 'deals as consumer'? Does the private buyer at an auction sale 'deal as consumer'? Does the seller, via the auctioneer, deal in the course of a business?
(b) G, a secretary, buys a word processor for use at home in a purely private capacity. Does G 'deal as consumer'? On whom is the burden of proving (or disproving) the point? **(21)**

13. To what extent is it possible for a party to a contract to exclude liability for misrepresentation? **(22)**

14. Comment on the legality of a notice displayed by a cash desk in a shop and stating: 'Money cannot be refunded on sale goods'. Would it make any difference if the notice read instead: 'Sale goods cannot be exchanged'? **(24)**

15. List the exemption clauses and non-contractual notices which are (*a*) totally void by virtue of the UCTA; and (*b*) valid only in so far as they satisfy the reasonableness test. **(12, 16–20, 22)**

7

Performance of consumer contracts for the sale of goods

Delivery

1. What constitutes delivery

Delivery (the 'voluntary transfer of possession from one person to another': s. 61 SGA) is usually effected by a simple physical transfer of the goods to the consumer. A common alternative is the transfer of the means of control, as where a car's ignition key is handed over to the buyer. Other methods of delivery are possible, but unlikely to arise in consumer transactions. The possibility of constructive delivery is worth noting, however. For example, the consumer may be in possession before the contract of sale is made, as where goods are sent on approval. Here, when the consumer adopts the transaction (cf. SGA s. 18, Rule 4), he thereupon possesses the goods as owner rather than as bailee; constructive delivery has been effected. Finally, it may be noted that were the seller is by the contract authorized to send the goods to the consumer by carrier, delivery to the carrier is prima facie delivery to the consumer: s. 32(1). In this case the seller must make such contract with the carrier on behalf of the consumer as is reasonable having regard to the nature of the goods and all the other circumstances. s. 32(2)

2. Delivery dates

The time of delivery will not generally be of the essence (i.e. condition) in a consumer contract, unless a contrary intention can be derived from the terms of the contract (cf. s. 10 SGA). If the delivery date is not met, or, in the absence of any specified delivery date, if delivery is not made within a reasonable time, the consumer can make time of the essence by giving reasonable notice to that effect to the trader. (The consumer can do this even if he had previously waived a delivery date in the hope of receiving the goods eventually.) If time is of the essence, or has by reasonable notice been made of the essence, failure by the trader to meet the delivery date is a breach of condition and entitles the consumer to repudiate the contract.

> NOTE: Similar rules as to making time of the essence apply to contracts for the supply of services. Cf. too s. 14 SGSA (*see* 5:**18**).

> *Charles Rickards Ltd* v. *Oppenheim* (1950): the plaintiffs contracted to build a car body on to a Rolls-Royce chassis, the work to be completed by 20th March. The car was not ready by that date. The defendant did not then repudiate the contract, but pressed for delivery. At the end of June the defendant gave four weeks' notice for delivery, failing which he would regard the contract as repudiated. Delivery was tendered in October. The defendant rejected the car, and was sued by the plaintiffs. HELD: The defendant was entitled to reject the car. Although he had waived the original delivery date, by giving reasonable notice he had made the new delivery date of the essence (Court of Appeal).

3. Place of delivery

Most retailers will deliver goods to the consumer's home when the goods are such that the consumer cannot reasonably be expected to take them away with him. Sometimes a charge is made for delivery. Nevertheless, the strict legal position is that unless otherwise agreed (expressly or impliedly), the place of delivery is the retailer's premises: s. 29(2). But where it is agreed that the goods are to be delivered to the consumer's home, this must be done within a reasonable time: s. 29(3), and the retailer and his servants or agents must exercise reasonable care. Delivery at the consumer's home may be made to anyone who appears to be authorized to receive the goods (*Galkbraith & Grant Ltd* v. *Block* (1922)). Delivery must be made at a reasonable hour: s. 29(5).

4. Expenses

The seller must bear the expenses of putting goods into a deliverable state, unless otherwise agreed: s. 29(6).

5. Delivery by instalments

The consumer is under no obligation to accept part only of the goods: s. 30(1). Further, unless otherwise agreed, the consumer is under no obligation to accept delivery by instalments: s. 31(1).

Acceptance

6. What constitutes acceptance

Acceptance and delivery are correlative concepts, yet delivery by the seller by no means necessarily involves acceptance by the consumer. Acceptance takes place when:

(a) the consumer tells the seller that he has accepted the goods; *or*

(b) the goods are delivered and the consumer either does an act inconsistent with the seller's ownership, or he retains the goods beyond a reasonable time without telling the seller that he rejects them: s. 35.

> NOTE: if the consumer signs an 'acceptance note' on delivery of the goods this is likely to amount to acceptance within rule (*a*) above. It is doubtful whether the Unfair Contract Terms Act 1977 can help the consumer here, as an acceptance note will probably not be a 'contract term' within the scope of the relevant sections of that Act.

7. Examination of the goods

The consumer is not deemed to have accepted the goods unless and until he has examined them or has had a reasonable opportunity of examining them: s. 34. By s. 35(1) of the Sale of Goods Act 1979, an act inconsistent with the seller's ownership will not amount to acceptance (*see* **6**) unless there has occurred the examination of the goods, or reasonable opportunity for the examination of them, envisaged by s. 34.

8.   Acceptance under the Consumer Guarantees Bill 1990

Had the 1990 Bill (*see* Chapter 5) successfully passed into law, the Law Commission's work on acceptance would have seen the legislative light of day. It is thought that these ideas will be reintroduced. If and when they do, the impact upon the doctrine of acceptance might well be as follows. Under s. 35 SGA the consumer will be deemed to have accepted the goods:

'subject to subsection (2) below —

(a) when he intimates to the seller that he has accepted them, *or*
(b) when the goods have been delivered to him and he does any act in relation to them which is inconsistent with the ownership of the seller.

(2) Where goods are delivered to the buyer, and he has not previously examined them, he is not deemed to have accepted them under subsection (1) above until he has had a reasonable opportunity of examining them for the purpose —

(a)   of ascertaining whether they are in conformity with the contract *and,*
(b) in the case of a contract for sale by sample, of comparing the bulk with the sample.

(3) Where the buyer deals as consumer or (in Scotland) the contract of sale is a consumer contract, the buyer cannot lose his right to rely on subsection (2) above by agreement, waiver or otherwise.

(4) The buyer is also deemed to have accepted the goods when after the lapse of a reasonable time he retains the goods without intimating to the seller that he has rejected them.

(5) The questions that are material in determining for the purposes of subsection (4) above whether a reasonable time has elapsed include whether the buyer has had a reasonable opportunity of examining the goods for the purpose mentioned in subsection (2) above.

(6) The buyer is not by virtue of this section deemed to have accepted the goods merely because (for example) —

(a) he asks for, or agrees to, their repair by or under an arrangement with the seller, *or*

(b) the goods are delivered to another under a sub-sale or other disposition.

(7) Where the contract is for the sale of goods making one or more commercial units, a buyer accepting any goods included in a unit is deemed to have accepted all the goods making the unit.

In this subsection, 'commercial unit' means a unit division of which would materially impair the value of the goods or the character of the unit.

9. Rejected goods

If the consumer refuses to accept the goods, having the right to do so, he does not have to return them to the seller but need only tell him that he refuses to accept them: s. 36. If the seller then fails to collect the goods and the consumer is put to expense in respect of them, that expense may be recovered by the consumer (*Kolfor Plant Ltd* v. *Tilbury Plant Ltd* (1977)).

10. Effect of acceptance

Once goods have been accepted in a non-severable contract, the consumer can no longer reject them: s. 11(4). This is so even if the grounds for rejection are breach of the Sale of Goods Act 'statutory rights'. The consumer's right to reject defective goods is thus severely restricted by s. 11(4), which when it applies leaves the consumer with a claim for damages only. Section 11(4) reads:

> 'Where a contract of sale is not severable, and the buyer has accepted the goods or part of them the breach of any condition to be fulfilled by the seller can only be treated as a breach of warranty, and not as a ground for rejecting the goods and treating the contract as repudiated, unless there is an express or implied term of the contract to that effect.

> NOTE: a contract is severable where it can be regarded as a series of 'mini-contracts' (e.g. a contract for delivery of goods by instalments will be severable if each instalment is to be paid for separately, but not where payment is to be by one lump sum: s. 31(2)).

11. 'Acceptance' of goods having latent defect

By the time a latent defect comes to light, the consumer may be held to have accepted the goods by having used them (an act inconsistent with the seller's ownership) or by having retained them beyond a reasonable time. The consumer could not then reject the goods, but could only claim damages. On the other hand, it could be argued:

(a) that use of the product is the only method of giving it the reasonable examination which is a prerequisite of acceptance; *and* (b) that use of itself would not be inconsistent with the seller's ownership unless it had the effect that the consumer could no longer return the goods in substantially the same condition as when purchased. English law is unclear on the point. In recent years the calculation of what amounts to be a reasonable time within which to exercise the right to reject (or lose it — *see* 11) has given rise to some extraordinary cases. The most notorious of these is probably *Bernstein* v. *Parsons Motors (Golders Green) Ltd* (1987) where driving a car for a little over 140 miles over a period of less than three weeks was held to be unreasonably long.

12. Repairs, replacements, credit notes

Another difficulty arises where a consumer complains about a defect and repeatedly submits the goods for repair, perhaps under a guarantee. The courts might interpret this as 'acceptance' (but cf. *Farnworth Finance Facilities Ltd* v. *Attryde: see* 13 though that case is not of direct authority on contracts of sale). The moral for the consumer is, if repairs are agreed upon, to make them without prejudice to the right to reject should the repair job prove to be unsatisfactory.

Equally problematical is the situation where the consumer complains and accepts a replacement article from the retailer for the defective one. If the replacement itself proves defective, is the consumer nevertheless deemed to have 'accepted' it? Probably not, if the replacement rescinds the original contract and substitutes a new one. Indeed, the replacement article is presumably obtained under a contract for the transfer of goods (contract of exchange: *see* 1:8) and is accordingly governed by Part I of the Supply of Goods and Services Act 1982. Part I contains no provision corresponding with s. 11(4) SGA and so the more generous common law rule that the right to reject is only lost on affirmation of the contract would apply: *see* **13.** Of course, if the consumer takes replacement goods under a manufacturer's guarantee without reference back to the retailer, that must amount to acceptance as an act inconsistent with the seller's ownership.

Where the consumer accepts a credit note in exchange for defective goods, that again would seem to rescind the original contract and to substitute a new one, presumably governed by the SGSA as a contract of barter, though the point is not free from doubt.

> NOTE: If the consumer can justifiably reject goods, he cannot be obliged to take a credit note, or repairs, or a replacement instead. Likewise, neither can the consumer insist upon repairs or a replacement (unless under a guarantee). Naturally the parties may always agree to the contrary.

13. Conditional sale and hire-purchase agreements
The consumer is better placed under these agreements so far as the right to reject goods and treat the contract as repudiated is concerned.

(a) *Conditional sale agreements.* Section 11(4) of the SGA does not apply to a conditional sale agreement where the buyer deals as consumer within the UCTA: s. 14(1) of the Supply of Goods (Implied Terms) Act 1973 (as amended).

(b) *Hire-purchase agreements.* These are not controlled by the Sale of Goods Act (*Helby* v. *Matthews* (1895) HL), and the common law rule about rejection in these cases is much less restrictive. In hire-purchase (and conditional sale) agreements the right to reject is lost on affirmation of the contract. But since hire-purchase involves continuing obligations, breach of contract for defective goods will be a continuing breach so long as the defects remain unremedied, and the right to treat the contract as repudiated will continue also (*Yeoman Credit Ltd* v. *Apps* (1962) CA).

> *Farnworth Finance Facilities Ltd* v. *Attryde* (1970): the consumer took a motor cycle on hire-purchase terms. Many things were defective and the machine was repeatedly returned for repairs. After more than four months and some 4,000 miles, the rear chain broke, whereupon the

consumer repudiated the contract. HELD: The consumer was entitled to do so. He had not affirmed the contract, but had indicated by his conduct that he would not accept the motor cycle unless the defects were remedied. The consumer therefore recovered all payments he had made, no deduction for use being imposed by the court as the consumer had been subject to a great deal of inconvenience (Court of Appeal).

Progress test 7

1. In April A ordered a new colour television set from B Ltd. No delivery date was specified. By July the set had still not been delivered. Advise A. Would it make any difference to your advice if the agreement had said: 'Delivery to be made in time for Wimbledon fortnight'? **(2)**

2. C buys a three piece suite of furniture from D Ltd. C pays the full purchase price. C is then told to collect the furniture himself. Advise C. If the facts were the D Ltd agreed to deliver the suite, but tendered only one piece on the day fixed for delivery with the promise to deliver the remaining pieces the next week, would C be entitled to (*a*) reject the part tendered; and (*b*) repudiate the whole contract? **(2, 3, 5)**

3. E buys a carpet from F & Co., who are to deliver it to E's home. When they do so E is out, so they leave it outside E's front door. Rain damages the carpet. Consider whether E can reject the carpet. If E can reject it, does E have to transport it back to F & Co.? **(3, 9)**

4. Explain when 'acceptance' of goods takes place. How would the Consumer Guarantees Bill 1990 have changed the position? **(6–8)**

5. L buys a refrigerator. The motor break down after three months' use. Can L reject the refrigerator and recover the purchase price? Would it make any difference if L had taken the refrigerator on either (*a*) conditional sale terms; or (*b*) hire-purchase terms?   **(11, 13)**

6.   M buys a watch from N & Co. The watch does not work so M has it repaired by N. It still does not work. N then replaces the watch with an identical one. The replacement works but cannot be made to keep good time despite N's attempts at regulating it when M repeatedly returns the watch to N for attention. Tired of the whole business, some four months after the initial purchase M returns the replacement watch to N and demands the return of the purchase price. Advise N.   **(12)**

8
Remedies

The trader at fault

1. Damages

The basic remedy for breach of contract is damages. The object of damages is to compensate the innocent party in monetary terms, so far as money can do this, and thereby to put him in the same position as he would have been in if the contract had been duly performed ('expectancy damages'). Damages for breach of contract may therefore include compensation for loss of bargain.

2. Remoteness of damage

As a matter of policy the law imposes a limit on the amount of damages recoverable in pursuit of the aim of monetary compensation. Certain kinds of loss will be held to be too remote to attract compensation. In contract the test for remoteness was laid down by the Court of Exchequer in *Hadley* v. *Baxendale* (1854):

> 'Where two parties have made a contract which one of them has broken, the damages which the other party ought to receive in respect of such breach of contract should be such as may fairly and reasonably be considered as either arising naturally, i.e., according to the usual course of things, from such breach of contract itself, or such as may reasonably be supposed to have been in the contemplation of both parties, at the time they made the contract, as the probable result of the breach of it.' (*per* Alderson B).

Explaining *Hadley* v. *Baxendale* in *Victoria Laundry (Windsor) Ltd* v. *Newman Industries Ltd* (1949), the Court of Appeal, *per* Asquith

LJ, identified two limbs to the rule, that is two types of recoverable loss arising from breach of contract:

(a) loss arising naturally (knowledge of the serious possibility of the occurrence of such loss being imputed to the contract-breaker); *and*

(b) loss arising in special circumstances where the contract-breaker had actual knowledge that breach of contract in those circumstances would be liable to result in special loss being suffered.

In *The Heron II, Koufos* v. *Czarnikow* (1969), the House of Lords stressed that the test for remoteness in contract was that the loss should be reasonably contemplated loss, which required a much higher degree of probability for its occurrence than that the loss should merely be 'reasonably foreseeable' — the test for remoteness in tort (*see* 9:**13**). The substantive validity of this distinction between the tests for remoteness of damage in contract and tort was doubted, however, by members of the Court of Appeal in *Parsons (Liverstock) Ltd* v. *Uttley Ingham & Co. Ltd* (1978). What the Court of Appeal did affirm in *Parsons* was that so long as the serious possibility of the occurrence of the kind of damage which did in fact occur was within the reasonable contemplation of the parties when they made their contract, then there is liability for all the loss of that kind, even if such loss was more extensive than was foreseeable. The facts of *Parsons* will illustrate the point.

> *Parsons (Liverstock) Ltd* v. *Uttley Ingham & Co. Ltd* (1978): the ventilator on a food hopper was not opened on installation, with the consequence that the food deteriorated, poisoning the pigs fed by the hopper and killing many of them.
> HELD: Some illness in the pigs was reasonably to be contemplated as probable in the circumstances, and so the party in breach of contract was liable for all the damage (i.e. death of the pigs) caused by the illness turning out to be much more severe than might have been contemplated. (But damages for loss of profits from future sales of pigs were too remote.)

NOTE: In *Parsons* Lord Denning MR, in a minority on this point, thought that a different test for remoteness (i.e. the 'foreseeability' test) was applicable in cases of physical loss (as distinct from loss of profit) arising from breach of contract.

3. Damages for disappointment

It used to be thought from *Addis* v. *Gramophone Co. Ltd* (1909) HL, that damages for breach of contract were confined to compensation for financial loss, that is loss quantifiable in monetary terms, but a series of cases, commencing with *Jarvis* v. *Swans Tours Ltd* (1973) CA, has allowed moderate damages in compensation for disappointment and distress suffered by the innocent party. (Of course, for such damages to be recoverable, the disappointment etc. must have been within the reasonable contemplation of the parties.)

> *Jarvis* v. *Swans Tours Ltd* (1973): the consumer, a solicitor, booked a skiing cum houseparty holiday in Switzerland for £63, in response to what was described by Edmund Davies LJ as the 'ecstatic text' of a brochure. The holiday was a disaster. Among other shortcomings, there were only thirteen guests in the first week and none at all in the second; no English was spoken by the owner; no full-length skis were available; there was no welcoming party on arrival, no Swiss cakes, and no proper yodeller — all of which had been promised. HELD: The plaintiff was entitled to damages for loss of enjoyment, assessed by the court at £125 (Court of Appeal).

> *Jackson* v. *Horizon Holidays Ltd* (1975): this was another case involving a disappointing holiday (in Sri Lanka) which failed to match the description given by the defendants. The price including air fares was £1,200. HELD: The plaintiff could recover damages for diminution in the value of the holiday and for disappointment, not only his own disappointment but also that of his wife and children (the damages once recovered being money had and received to their use). On this basis, the total sum awarded as damages amounted to £1,100 (say £600 for diminution in value and £500 for mental distress) (Court of Appeal).

NOTE: *Jackson* does not abrogate the doctrine of privity of contract (*see* 9:2), but 'may be supported either as a broad decision on the measure of damages . . . or possibly as an example of a type of contract, examples of which are persons contracting for family holidays, ordering meals in restaurants for a party, hiring a taxi for a group, calling for special treatment' (Lord Wilberforce in *Woodar Investment* v. *Wimpey Ltd* (1980) HL).

Perry v. *Sidney Phillips & Son* (1982): surveyors negligently reported a house to be in good order, whereas major repairs were needed. HELD: The purchaser's damages would include a 'modest' sum (to be assessed in subsequent proceedings) for his inconvenience, distress and discomfort (Court of Appeal).

Heywood v. *Wellers* (1976): the plaintiff instructed solicitors to apply for an injunction to restrain a man from molesting her. The solicitors were negligently slow in obtaining and enforcing the injunction, so that the plaintiff suffered mental distress and was molested on three or four occasions. HELD: The mental distress suffered was within the solicitor's contemplation, and damages for the molestation and distress were assessed in total at £150, less the £25 the plaintiff would have paid had the solicitors done their duty (Court of Appeal).

Woodman v. *Photo-Trade Processing* (1981) (*see* 6:**14**): here a film processing laboratory lost a film containing wedding photographs. £75 was added to the award for the inevitable, predictable disappointment.

4. Mitigation of damages

The plaintiff claiming damages for breach of contract (whether as consumer or trader) must take reasonable steps to mitigate the loss, otherwise damages will be reduced. For example, where the consumer justifiably rejects defective goods, or where the trader fails to deliver the goods in the first place, the consumer must whenever possible buy similar goods elsewhere at the lowest price reasonably obtainable. On the other hand, if the consumer has accepted defective goods, or chooses to accept them, and by reason of s. 11(4) SGA can no longer reject them (*see* 7:**10–12**), then the consumer must avail himself of any reasonable offers of repairs or replacement by the trader (cf. *Payzu Ltd* v. *Saunders* (1919) — a commercial case) — or alternatively the consumer should avail himself of any manufacturer's guarantee. The consumer need not have the goods repaired by the trader, however, where he has reasonably lost confidence in the trader's ability to effect the repairs satisfactorily. Nor need the consumer take a replacement where he has reasonably lost confidence in the product itself. Similar rules as to mitigation of loss by submitting to repairs apply to contracts for the supply of a service. Where the plaintiff does act reasonably in an attempt to mitigate loss, the cost of the attempt will be recoverable even if the effect of the attempt is to increase the total damages incurred (*Hoffberger* v. *Ascot International Bloodstock Bureau Ltd* (1976)).

> NOTE: Nothing in the above rules prevents a consumer who has not 'accepted' goods from rejecting them if they are defective in breach of the statutory rights and from claiming the return of the price (*see* 5(**c**) and (**d**)). But once the consumer claims *damages* (e.g. for consequential loss) he must mitigate that loss where reasonable along the lines indicated above.

5. Contracts for the sale of goods

The principles considered in the foregoing paragraphs are applicable to all types of contract. But it will be useful to summarize the various remedies available to the consumer in sale of goods cases.

(a) *Damages for non-delivery.* The Sale of Goods Act in effect codifies *Hadley* v. *Baxendale*. Thus, 'the measure of damages is the estimated loss directly and naturally resulting, in the ordinary course of events, from the seller's breach of contract': s. 51(2), which corresponds to the first limb of *Hadley* v. *Baxendale*. Spelling the matter out further, the Act continues: 'Where there is an available market for the goods in question the measure of damages is prima facie to be ascertained by the difference between the contract price and the market or current price of the goods at the time or times when they ought to have been delivered, or (if no time was fixed) then at the time of the refusal to deliver': s. 51(3), which envisages that the buyer will mitigate his loss by purchasing elsewhere. The meaning of 'available market' is considered below (*see* 8).

Section 51(3) is only a prima facie rule. If the serious possibility of special loss was within the reasonable contemplation of the contract-breaker, damages for such loss will be recoverable in accordance with the second limb of *Hadley* v. *Baxendale*, for the s. 54 of the SGA, nothing in the Act is to affect the consumer's (or trader's) right to recover special damages. Nevertheless, the normal outcome of breach of contract by the seller will be that the consumer will be able to buy the goods elsewhere and recover any additional expenditure incurred.

> NOTE: Non-delivery for the purpose of the above-mentioned rules includes cases where the consumer justifiably rejects the goods.

(b) *Specific performance.* This is an equitable remedy and accordingly will be available subject to the usual rules. In particular, damages must be an inadequate remedy. The consequence of this requirement is that the trader would only be directed to perform the contract specifically where the goods were in some way unique (e.g. an antique) and not otherwise available — an unusual thing in run-of-the-mill consumer contracts. Other bars to obtaining a decree of specific performance include undue delay prejudicial to the defendant; undue hardship caused to the defendant; prejudice to an innocent third party. Where specific performance is obtained, this does not necessarily preclude an award of damages as well: s. 52.

(c) *Action for return of the price* if the consideration has wholly failed: s. 54.

(d) *Rejection of goods* for breach of condition (subject to s. 11(4) of the SGA: *see* 7:10). To be effective, the rejection must be unequivocal (*Lee* v. *York Coach and Marine* (1977) CA). Damages will be available in appropriate cases as well as the remedy of rejection of the goods and consequent return of the price under s. 54. Where the buyer justifiably rejects goods he need not return them to the seller, unless otherwise agreed, but may simply tell the seller he rejects them: s. 36. Nevertheless it would normally be advisable for the consumer to return goods which are portable and to claim any incidental expenses incurred.

(e) *Damages for breach of warranty.* In the case of breach of warranty of quality, the damages will prima facie be the difference in value of the goods at the time of delivery to the consumer and the value they would have had if they had fulfilled the warranty: s. 53(3). If the price has not yet been paid, damages on this basis can be deducted from the amount payable: s. 53(1).

NOTE: Section 53(3) is only a *prima facie* rule, so that in a consumer contract the actual cost of repairs may be recoverable where defective goods are reasonably repairable. In *Keeley* v. *Guy McDonald Ltd* (1984), the cost of repairs for an unmerchantable second-hand Rolls Royce were recoverable under s. 53(3) as the difference between the actual unrepaired value of the car and the value it would have possessed if the implied condition had not been broken. Cf. *Perry* v. *Sidney Phillips & Son* (1982) (*see* **3**) — not a sale of goods case — where the plaintiff was awarded the difference between the price actually paid and the market value of the house at the date of purchase (plus interest); here the cost of repairs, which was greater, was not recoverable even had the plaintiff remained in the property (he had in fact sold it in desperation).

6. Entire contracts

An entire contract is one where the consideration is indivisible (e.g. payment by one lump sum) and is not intended by the parties to pass until the other party has completely performed his side of the contract. This is known as the rule in *Cutter* v. *Powell* (1795). It means that complete performance of the contract will be a condition precedent to payment, and it is therefore an important common law doctrine which the consumer can take advantage of in cases of partial or defective performance by the supplier of goods or services. Take a lump sum building contract, for example. If the builder fails to complete the job after time has been made of the essence (*see* **7:2**), then the consumer will not have to pay anything at all — at least not unless the contract has before expiry of the deadline been *substantially performed*. Consider the following two cases by way of illustration of the doctrine:

Hoenig v. *Isaacs* (1952): the plaintiff agreed to redecorate and furnish a flat for £750. The work was defective in certain minor respects and cost the flat owner £55 to put right. HELD: The contract had been substantially performed and the decorator was entitled to the contract price less the cost of making good the defects (Court of Appeal).

Bolton v. *Mahadeva* (1972): a central heating system at an agreed price of £560 was installed by a contractor. There were serious defects which the contractor refused to remedy. The deficiencies were assessed at £174. HELD: The contract had not been substantially performed and the contractor was not entitled to the contract price or any part of it (Court of Appeal).

The consumer at fault

7. General principles

The rules as to measure of damages, remoteness and mitigation of loss, considered above, will be equally applicable in cases where it is the consumer who is in breach of contract, whether the contract is for the sale of goods or the supply of services.

8. Contracts for the sale of goods

The consumer at fault may find himself faced with one of the following personal actions brought by the trader.

(a) *Action for the price.* This action is open to the trader where property in the goods has passed to the consumer: s. 49 SGA. The consumer will not of course be liable to pay the price if there is an unexpired credit period, or if the consumer can validly reject the goods. Further, the trader can sue for the price only if he is ready and willing to deliver the goods.

NOTE: Cf. s. 49 with the common law rule that where the supplier of a service can perform his side of the contract without the co-operation of his customer, then the supplier can ignore a wrongful cancellation by the customer and go ahead and perform the service and claim the *full contract price* — though not if the customer can show that the supplier had 'no legitimate interest, financial or otherwise' in performing the contract rather than in merely claiming damages: *see White & Carter (Councils) Ltd* v. *McGregor* (1961) HL and *Clea Shipping* v. *Bulk Oil* (1984).

(b) *Action for damages for non-acceptance*, where the consumer wrongfully refuses to accept and pay for the goods: s. 50(1). Damages may include a reasonable charge for the care and custody of the goods: s. 37. The measure of damages for non-acceptance is the estimated loss directly and naturally resulting, in ordinary course of events, from the consumer's breach of contract: s. 50(2). Further, s. 50(3) provides: 'Where there is an available market for the goods in question the measure of damages is *prima facie* to be ascertained by the difference between the contract price and the market or current price at the time or times when the goods ought to have been accepted, or (if no time was fixed for acceptance) then at the time of the refusal to accept.' The correspondence of these provisions with those contained in s. 51 (*see* **5**) will not escape the reader. As for the meaning of 'available market', this expression has been discussed by the courts without final conclusions being reached. Probably the expression means no more than that the goods may be freely sold in a situation in which the price is fixed by supply and demand.

> *W. L. Thompson Ltd* v. *Robinson (Gunmakers) Ltd* (1955): the defendants ordered a Vanguard car from the plaintiffs, but refused to accept delivery of it. The plaintiffs claimed damages for loss of profit. There was then a fixed retail price for the car, and the contract price and the market price at the date of breach were the same. The defendants therefore claimed that they were liable only for nominal damages. HELD: Section 50(3) of the SGA did not apply, because there could be no 'available market' in a situation (which then existed) where supply exceeded demand. The plaintiffs' damages were not merely nominal; they had lost their bargain and were entitled to recover their loss of profit.

> *Charter* v. *Sullivan* (1957): here it was a Hillman car which the buyer ordered but later refused to accept. The facts were different from *Thompson* v. *Robinson* in that demand exceeded supply, there being a shortage of Hillman cars. HELD: The plaintiff dealer could obtain only nominal damages. Even if there was an 'available market' (which the court doubted in view of the then fixed retail price), the *prima facie* rule as to damages in s. 50(3) of the SGA was to

be rejected where demand exceeded supply. This was because the dealer could mitigate his loss by a resale. The dealer lost no profit on any abortive sale, for he simply sold to the next customer. Further, applying s. 50(2) of the SGA the plaintiff had suffered no 'loss directly and naturally resulting, in the ordinary course of events, from the buyer's breach of contract' (Court of Appeal).

Lazenby Garages Ltd v. Wright (1976): the defendant consumer agreed to buy a used BMW car from dealers for £1,670. The defendant then repudiated the contract. The dealers had bought the BMW for £1,325, and they claimed £345 loss of profit, although two months after the defendant's repudiation of the contract they had sold the car for £1, 770. HELD: There could be no 'available market' for unique goods such as second-hand cars. Section 50(3) of the SGA was therefore inapplicable. Applying s. 50(2), the most that the buyer would have contemplated was that he would be liable for the difference if the car was resold at a loss on breach of contract. Loss of profit was not recoverable as no loss had been suffered on the particular transaction (Court of Appeal).

Shearson Lehman Hutton Inc. v. *Maclaine Watson & Co. Ltd* (1989): this was a commercial case about the sale of 7,755 tonnes of tin. The court held that the test for determining the market or current price (s. 50(3)) is objective and should not be coloured by any lack of negotiating skill on the part of the seller.

9. Remedies against the goods

The two actions considered in the preceding paragraph are personal actions against the consumer. An unpaid seller also has certain 'real' remedies, i.e. remedies against the goods themselves. A seller is 'unpaid' if either the whole of the price has not been paid or tendered, or a negotiable instrument taken as conditional payment has not been honoured: s. 38 of the SGA. Included among the unpaid seller's 'real' remedies are the following remedies of interest to the consumer.

(a) *Lien,* i.e. the right to retain goods until the price has been paid. Lien arises if:

(*i*) there is no provision as to credit; *or*

(*ii*) the credit term has expired; *or*

(*iii*) the buyer becomes insolvent: s. 41.

The right of lien reflects the rule that delivery of goods and payment are concurrent conditions, which means that the consumer must pay for the goods on delivery, unless credit is given: s. 28. The lien is lost if the seller delivers the goods or waives the lien: s. 43.

NOTE: Lien presupposes that property in the goods remains with the seller. Where property in the goods has passed to the consumer, however, the unpaid seller has a right of retention co-extensive to the right of lien: s. 39(2).

(b) *Right of resale.* The unpaid seller who has exercised the right of lien or retention can give notice to the consumer of his intention to resell. If the consumer does not pay within a reasonable time, the seller can sell and in addition recover from the consumer any loss occasioned by the breach of contract: s. 48(3). The effect of a resale is to give the second buyer a good title as against the original consumer: s. 48(2). This is so even if the original consumer was not given reasonable notice of the resale.

10. Deposits

Once the consumer enters into the contract (whether for the sale of goods or the supply of services), any deposit paid or payable by him will, subject to contrary agreement, be forfeited if he wrongly repudiates the contract. Similarly, goods given in part-exchange in lieu of a deposit would be forfeited. Where the seller exercises his right of resale of goods under s. 48(3) (*see* **9(b)**), the first consumer's deposit will be forfeited. In any of these cases, if the seller sues for damages the deposit will be taken into account in assessing the seller's loss. Of course, the seller will not necessarily make a loss. He may indeed succeed in selling the goods at a higher price to a third party. Even so, any deposit paid by the original consumer does not as a matter of law have to be returned.

NOTE: A deposit (i.e. a guarantee of performance, say 10 per cent of the price) must be distinguished from a *part payment,* which will normally be recoverable on breach of contract by the payer, subject to any deduction for damages assessed under the ordinary principles.

Progress test 8

1. What is the object of an award of damages as a remedy for breach of contract? **(1)**

2. What is the test for remoteness of damage in contract? How (if at all) does this test differ from the test for remoteness in tort? **(2)**

3. A buys an oil-filled electric heater. It is faulty and starts an electrical fire, burning down A's house and destroying in the process some valuable pictures worth over £100,000. Will the damages to be awarded to A include (*a*) the value of the house (£50,000); and (*b*) the value of the pictures? **(2)**

4. B, a builder, entered into a lump sum contract to build an extension to C's house, the work to be completed in three months. Time was expressly made of the essence. B took nine months over the work, and during the extra six months part of the inside of C's house was left exposed to the weather and was uninhabitable. C now wishes to deduct from B's final account £50 per month for six months as compensation for the vexation caused to C by the delay. Advise C. **(3)** If the facts were that B had simply refused to complete the job, leaving the extension unroofed, what would C's legal position have been? **(6)**

5. D engages a photographer to take photographs at his daughter's wedding. The photographer fails to turn up. Can D sue the photographer for damages for his own disappointment and that of his wife and daughter? If so, what kind of sum do you think a court might award? If the facts were that the wedding had been cancelled and that the photographer had

turned up nevertheless. Could he claim the full contract price?
(**3, 8**)

6. E orders a new car from F, a dealer. The car is defective in
many respects and E rejects it. E then buys the same model
from another dealer who has it already in stock, but meanwhile
there has been a price increase. Can E recover the difference
from F? (**5**)

7. G and H booked a holiday at a two-star hotel in a popular
resort. Their room was to have a sea view but when they arrived
at the hotel there was no such room available. G and H stayed
at another hotel, which had the required accommodation,
although they paid much more for their holiday as it was a
luxury four-star hotel. There were numerous other hotels in the
resort which appeared to afford a view of the sea, but G and H
did not trouble to enquire whether these hotels had any
vacancies. Can G and H recover the difference in tariff between
the two-star and four-star hotel? (**4**)

8. J agreed to buy an antique Sheraton parlour chair from K, a
dealer. K later sold the chair to L because L offered K an extra
£200 for the chair. The chair is till in K's possession. Is J likely
to be able to obtain a decree of specific performance? If instead
J sues for damages, on what basis would they be assessed? (**5**)

9. M orders a new sofa. When it is delivered M discovers that
part of the fabric is badly soiled. The trader refuses to do
anything about the matter. Advise M whether he can bring an
action for the return of the price which M has paid. If M decides
to keep the sofa, can he recover the cost of repairing it? (**5**)

10. In what circumstances can a trader bring an action for the
price against a consumer? (**8**)

11. N commissions his portrait from O, an artist, for £200. N
unjustifiably refuses to accept the finished work. O is able to sell
the picture to P for £30. What damages will N be liable to pay?
Would it make any difference if instead of P it was Q, an

eccentric collector, who bought the picture from O, and at a price of £300?   **(8)**

12. R orders a colour television set from S, a retailer, for £350. R pays a deposit of £50. Nothing is said about payment of the balance. When the set arrives at S's premises from the manufacturers, S informs R and requires payment of the balance. R refuses to pay until the set has been delivered and tested over a period of one week in R's house.

(a) Does S have to deliver the set?
(b) If R continues in his demands, can S sell the set to someone else? If so, will S have to return R's deposit?
(9, 10)

9
Product liability

The consumer's contractual rights

1. The statutory rights

It will be recalled that in respect of defect in title and defective goods the consumer has certain inalienable rights (or 'statutory rights') under the Sale of Goods Act and other legislation by virtue of the Unfair Contract Terms Act (*see* 6:**19, 20**). These rights will be available to the consumer as against the manufacturer of the defective product if, and only if, the manufacturer is also the seller of the product direct to the consumer. Normally, of course, the product will reach the consumer indirectly, through a retailer, with whom the consumer makes the contract of sale. This result, that the statutory rights avail the consumer against the seller alone, arises by virtue of the doctrine of privity of contract.

2. Privity of contract

The doctrine asserts that only a party to a contract can take rights (or for that matter, obligations) under it. Therefore only a party to a contract can sue or be sued on it. In practical terms, this means that in respect of a breach of the statutory rights, the consumer can sue only the seller, and even this action is not open to the consumer unless he is also the buyer. It is not possible for a non-contracting party, such as a member of the consumer's family, or a friend, or the recipient of the goods as a gift, or a subsequent private purchaser from the consumer, to sue the original seller, unless the buyer can be construed as acting as the agent for the non-contracting party (e.g. where a wife acts as agent for her husband). The doctrine of privity is thus a severe limitation on the efficacy of the consumer's statutory rights. The consequence is that an action by the consumer against the manufacturer will normally have to be based either in contract on the manufacturer's guarantee (if any) or in tort.

> *Daniels* v. *White and Tarbard* (1938): Mr Daniels purchased some lemonade from Mrs Tarbard. The lemonade, manufactured and bottled by R. White & Sons Ltd. had somehow been contaminated by carbolic acid, which made both Mr and Mrs Daniels ill. It was held that Mr Daniels could succeed on a claim against Mrs Tarbard under the Sale of Goods Act. But note that Mrs Daniels had no claim against Mrs Tarbard as she had not bought the lemonade and so was not a party to the contract. (For her claim against the manufacturers, *see* 11.)

> NOTE: A retailer who is liable to a customer for breach of the statutory rights in the Sale of Goods Act can normally seek an indemnity from his own supplier for breach of the Act, who in turn can claim against his supplier and so on back through each link in the chain of distribution to the manufacturers (*see Godley* v. *Perry* (5:11)).

3. Manufacturers' guarantees

Provided that the consumer knows about the guarantee before he makes the contract with the retailer, and that he fulfils any requirements imposed by the manufacturer (e.g. return of a guarantee card), then the consumer can establish a 'collateral' contract with the manufacturer and can sue on it. To adopt the technical language of the law of contract, the 'offer' is found in the terms of the guarantee (which have to be communicated to the consumer before acceptance), while the act of purchasing the goods from the retailer, and the fulfilment of any other requirements of the guarantee, constitute both the 'acceptance' of and the 'consideration' for the contract of guarantee. The consumer has become privy to a contract with the manufacturer. In other words, the parties have entered into a direct and enforceable contractual relationship together. Some argue that even if the consumer's first notion of the 'offer', say the registration card from the manufacturer, is when he or she opens the box, the affixing of a stamp and the completion of all the many and detailed questions often found upon it will constitute the mechanics of a contract. Of course, they may also guarantee the inclusion of the consumer on so-called 'junk' mailing lists!

NOTE: A manufacturer's guarantee is often called a 'warranty'. This use of the word 'warranty' must not be confused with the same word 'warranty' in its alternative meaning of minor contractual term, as opposed to a 'condition'. The meaning which the word carries will be clear from the context in which it is employed.

Carlill v. *Carbolic Smoke Ball Co.* (1893): this famous case is a forerunner of the enforceability of guarantees. Mrs Carlill bought a smoke ball on the strength of an advertisement by the defendants in which they offered to pay £100 to anyone who caught influenza after using one of their smoke balls in the prescribed way. 'To show their sincerity' the defendants deposited £1,000 with named bankers. Mrs Carlill used the smoke ball in the prescribed way but nevertheless caught influenza. She sued for the £100. HELD: She was entitled to succeed. The advertisement was an offer to the world at large, which Mrs Carlill had accepted by buying and using the smoke ball as prescribed; in the absence of any requirement to the contrary, there was no need to communicate 'acceptance' of the guarantee to the defendants.

It should be clearly understood that if the consumer does sue on a guarantee, his only rights are those granted by the guarantee itself. Thus if the guarantee provides for repair of goods and replacement of defective parts, then that is all that the consumer is entitled to under the guarantee; he cannot claim as against the manufacturer that his statutory rights have been infringed, a point often misunderstood.

NOTE: It is increasingly common to find the sellers of 'white' goods (refrigerators, cookers, freezers, etc.) and 'brown' goods (TVs, hi-fis, etc.) offering so-called 'extended guarantees', e.g. 'five years of trouble-free viewing'. In reality these are no more than insurance contracts. They are usually expensive, say 25% of the purchase price of the goods. The wise consumer will consider the value of such a deal in the light of the likelihood of failure of the goods, and the cost of repair, at a time beyond the consumer rights attached by the SGA and whatever manufacturer's guarantee may be available to him.

4.   Unfair Contract Terms Act

Section 5 of the Act provides that where goods are of a type ordinarily supplied for private use or consumption, a manufacturer's guarantee cannot exclude or restrict liability for defects in the goods while in consumer use, resulting from negligence during manufacture or distribution of the goods. Goods are to be regarded as 'in consumer use' when in use otherwise than exclusively for the purposes of a business. Section 5 does not apply to a dealer's guarantee (*see* 6:**18**).

Prior to the enactment of s. 5, manufacturers' guarantees sometimes took away more rights than they actually awarded, in which case a consumer would have been well advised not to accept the guarantee by returning the guarantee card (if any). Now, however, it is impossible for the consumer, in consequence of accepting a guarantee, to lose the right to sue the manufacturer or a distributor in the tort of negligence. But s. 5 does not strictly speaking create new rights; it merely prevents the consumer from being deprived of his common law right to sue a negligent manufacturer or distributor. The manufacturer is not subjected to strict liability for defective products — negligence must still be proved as a condition of liability. Further, nothing in s. 5 alters the rule that the manufacturer is not liable (apart from any obligations specifically assumed under the guarantee) in contract, whether for breach of the statutory rights or for breach of any other contractual obligations of the seller.

5.   Criminal law sanction

The Consumer Transactions (Restrictions on Statements) Order 1976 makes it a criminal offence for a guarantee to contain a statement describing or limiting obligations (whether legally enforceable or not) accepted by the manufacturer in relation to goods, without accompanying that statement by a further statement clearly and conspicuously to the effect that the statutory rights of the consumer against the seller are not affected (Art. 5). The law's policy here is to resort to the threat of criminal law sanctions in an attempt to prevent consumer ignorance of the statutory rights from being exploited, for example by the display of a 'no refunds' sign (*see* 6:**24**).

The consumer's rights in tort

6. Negligence

So far as an action against the manufacturer is concerned, the alternative to suing on the guarantee (if there is one) is to sue in tort — the tort of negligence. In order to succeed in a negligence action, the plaintiff must prove more than the mere existence of carelessness. He must prove:

(a) that the defendant was under a duty of care to him; *and*
(b) that there has been a breach of that duty; *and*
(c) that as a result the plaintiff has suffered damage which is not too remote.

7. The duty of care

The leading case is *Donoghue* v. *Stevenson.*

Donoghue v. *Stevenson* (1932): the assumed facts (i.e. they may never have happened!) on which the decision as to legal principle was based were that Mrs Donoghue visited a cafe and there drank from a bottle of ginger beer which had been bought for her by a friend. Among the contents of the bottle Mrs Donoghue then discovered a decomposing snail, previously hidden by the opaque glass of the bottle. Mrs Donoghue became ill and claimed damages from the manufacturer. HELD (but only 3:2): The manufacturer of goods sold by him to a retailer or other distributor in circumstances which prevent the retailer or ultimate consumer from discovering by inspection any defect, is under a legal duty of care to the ultimate consumer to take reasonable care that the goods are free from any defect likely to cause injury or damage (House of Lords).

NOTE: (1) The 'ultimate consumer' need not necessarily be a purchaser but could be anyone foreseeably injured by a dangerous product. (2) The defect need not necessarily be a defect in the actual manufacturing process; it may equally be in the design, or in the container, or even in the labelling of the goods.

Donoghue v. *Stevenson* is authority for the much wider proposition underlying the development of the whole concept of the duty of care in negligence, namely that . . . 'You must take reasonable care to avoid acts or omissions which you can reasonably foresee would be likely to injure your neighbour. Who, then, in law is my neighbour? The answer seems to be — persons who are so closely and directly affected by my act that I ought reasonably to have them in contemplation as being so affected when I am directing my mind to the acts or omissions which are called in question' (Lord Atkin). Students of tort, being aware of this wider 'neighbour principle', often overlook that *Donoghue* v. *Stevenson* is in essence a product liability case, authority for the narrower proposition given in the text above that a negligent manufacturer is liable to an ultimate consumer who suffers damage.

8.   Product must be dangerous

The extent of the duty of care owed by the manufacturer to the ultimate consumer is limited by the rule that the defect must be such that it may result in 'injury to the consumer's life or property' (Lord Atkin in *Donoghue* v. *Stevenson*). It is not enough for the product merely to be defective; it must also be dangerous. For example, if the consumer buys an iron which will not heat up, the manufacturer has no liability in the tort of negligence, whereas if the iron overheats and causes a fire, then the manufacturer, if negligent, will be liable. Stamp LJ in *Dutton* v. *Bognor Regis UDC* (1972) CA put the matter this way: 'I may be liable to one who purchases in the market a bottle of ginger beer which I carelessly manufactured and which is dangerous and causes injury to person or property; but it is not the law that I am liable to him for the loss he suffers because what is found inside the bottle and for which he has paid money is not ginger beer but water.'

Junior Books Ltd v. *Veitchi* (1982): JB engaged a building company to build a factory for them. Their architect nominated specialist sub-contractors (V) to lay a concrete floor. There was no contractual relationship between JB and V. Owing to V's negligence the floor developed cracks. It was not dangerous, but it would require expensive maintenance. JB claimed the cost of replacing the floor and consequential financial loss including loss of profits from V. HELD by a majority of the House of Lords: Where, as here, the proximity between the producer of faulty work or a faulty product and the user was sufficiently close, the duty of care owed by the producer extended beyond a duty merely to prevent harm to the user's person or property but included a duty to avoid defects in the work or product itself. In such a case the cost of remedying the defects in the work or product or of replacing it, and any consequential financial loss, was recoverable by the user, notwithstanding the lack of a contractual relationship between producer and user.

NOTE: *Junior Books* was regarded by many as a landmark in the development of the law of tort, extending the circumstances in which damages for pure economic loss, not consequential on personal injury or damage to property, will be recoverable (if foreseeable: *see* **13**). But at present the law still stops short of creating a general manufacturer's warranty of quality in tort for a defective article which is not at the same time dangerous. 'The concept of proximity must always involve, at least in most cases, some degree of reliance . . . between an ultimate purchaser and a manufacturer [it] would not easily be found to exist in the ordinary everyday transaction of purchasing chattels when it is obvious that in truth the real reliance was on the immediate vendor and not on the manufacturer' (Lord Roskill). However, the House seems to have gone smartly into reverse on the *Junior Books* decision: *Leigh and Sullivan* v. *Aliakmon Shipping* (1986), and the Privy Council too: *Candlewood Navigation Corporation* v. *Mistui OSK Lines* (1985). In *Simaan General Contracting* v. *Pilkington Glass* (1988), Dillon LJ said that the *Junior Books* decision had been 'the subject of so much analysis and discussion that it cannot now be regarded as a useful pointer to any development of the law', and in *D & F Estates* v. *Church Commissioners* (1988) the House of Lords has reverted to the original position regarding pure economic loss — that unless it is consequent upon physical damage it is not recoverable in tort. This has now been applied in *Department of the Environment* v. *Bates* (1989) and most importantly by a seven-member House of Lords in *Murphy* v. *Brentwood DC* (1990), where it was firmly emphasised that matters of pure economic loss are to be left to contract law principles. Product liability issues involving defective goods causing personal injury or causing economic loss consequent upon personal or property injury remain in the sphere of tort law. (Furthermore this case overrules the decision in *Dutton* v. *Bognor Regis UDC* (1972) and *Anns* v. *London Borough of Merton* (1977).

9. Intermediate examination

For the duty of care to arise, the defect must not be such that the manufacturer could reasonably have expected the consumer or retailer to discover and remedy it before loss was caused. There must be 'no reasonable possibility of intermediate examination' (Lord Atkin in *Donoghue* v. *Stevenson*; it will be remembered that the ginger beer bottle was opaque and so precluded intermediate examination). Where there does exist a reasonable opportunity of intermediate examination of the goods, the retailer will bear liability in negligence for defective goods. But in today's legal climate it is clear that if the manufacturer for his part is to escape liability, Lord Atkin's 'reasonable possibility of intermediate examination' requires that there is a reasonable expectation of intermediate examination.

Grant v. *Australian Knitting Mills Ltd* (1936): the purchaser of a pair of underpants contracted dermatitis because the garment contained excessive sulphite. Could the consumer reasonably have been expected to wash the underpants before wearing them for the first time, and so wash out the excess sulphite? HELD: This was not to be expected.

Holmes v. *Ashford* (1950): the plaintiff contracted dermatitis from hair dye. Instructions had been issued by the manufactures that the dye might be dangerous to certain skins, and they advised a test. The hairdresser read the warning but ignored it and made no test. HELD: The hairdresser was liable but not the manufacturer.

Evans v. *Triplex Glass Co. Ltd* (1936): a car windscreen suddenly and for no apparent reason shattered one year after purchase of the car, causing injury. HELD: The manufacturers of the windscreen were not liable as there was the likelihood of an intermediate examination by the makers of the car. Nor had the windscreen been proved to be defective when its manufacturers put the product into circulation.

10. Joint liability

Liability for a defective product may rest jointly upon both manufacturer and retailer. This possibility will be an important consideration where one defendant's financial resources are greater than the other's. The retailer will, for instance, be jointly liable in negligence (quite apart from any liability of the retailer under the Sale of Goods Act) where he sells an untested product which he has acquired from an unreliable source. In these circumstances liability would be joint and several, i.e. either or both parties could be sued. Of course the plaintiff would not obtain double damages by suing both parties. But he would have the tactical advantage of being able to obtain his damages from the defendant most likely to pay up, leaving it to the two defending parties to seek an indemnity or apportionment of loss between themselves under the Civil Liability (Contribution) Act 1978.

Fisher v. *Harrods Ltd* (1966): the plaintiff was injured by a bottle of cleaning fluid which exploded. The doctrine of privity of contract meant that the plaintiff had no action for breach of the statutory rights, the bottle having been purchased by a friend. But HELD: The sellers were liable in negligence for selling an untested product which they had obtained from an unreliable source. The manufacturers were not sued, otherwise they would have been found liable too. This case shows a clear policy toward retailers — that they should choose their suppliers with care.

11. Breach of duty of care

Given that a duty of care exists within the limitations specified in **8** and **9** above, it still does not follow that the consumer will succeed in an action for negligence against the manufacturer. He must prove that the manufacturer failed to exercise reasonable care. The test of such failure is whether, on balance of probabilities, it is a reasonable inference to be drawn from the evidence that the harm was so caused. Thus in *Grant* v. *Australian Knitting Mills Ltd* 'If excess sulphites were left in the garment, that could only be because someone was at fault. The appellant is not required to lay his finger on the exact person in all the chain who was responsible, or to specify what he did wrong. Negligence is found as a matter of inference from the existence of the defects taken in connection with all the known circumstances . . .' The point is that it would be an impossible task for a consumer to identify exactly how the defect occurred, for he has no knowledge of the defendant's manufacturing process. It is enough that the consumer can identify a defect which *prima facie* ought not to be there.

The burden of proof is then shifted on to the manufacturer to answer the inference of negligence and satisfy the court that he took reasonable care. This reversal in practice of the burden of proof led the Royal Commission on *Civil Liability and Compensation for Personal Injury* (*see* **16**) to conclude that reversal of the burden by legislation would usually make no difference to the consumer. Yet even so the problem of proving breach of duty can defeat the claimant in a consumer case. In *Daniels* v. *White* (*see* **2**), Mrs Daniels failed in her claim against the manufacturers because the court was satisfied, too easily perhaps, that they had answered the inference of negligence by proving the existence of a good system of work under proper supervision at their factory. So Mrs Daniels recovered no compensation from either the seller or the manufacturers.

NOTE: *Daniels* v. *White* was not followed in *Hill* v. *James Crowe (Cases) Ltd* (1978), where Mackenna J held that it was not enough for the manufacturer of a badly made wooden packing case to prove that he had a good system of work and proper supervision at his factory. In the circumstances one of the manufacturer's workmen must have been negligent, and the manufacturer was vicariously liable. *Daniels* v. *White* must now be viewed as wrongly decided, at least to the extent that it omitted to consider the issue of vicarious liability for negligence by a member or members of the workforce, after all, it seems that the judge was satisfied in that case that a proper system of checking could consist of a 14-year-old girl sniffing the bottles emerging from a cleansing process! Admittedly, it is always dangerous to judge 1930s circumstances through 1990s spectacles.

12. Breach of statutory duty

Contravention by manufacturer or retailer of safety regulations, etc., under the Consumer Protection Act 1987, Part II, will not only be a criminal offence but will also allow any person affected by the contravention to bring an action for breach of statutory duty. Chapter 18 treats this aspect of product liability in detail.

13. Remoteness of damage

The final fact that the plaintiff has to prove in a negligence action, having proved the existence of a duty of care and breach of that duty, is damage which is not too remote. In tort this means that loss will be irrecoverable unless reasonably foreseeable as a consequence of the breach of duty (the rule established by *The Wagon Mound* (1961)). But the defendant does not have to be able to foresee the precise circumstances in which the damage occurs in order to be fixed with liability. It is enough that the manufacturer or retailer foresees, or ought reasonably to foresee, the general kind of damage against which he should guard. If the damage of that kind which actually occurs is then simply more extensive than could have been anticipated, this is no defence; nor is it a defence that the precise manner in which the damage was inflicted could not have been anticipated. Damage in tort will be 'foreseeable' and not too remote, even if 'very improbable', or only 'liable to happen in the most unusual case' (to adopt expressions used by the House of Lords in *The Heron II, Koufos* v. *Czarnikow* (1969)). Again, the fact that an individual consumer may be particularly susceptible to certain kinds of injury, because he has (say) an unusually thin skull or an unusually weak heart, does not exculpate the defendant (the 'egg-shell skull' principle, which, expressed colloquially, means that 'you take your victim as you find him').

Subject to these rules, then, damages (including where appropriate loss of earnings and damages for pain and suffering) will be recoverable in respect of personal injury and death, and property damage. The measure of damages will be on an indemnity basis, i.e. the compensation needed to restore the consumer to the financial position he would have been in had the breach of duty never occurred. (Contrast this basis of assessment of damages in tort with 'expectancy damages' in contract: *see* 8:**1**.)

14. Contract or tort?

The great advantage of a negligence action is that it is not restricted by the doctrine of privity. On the other hand its great disadvantage is that the manufacturer may succeed in rebutting the inference of negligence (i.e. that he was not to blame, he acted reasonably). Contrast a contractual action for breach of the statutory rights. While subject to limitations by the doctrine of privity, this has the great advantage that once the breach is established liability is strict, i.e. it exists whether the seller has been negligent or not. But it seems that there is no difference between contract and tort is far as the question of remoteness of damage is concerned (*see* 8:**2**).

> *Frost* v. *Aylesbury Dairy Co.* (1905): typhoid germs were found in milk. The dairy as seller was held liable under what is now s. 14(3) of the Sale of Goods Act, even though the exercise of all reasonable skill by the dairy could not have detected the defect which caused the germs.

Law reform proposals

15. Strict liability

As the foregoing paragraphs have noted, a consumer may have no remedy at all in respect of loss caused by defective goods. This may be because there is no privity of contract and the manufacturer cannot be demonstrated to have been negligent. But whatever the reason, the possible absence of an adequate remedy has led to demands for reform of the law relating to product liability. These demands reflect developments in the United States, where judicial activity has imposed strict liability on manufacturers and distributors for death or injury caused by defective products.

16. Proposals
Four proposals should be noted:

(a) Strasbourg Convention on Products Liability in regard to Personal Injury and Death (open for signature from 1977);
(b) Directive on Liability for Defective Products, presented by the Commission of the EEC to the Council adopted in 1985 and implemented in the UK by the Consumer Protection Act 1987, Part I.
(c) Report on Liability for Defective Products by the Law Commission (Cmnd 6831, 1977);
(d) Report of the Royal Commission on Civil Liability and Compensation for Personal Injury (under the chairmanship of Lord Pearson, Cmnd 7054, 1978).

17. Recommendations of the proposals
Broadly, these proposals advocate the following.

(a) Producers (both of finished products and components) should be subject to strict liability in tort for death or personal injury caused by defective products. A product is to be regarded as 'defective' when it does not provide the safety which a person is entitled to expect, having regard to all the circumstances including the presentation of the product.
(b) Distributors should not be strictly liable, except where they fail to disclose the identity of the supplier of the defective goods, or where they sell them exclusively under their own brand name, or where they import the goods.
(c) The producer should have a defence where the product was not defective when he put it into circulation. His strict liability should in any event be subject to a cut-off period of ten years from the circulation of the product.

18. The EC Directive on Product Liability
This was implemented by Part I of the Consumer Protection Act 1987 (hereafter CPA) which was brought into force on 1 March 1988. Part I of the CPA does not apply to any product supplied by its producer before Part I was brought into force: s. 50(7).

19. The Part I strict liability regime
Strict civil liability — i.e. liability without proof of negligence

or fault and aside from any limitations imposed by privity of contract principles — is imposed on the producer of a defective product which causes loss or damage: s. 2.

'Product' means all goods (including components or raw materials comprised in another product, but not 'primary agricultural goods' — *see* **20**) and electricity: s. 1(2). But a person who supplies a product in which components or raw materials are comprised is not to be treated by reason only of his supply of the finished product as supplying any of the components or raw materials: s. 1(3).

> NOTE: Unlike the new general safety requirement created in Part II of the CPA (s. 10) — which makes it a criminal offence to supply any consumer goods which are not safe having regard to all the circumstances — civil liability under Part I covers all goods (as defined above) and is not restricted to consumer goods.

20. Liability of 'producer' and others

Liability under s. 2 is imposed primarily on the 'producer' of the product, a term which includes within its ambit not just manufacturers but also producers of raw materials and those who carry out an industrial process on goods: s. 1(2).

Furthermore, liability under s. 2 extends beyond producers to certain other traders, namely:

(a) any person who holds himself out as the producer by putting his name or mark on the product ('own-brand' products);
(b) any person who imports the product into the Community (note not into the UK, so an injured consumer might find himself able to sue a company which imported the product from the Far East into France, from where they were further traded into England).
(c) the supplier of the product where he cannot identify the producer or importer or his own supplier (e.g. because his bookwork is slovenly): s. 2(2), (3).

Where two or more persons are liable under Part I for the same damage, their liability is joint and several: s. 2(5).

> NOTE: Liability under s. 2 does not extend to producers of

game or agricultural produce not industrially processed: s. 2(4). The UK has chosen *not* to exercise the option of derogating from the Directive here by including unprocessed agricultural produce or game within the scope of the strict liability regime.

21. Meaning of 'defect'

A product is defective 'if the safety of the product is not such as persons generally are entitled to expect': s. 3. In determining this question all the circumstances are to be taken into account, including:

(a) the manner in which, and purposes for which, the product has been marketed, its get-up, the use of any mark in relation to the product and any instructions or warnings about the use of the product;

(b) the use to which it could reasonably be expected that the product would be put;

(c) the time when the product was supplied by its producer.

A defect is not to be inferred from the fact alone that the safety of a product which is supplied after that time is greater than the safety of the product in question.

22. Defences

By virtue of s. 4, in any proceedings under Part I it is a defence for the defendant to show:

(a) that the defect is attributable to compliance with any requirement imposed by or under any enactment or with any Community obligation;

(b) that the defendant did not at any time supply the product in question;

(c) that the product was not supplied in the course of a business;

(d) that the defect did not exist in the product at the time of supply;

(e) 'that the state of scientific and technical knowledge' when the actual product was supplied 'was not such that a producer of products of the same description as the product in question might be expected to have discovered the defect if it had existed in his products while they were under his control': s. 4(1)(e);

(f) that, in the case of a manufacturer of a component, the defect was wholly attributable to the design of the product in which the component has been fitted or to compliance with instructions given by the producer of that product.

> NOTE: The defence in s. 4(1)(*e*) above is the so-called 'development risks' or 'state of the art' defence, which the UK has chosen to include among the defences, having declined to exercise the option given in the Directive of derogating from the Directive on this point by disallowing the development risks defence. Some commentators have seen this defence as reintroducing the concept of fault by the back door. Product liability is about loss distribution (an economic concept), not fault (a moral one). It has been argued that, had this law been in force, and had the many cases been litigated, the 'Thalidomide Children' might well not have been able to sue successfully. Further, it was reported in March 1990 that the European Commission plan to take the UK before the European Court, arguing that this implementation of the so-called 'state-of-the-art' defence falls short of the requirements of the Directive in that the idea was that the defect ought to have been *impossible* to discover, not merely that it *might* not have been discovered.

If may be added that a producer cannot avoid or reduce his liability merely because damage was caused both by a defect in his product and by the act of omission of a third party (e.g. a negligent supplier handling a defective product); but in such a case the producer may have recourse against the third party for apportionment of loss as between themselves.

23. Damage giving rise to liability under Part I
By virtue of s. 5 this is limited to:

(a) death or personal injury;
(b) any loss of or damage to any property (including land) which at the time of the loss or damage is (*i*) of a description of property ordinarily intended for private use, occupation or consumption, and (*ii*) intended by the person suffering the loss or damage mainly for his own private use, occupation or consumption. No damages can be awarded under Part I in respect of loss or of damage to such property unless the amount to be so awarded exceeds £275.

No liability exists under Part I in respect of any loss of or damage to the defective product itself or to the whole or any part of any product which has been supplied with the defective product comprised in it.

NOTE: Article 16 of the Directive gives Member States an option of introducing an upper financial limit on liability, resulting from the same defect in identical items, of not less than 70 million ECU (about £40 million). The UK has decided *not* to exercise this option.

24. Contributory negligence
Where the person suffering the loss or damage has been contributorily negligent, damages may be reduced or disallowed under the Law Reform (Contributory Negligence) Act 1943: s. 6(4) CPA.

25. Limitation of actions
There is a limitation period of three years for the bringing of proceedings, commencing the day on which the claimant became aware, or should reasonably have become aware, of the damage, the defect, and the identity of the producer. There is an absolute cut-off period of ten years from the date on which the actual product was supplied, unless the claimant has in the meantime instituted proceedings: s. 6 and Sched. 1.

26. Exclusion clauses
The producer (or other defendant) is prevented from limiting or excluding his liability under Part I by any contract term, notice or other provision: s. 7.

27. Causation
While Part I of the CPA means that the claimant no longer has to prove negligence or fault in respect of damage covered by Part I, it will be appreciated that the claimant still has to prove that the product was defective (as defined in **21** above), and that the damage was caused by the defect.

28. Existing rights unaffected
The producer's liability under Part I is without prejudice to

any right of the victim to bring a claim under the existing laws of contract or tort: s. 2(6). That is, CPA Part I is an addition to consumer protection, it does not repeal or replace rights ('as well', not 'instead').

Progress test 9

1. What is the doctrine of privity of contract? How does it operate to restrict the consumer in seeking redress for loss caused by defective goods? **(2)**

2. In what circumstances will a manufacturer's guarantee be enforceable against him by a consumer? **(3)**

3. A manufacturer's guarantee reads: 'Should these goods prove to be defective in any way within twelve months from date of purchase, the manufacturer will repair them or, at his option, replace them free of charge. No further liability whatsoever can be accepted'

    (a) Is the exclusion cause effective?
    (b) Does the issue of the guarantee with the goods
    constitute a criminal offence? **(4, 5)**

4. What does the consumer have to prove in order to succeed in an action in negligence against a manufacturer? **(6)**

5. In what circumstances will a retailer (but not the manufacturer) be liable to the consumer in negligence? When will the retailer be jointly liable with the manufacturer? Precisely describe the nature of this claim, if one exists. **(9, 10)**

6. A student buys a pocket electronic calculator, which he is allowed to use in his examinations. The calculator does not perform certain mathematical functions properly, with the consequence that the student fails his examinations. Does the student have a good claim in law against the manufacturer? **(8, 13)**

7. Does the consumer have to prove negligence on the part of the manufacturer, or does the manufacturer bear the burden of disproving it? **(11)**

8. What additional remedy does the consumer have in respect of a contravention of safety regulations made under the Consumer Protection Act 1987? **(12)**

9. When will damages in negligence be too 'remote' to be recoverable? **(13)**

10. What are the advantages and disadvantages of an action against a retailer in negligence, as opposed to an action against him for breach of the statutory rights under the Sale of Goods Act? **(14)** How has the position been improved by the implementation of CPA Part I? **(18–28)**

11. What is meant by the 'state-of-the-art' defence within CPA Part I? Why is it to be subjected to the scrutiny of the European Court? **(22)**

10
Consumer credit: introductory

Introduction to the Consumer Credit Act

1. Crowther Committee Report on Consumer Credit

English law regulating credit had developed in a characteristically *ad hoc* way, with the consequence that much depended on the legal technicalities in which a particular credit transaction was framed, irrespective of the real substance of that transaction. The Crowther Committee was appointed by the government to review the whole field of consumer credit and it reported in 1971 (Cmnd 4596). The Committee were concerned at 'the serious anomalies arising from the division of credit transactions into legally distinct compartments and from failure to accord a uniform treatment to a range of security devices all designed to achieve the same objective'. The Report's recommendations so far as they concerned the consumer credit law — as distinct from its recommendations for a separate Lending and Security Act rationalizing the law of security — received government approval in the White Paper *The Reform of the Law on Consumer Credit* (Cmnd 5472, 1973), and were duly enacted (with modifications) in the Consumer Credit Act 1974. The provisions of the Act were brought into force in stages over a period of years, the process not finally being completed until 19 May 1985. (In this and subsequent chapters the Consumer Credit Act is referred to as 'the Act' or 'CCA'.)

2. Scope of the Act

The Act comprehensively regulates the provision of any form

of financial accommodation to individuals (including unincorporated firms), subject to a ceiling of £15,000. (On questions concerning 'extortionate credit bargains' this limit does not apply.) All methods of supplying credit are controlled. Banks, finance houses, mail order firms, retailers, moneylenders, pawnbrokers, ancillary credit businesses (credit-brokers, debt adjusters, debt counsellors, debt collectors, credit reference agencies: cf. s. 145 CCA), etc. — all are controlled by the Act and subjected to the licensing system (*see* 16:6) which it establishes.

The Act may be described as a skeleton in that it comprises the fundamental structure of the control over consumer credit, but requires for its flesh the detailed further provisions as to its operation contained in the many regulations and orders made under the Act.

3. Find one's way round the Act
The Act contains several helpful features of draftsmanship. These include the following.

(a) A comprehensive definition section (s. 189) defining, or directing the reader to the definition of, the terms used by the Act.
(b) A summary (Sched. 1) of the thirty-five offences created by the Act, together with an indication of the appropriate sanction to which contravention renders the wrongdoer liable.

> NOTE: When construing a statue it is frequently difficult to determine whether infringement of any particular requirement allows the victim to bring a civil action against the wrongdoer for, e.g. breach of statutory duty. In this respect the Act gives specific guidance: 'A breach of any requirement made (otherwise than by any court) by or under this Act shall incur no civil or criminal sanction as being such a breach, except to the extent (if any) expressly provided by or under this Act': s. 170(1). It may be added that while breach of the CCA may carry with it no further sanction, such breach (or breaches) will be a factor to be taken into account by the Director General of Fair Trading in exercising his licensing functions under the Act: s. 170(2).

(c) A series of examples (Sched. 2) illustrating by a full analysis the use of the terminology employed by the Act. In the case of conflict between Sched. 2 and any other provision of the Act, that other provision prevails: s. 188(3).

Basic concepts and definitions

4.   Consumer credit agreement

A consumer credit agreement is a personal credit agreement by which the creditor provides the debtor with Credit not exceeding £15,000: s. 8(2). A personal credit agreement involves the granting of credit by the creditor to an individual (which includes a partnership or other unincorporated body: s. 189, s. 8(1)). 'Credit' includes any form of financial accommodation: s. 9(1).

5.   Consumer hire agreement

The Act also controls consumer hire agreements because in substance a hire agreement often amounts to the giving of financial accommodation. Furthermore, many hire agreements, such as the rental of TVs, often give the hirer the use of the equipment for all, or at least most of, its useful life. A consumer hire agreement is an agreement by which goods are bailed to an individual (the 'hirer', which includes a partnership or other unincorporated body: s. 189), where the agreement is such that it:

(a)   is not a hire-purchase agreement; *and*
(b)   is capable of subsisting for more than three months; *and*
(c)   does not require the hirer to make payments exceeding £15,000: s. 15.

> NOTE: (1) A consumer hire agreement need only be *capable* of lasting for more than three months — it need not necessarily do so. (2) Hire-purchase agreements fall within the definition of consumer credit agreements.

6.   Regulated agreements

This is the key concept in the Act, for the Act controls only regulated agreements (except for the controls over advertising and extortionate credit bargains, which are of wider application). A 'regulated agreement' is a consumer credit agreement, or consumer hire agreement, other than an exempt agreement: s. 189.

Before turning to the meaning of exempt agreement (*see* **7**), we may note that the effect of the definitions considered so far is to subject to the Act's control agreements involving financial accommodation where the party accommodated is an individual (as defined above) and where the amount of the credit does not exceed £15,000. The ceiling of £15,000 refers to the amount of the credit granted, and does not take into account the interest thereon. With regard to hire-purchase agreements (defined below: *see* **14**) the Act specifically provides for the amount of credit to be computed as the total price of the goods less the aggregate of any deposit or down-payment and the total charge for credit: s. 9(3).

> NOTE: (1) By s. 189, 'total price' means 'total sum payable by the debtor under a hire-purchase agreement or a conditional sale agreement including any sum payable on the exercise of an option to purchase, but excluding any sum payable as a penalty or as compensation or damages for a breach of the agreement'; and (2) by the same provision 'total charge for credit' means a sum calculated in accordance with regulations under s. 20(1). (The regulations referred to are the Consumer Credit (Total Charge for Credit) Regulations 1980).

In the case of conditional sale and credit-sale agreements (defined below: *see* **15, 16**) the amount of credit is similarly computed. The amount of credit provided will be the total price less any deposit and the total charge for credit. In the case of cash loans of a fixed sum the amount of credit is simply the amount of the loan.

7. Exempt agreements

As has just been seen, the meaning of exempt agreement is an important element in the definition of regulated agreement. An exempt agreement is not regulated by the Act. Exempt agreements are defined in s. 16 of the CCA, and fall into one of two broad categories.

(a) Section 16(2) exempts mortgages for the purchase of land or the provision of dwellings on land where the mortgage is granted either (*i*) by a local authority or building society; or (*ii*) by an insurance company, friendly society, organization of employers or organization of workers, charity, land improvement company, or body corporate named or specifically referred to in any public general Act. The institutions listed in (*ii*) have to be specified in an order made by the Secretary of State if they are to be exempted. The relevant order is the Consumer Credit (Exempt Agreements) Order 1989 (as amended).

(b) Section 16 also gives the Secretary of State power to exempt certain other agreements where the number of payments does not exceed a specified number or the rate of interest does not exceed a specified maximum: s. 16(5). Section 16 further provides for the exemption by order from regulated consumer hire agreements of agreements covering the hire of meters for gas, electricity, or water, or British Telecom telephones: s. 16(6). The Consumer Credit (Exempt Agreements) Order 1989 gives effect to these exemptions and spells out the details (*see* 8). The very need for such exemptions to be specified emphasizes the exhaustive nature of the Act's control over consumer credit.

8.   The Consumer Credit (Exempt Agreements) 1989
Under this Order exempt agreements include the following.

(a) Debtor-creditor-supplier agreements for fixed-sum credit where payment is to be made in not more than four instalments. (The terms 'debtor-creditor-supplier' and 'fixed-sum credit' are defined below: *see* **10, 11**.) This exemption covers ordinary account or trade credit, e.g. the milkman's or newsagent's bill or the retailer's account to be settled at the end of the month. The exemption does not apply to any hire-purchase, conditional sale or pledge agreements.

(b) Debtor-creditor-supplier agreements for running-account credit where repayment of the whole amount of the credit taken up in each accounting period has to be made by a single payment. ('Running-account credit' is defined below: *see* **11**.) Credit cards are an example of running-account credit, and this exemption covers, for instance, Diners Club and the American Express green card (but not, e.g., Barclaycard, Access, or the American Express gold card) precisely because the terms on which the first-named cards are issued require settlement of the entire periodical account by a single payment with no facility for extended credit. The exemption would also cover, for instance, a credit account at a shop of the kind where the consumer is sent a monthly statement to be settled in full by a single payment.

(c) Agreements where the maximum interest does not exceed 13 per cent or 1 per cent above the highest of the London and Scottish Clearing Banks' base rates 28 days before the agreement is made, whichever is higher. This exemption is designed to cover cheap loans extended by business to employees. It applies only to debtor-creditor agreements (defined below: *see* **10**), i.e. it does not apply in cases where the credit supplied is linked with the supply of goods or services by a seller who has a business connection with the creditor. So a credit sale where, say, the retailer allows the consumer to pay off the purchase price over several months without imposing a charge for credit will be exempt (if exempt at all) under the exemption mentioned in **(a)** above.

9. No contracting out

By s. 173(1) of the CCA, any term in any agreement inconsistent with a provision in the Act for the protection of the debtor or hirer or his relative or surety, is void. But nothing in s. 173(1) prevents a thing from being done in relation to any person which would normally require the authority of an order of the court or the Director General of Fair Trading, if that person consents at the time to its being done: s. 173(3).

10. Debtor-creditor-supplier agreements and debtor-creditor agreements

These expressions look formidable and indeed, the definitions (ss. 12, 13) are rather complex. They have been described as impenetrably obscure! But the essence of the matter is as follows. A debtor-creditor-supplier agreement is one where the creditor is also the supplier of the goods or services or has an existing or contemplated business connection with the supplier. A debtor-creditor agreement, on the other hand, is one where the creditor is not also the supplier and has no existing or contemplated business connection with him. In a debtor-creditor agreement the creditor merely provides the debtor with the needed credit facilities.

Examples of debtor-creditor-supplier agreements include

hire-purchase, conditional sale and credit-sale agreements, and transactions whereby good or services are paid for by credit card. Example of debtor-creditor agreements include the ordinary bank loan or overdraft, and personal loans by finance houses in cases where there is no business connection between the creditor and the supplier of any goods or services financed by the loan (i.e. the lender has no particular interest in the way the 'financial accommodation' is used).

11. Running-account credit and fixed-sum credit

Running-account credit is credit which is made available under a personal credit agreement where the credit fluctuates up to a permitted maximum, as is the case, for example, with credit cards. Periodical payments made by the debtor 'top-up' the amount of credit available: s. 10(1)(a). All credit other than running-account credit is fixed-sum credit: s. 10(1)(b). Hire-purchase, conditional sale and credit-sale agreements all involve fixed-sum credit.

12. Restricted-use credit and unrestricted-use credit

The definitions of these in s. 11 express a fairly simple concept. Restricted-use credit is a regulated consumer credit agreement involving credit which is earmarked to finance a particular transaction and the money is paid direct to the supplier of the goods or services (as for instance under hire-purchase, conditional sale and credit-sale agreements). Unrestricted-use credit involves cases where the money goes through the hands of the debtor (as for instance when a finance house gives the debtor a personal loan). In such cases the credit will still be unrestricted-use credit even though a term of the agreement requires the debtor to use the money in a certain way and any other use would be a breach of contract. For example, suppose that a finance house makes a personal loan to the debtor on condition that the money be used to finance an extension to the debtor's house. If the money is paid direct to the builder it will be restricted-use credit; whereas if the money is paid to the debtor in the first instance it will be unrestricted-use credit, and it would still be so even if another use of the money (e.g. to finance a holiday) by the debtor would amount to a breach of contract.

13. Linked transactions

The definition of linked transaction (s. 19) is complex. Basically, however, a linked transaction is one which is ancillary to the regulated agreement. The idea is that a linked transaction is to be treated under the Act as if it had been part of the regulated agreement itself. In particular, the debtor's right of cancellation (*see* 12:**14**) is to apply to a linked transaction in the same way as it applies to the regulated agreement: s. 69(1). Further, a linked transaction entered into before the making of the principal agreement has no effect until such time (if any) as that agreement is made: s. 19(3).

> NOTE: By virtue of the Consumer Credit (Linked Transactions) (Exemptions) Regulations 1983, certain linked transactions are excluded from the operation of ss. 19(3) and 69(1). The exempted linked transactions are contracts of insurance; other contracts in so far as they contain a guarantee of goods; and transactions comprising or effected under agreements for the operation of deposit and current accounts.

One type of situation caught by s. 19 is where the ancillary transaction is entered into in compliance with a term of the principal (regulated) agreement. For example, where the debtor is obligated by the principal agreement to enter into a maintenance contract in respect of consumer durables which he is acquiring under a regulated hire-purchase or conditional sale agreement, that maintenance contract would be a linked transaction. It would, therefore, be cancelled or terminated along with the principal agreement should that occur.

Another type of situation caught by s. 19 is where the principal agreement is a debtor-creditor-supplier agreement and the ancillary transaction in question is financed or to be financed by the principal agreement. For example, if the debtor uses a credit card to obtain goods or services, the contract by which he obtains them is a linked transaction.

The concept of a limited transaction is important for at least two reasons: if and when a regulated agreement can be cancelled, the limited transaction falls too, and when an evaluation is being made as to whether a credit transaction is extortionate, any linked transactions will be taken into account.

Hire-purchase, conditional sale and credit-sale agreements

14. Hire-purchase agreement

This is an agreement, other than a conditional sale agreement, under which:

(a) goods are bailed in return for periodical payments by the bailee; *and*
(b) the property in the goods will pass to the bailee if the terms of the agreement are complied with and the bailee exercises an option to purchase the goods: s. 189.

The retailer may finance the hire-purchase agreement himself, but often the arrangement is a tripartite one. That is, the retailer sells goods to a finance house and the finance house lets the goods out on hire-purchase terms to the consumer. The finance house has, in effect, made a secured loan to the debtor.

15. Conditional sale agreement

This is an agreement for the sale of goods (or land) under which the purchase price or part of it is payable by instalments, and property is to remain in the seller (notwithstanding that the buyer is to be in possession) until such conditions as to the payment of instalments or otherwise as may be specified in the agreement are fulfilled: s. 189.

While a conditional sale at common law technically involves an agreement for *sale*, the policy of the CCA, is to assimilate the legal incidents of hire-purchase and conditional sale. So far as regulated consumer credit agreements are concerned, the consumer is placed in the same position irrespective of whether the contract is technically hire-purchase or conditional sale.

16. Credit-sale agreement

This is 'an agreement for the sale of goods, under which the purchase price or part of it is payable by instalments, but which is not a conditional sale agreement': s. 189.

It will be noted that under a credit-sale agreement the consumer acquires title to the goods immediately upon making the contract. The creditor has, in effect, made an unsecured loan.

NOTE: Hire-purchase, conditional sale and credit-sale agreements will always be debtor-creditor-supplier agreements for fixed sum, restricted-use credit (*see* **10–12**).

17. Meaning of 'debtor' and 'creditor'
The CCA uses the term 'debtor' as meaning the individual receiving credit under a consumer credit agreement (s. 189), and therefore the term includes the hirer under a hire-purchase agreement and the buyer under a conditional sale or credit-sale agreement. Similarly the term 'creditor' means the person providing credit under a consumer credit agreement, and therefore includes the legal supplier of the goods (i.e. the retailer, or the finance house where the transaction is the typical tripartite one) in contracts of hire-purchase, conditional sale and credit sale.

18. Terms control
Quite separate from the controls over hire-purchase, conditional sale and credit-sale agreements found in the CCA is the control over credit terms exercised by the government from time to time by orders made under the Emergency Laws (Re-enactments and Repeals) Act 1964 (as amended by Schedule 4, para. 23 of the CCA). Hire agreements are also controlled under the 1964 Act. The control is achieved by the stipulation of minimum deposits and by the limitation of the period over which repayment may be made. The object of exercising this control over credit terms is not to protect consumers by discouraging them from over-committing themselves, but rather to achieve a measure of monetary control over the economy. No credit restrictions under the 1964 legislation are currently in force.

Progress test 10

1. How many offences does the CCA create? Where may a summary of them be found? Can the legal adviser know for certain whether contravention of any of the offences will allow the consumer to sue for breach of statutory duty? **(3)**

2. Define (*a*) 'consumer credit agreement'; and (*b*) consumer hire agreement'. **(4, 5)**

3.   C agrees to bail goods to D (an individual) in return for periodical payments. The agreement provides for the property in the goods to pass to D on payment of a total a £22,500 and the exercise by D of an option to purchase. The sum of £22,500 includes a down-payment of £3,000. It also includes an amount which, according to the regulations made under s. 20(1) of the CCA constitutes a total charge for credit of £4,500.

  (a) Is this a hire-purchase, credit-sale, or conditional sale agreement?
  (b) How much credit is provided under the agreement?
  (c) Is the agreement a consumer credit agreement?
  (**4, 6, 14**) (Cf. example 10, Sched. 2, CCA.)

4.   Define 'regulated agreement', and consider whether the agreement in question 3, above, is such an agreement.   (**6**)

5.   Consider whether the following agreements are regulated under the CCA:

  (a) a building society mortgage;
  (b) rental of a British Telecom telephone;
  (c) newspaper deliveries, the account for which is presented monthly;
  (d) agreement for the use of a credit card;
  (e) a credit-sale agreement where the consumer has to pay the purchase price in six equal monthly instalments, no charge being made for credit.   (**7, 8**)

6.   Is it possible to contract out of the provisions of the CCA? (**9**)

7.   Explain the distinction between debtor-creditor-supplier agreements and debtor-creditor agreements.   (**10**)

8.   (a) Consider whether the following agreements are debtor-creditor-supplier agreements or debtor-creditor agreements: (*i*) hire-purchase agreement; (*ii*) agreement for the use of a credit card; (*iii*) a bank overdraft.
  (b) Consider whether the agreements in (*i*), (*ii*) and (*iii*) above will involve running-account credit or fixed-sum credit.

(c) Consider whether the agreements in (*i*), (*ii*) and (*iii*) above will involve restricted-use credit or unrestricted-use credit.   **(10–12)** (Cf. examples 10, 16–18, Sched. 2, CCA.)

9. Give an example of a linked transaction and explain the significance of the concept.   **(13)**

10. Define and distinguish between (*a*) hire-purchase agreement; (*b*) conditional sale agreement; (*c*) credit-sale agreement.   **(14–16)**

11
Seeking credit business

The control of advertising generally

1. Legal sanctions

English law contains no generalized provisions controlling advertising. There are, however, numerous statutes which bear upon advertising. Perhaps most significant are the Consumer Credit Act 1974 (*see* **5–8**) and the Trade Descriptions Act 1968. The 1968 Act in prohibiting false trade descriptions at the same time necessarily prohibits false and misleading advertisements. False statements about the quality or price of goods, or the existence of facilities or services, can be attacked in this way. Moreover the consumer, aided by Misrepresentation Act 1967, may be able to bring a civil claim in respect of misrepresentation if such is the effect of the advertisement. But English law is ill-adapted to deal with the more subtle case of misleading advertising — the undue emphasis, ambiguity, suggestion by association, etc. Nor is the advertising 'puff' controlled.

2. Self-regulation

The wider control over advertising in the UK is presently achieved by a voluntary code of practice: the British Code of Advertising Practice, first published in 1962 and subsequently revised several times, most recently in December 1988. The main burden of the Code from the consumer's viewpoint is to ensure that advertisements are:

(a) 'legal, decent, honest and truthful';

(b) prepared 'with a sense of responsibility to the consumer and to society'; *and*
(c) 'all advertisements should conform to the principles of fair competition generally accepted in business'.

The Code is administered by the CAP Committee (Committee of Advertising Practice), whose members are drawn from the advertising industry. Complaints from consumers, or bodies representing consumer interests, go to the Advertising Standards Authority, which was set up by the advertising industry. The ASA has an independent chairman, and two-thirds of its members are drawn from outside advertising.

Sanctions for breach of the Code include adverse publicity from the reports issued by the ASA in respect of complaints investigated. Ultimately the media may deny defaulting advertisers advertising space, and defaulting agencies may be denied trading facilities. Nevertheless the weakness of the Code, a weakness common to all self-regulatory codes, is that in the last resort the code is voluntary and lacks the force of law (but *see* **3**).

> NOTE: *Broadcast* advertising is regulated solely by the Independent Broadcasting Authority under the Broadcasting Act 1981 and the Cable Authority under the Cable and Broadcasting Act 1984. The detail, although probably not the general policy, of this regulation will alter with the implementation of the Broadcasting Act 1990, the demise of the IBA, and the creation of the Independent Television Commission (ITC).

3. Directive on Misleading Advertising
This Directive was adopted by the EEC Council of Minsters in June 1984 (84/450/EEC), and implemented in the UK by means of the Control of Misleading Advertisements Regulations 1988. The Regulations are intended to protect consumers, traders and the public interest from misleading advertising, defined as 'any advertising which in any way, including its presentation, deceives or is likely to deceive the persons to whom it is addressed or whom it reaches and which, by reason of its deceptive nature, is or is likely to injure a competitor of the person whose interests the advertisement seeks to promote'.

The UK has given effect to the Directive through

strengthening the existing system of self-regulation. The Director General of Fair Trading now has the power, as a last resort, to seek a court order banning misleading advertising under the self-regulatory system. That is, complaints are routed through the ASA and if their self-regulatory mechanisms fail, the Director can and has acted. There have been at lease three interesting cases so far: a misleading slimming advertisement (Tobyward) and homeworking schemes (Blinkhorn) where injunctions were obtained, and a timeshare development sales campaign (Home Ownership Exchange) where the Director accepted an assurance of future good conduct drawn in the same terms as he would have requested an injunction.

4.   Fair trading
The Director General of Fair Trading is responsible for reviewing practices which may adversely affect the economic interest of consumers and this responsibility includes review of advertising practices. The Director has in fact taken action against bargain offer claims and an Order has been made. (*See* 17:**3**.)

Advertising credit facilities

5.   Part IV Consumer Credit Act: its scope
Part IV applies to persons who:

(a)   carry on a consumer credit business; *or*
(b)   carry on a consumer hire business; *or*
(c)   carry on a business in the course of which they provide credit to individuals secured on land: s. 43(2).

Part IV controls advertisements by such persons for business purposes, where the advertisement indicates that the advertiser is willing (*i*) to provide credit, or (*ii*) to enter into agreements for the bailment of goods by him: s. 43(1).

NOTE: 'Advertisement' is very broadly defined in s. 189 to include every form of advertising.

6.   Exempt advertisements
Part IV does not control advertisements which indicate that

the credit must exceed £15,000 and that no security is required, or that the security is to consist of property other than land, or that the credit is available only to a body corporate: s. 43(3). (Note that, subject to s. 43(3), the advertisement will be controlled under Part IV even if it does not relate to a regulated agreement.) An advertisement for the bailment of goods (i.e. for hire facilities) is outside Part IV if it indicates that the advertiser is not willing to enter into a consumer hire agreement: s. 43(4). The Secretary of State may by order provide that Part IV shall not apply to other advertisements of a description specified in the order: s. 43(5). Broadly, regulations have exempted advertisements relating to agreements which are exempt agreements —

(a) by virtue of s. 16(2) CCA, *or*

(b) by virtue of the Consumer Credit (Exempt Agreements) Order 1989 (*see* 10:**7, 8**).

> NOTE: The exemptions mentioned in (a) and (b) above are conferred by the Consumer Credit (Advertisements) Regulations 1980, reg. 2, and the Consumer Credit (Exempt Advertisements) Order 1985 respectively. It may be added that the figure of £15,000 mentioned above was raised from the original figure of £5,000 by the Consumer Credit (Increase of Monetary Limits) Order 1983.

7. Part IV controls

The controls, designed to secure 'truth in lending' (the basic policy behind the whole CCA), comprise the following.

(a) The Secretary of State is required to make regulations concerning the form and content of advertisements to which Part IV applies, with a view to ensuring that the advertisement conveys a fair and reasonably comprehensive indication of the nature of the credit or hire facilities offered by the advertiser and of their true cost to persons using them: s. 44(1).

> NOTE: Detailed regulations have been made pursuant to s. 44(1), namely the Consumer Credit (Advertisements) Regulations 1989. These regulations control the form and content of credit advertisements, dividing them into three distinct categories: simple, intermediate and full. They replaced earlier regulations and introduced new provisions which require advertisers to publish specified warnings in relation to loans secured on the debtor's home. In particular

the warning: 'YOUR HOME IS AT RISK IF YOU DO NOT KEEP UP REPAYMENTS ON A MORTGAGE OR OTHER LOAN SECURED ON IT'. This, obviously, is designed to warn borrowers of the potentially dire consequences which can arise if they fail to repay a secured loan.

(b) In addition to the particularized disclosure requirements to be imposed under the regulations referred to in **(a)** above, the Act makes it an offence for advertisements to convey information which is in a material respect false or misleading: s. 46(1). Information stating or implying an intention on the advertiser's part which he has not got will be 'false' for this purpose: s. 46(2).

(c) It is an offence for an advertisement to which Part IV applies to indicate that the advertiser is willing to provide credit under a restricted-use credit agreement relating to goods or services, if the advertiser does not hold himself out as prepared to supply the goods or services for cash: s. 45.

(d) advertisements by ancillary credit businesses (*see* 10:2) are covered (subject to exemptions) by the relevant parts of the above-mentioned controls: s. 151.

8. Advertising infringements

Where the advertiser commits an offence, a like offence is committed by the publisher, the deviser, and the person who procured the publication of the advertisement: s. 47(1). The publisher will have a defence if he proves that the advertisement was published by him in the course of a business and that he did not know or suspect that its publication would be an offence: s. 47(2). Further, the CCA contains the usual 'due diligence' type of defence (applicable generally to offences under the Act), i.e. it is a defence for the person charged to prove:

(a) that his act or omission was due to a mistake, or to reliance on information supplied to him, or to an act or omission by another person, or to an accident or some other cause beyond his control; *and*

(b) that he took all reasonable precautions and exercised all due diligence to avoid such act or omissions: s. 168(1).

Infringement does not affect the validity of any agreement subsequently entered into by the consumer (*see* s. 170(1)), unless of course the advertisement constitutes a misrepresentation or misdescription.

Canvassing

9. Canvassing off trade premises

The Act contains provisions designed to control the doorstep selling of credit. It is an offence to canvass debtor-creditor agreements off trade premises: s. 49(1). Canvassing involves making oral representations during visits made otherwise than in response to a previous request: s. 48(1). The request should also be in writing and signed, otherwise the salesman commits the offence of soliciting debtor-creditor agreements during visits made in response to a previous oral request: s. 49(2). Section 49 does not apply to debtor-creditor-supplier agreements, so canvassing of such agreements off trade premises is permissible, but only if the supplier of the credit has a licence specifically so providing: s. 23(3). (The debtor will have the benefit of the statutory 'cooling-off' period in cases where he signs a regulated agreement elsewhere than on business premises: *see* 12:**15**.)

10. Circulars to minors

A person commits an offence if, with a view to financial gain, he sends to a minor (i.e. someone under age eighteen) any document inviting him to:

(a) borrow money; *or*
(b) obtain goods on credit or hire; *or*
(c) obtain services on credit; *or*
(d) apply for information or advice on borrowing money or otherwise obtaining credit, or hiring goods: s. 50(1).

It is a defence for the person charged to prove that he did not know, and had no reasonable cause to suspect, that the recipient of the document was a minor: s. 50(2).

11. Unsolicited credit-tokens

It is an offence to deliver or send by post an unsolicited credit-token to a person: s. 51(1). This means that now it is, for instance, an offence for a bank to post unsolicited credit cards to its customers. (Credit-tokens also include checks, vouchers, coupons, stamps, etc., as defined in s. 14 of the CCA, and *see Re Charge Card Services Ltd* (1988).) Except in the case of a small (*see* 12:**4**, NOTE) debtor-creditor-supplier agreement, the credit-token will be unsolicited unless the recipient has made a prior request for the token in a document signed by him: s. 51(2). Unsolicited credit-tokens are permissible, however, where the credit-token is for use under an existing agreement or in renewal or replacement of a previous token: s. 51(3).

> *Elliott* v. *DGFT* (1980): the Divisional Court upheld the conviction under s. 51(1) of footwear retailers who mailed to prospective customers an unsolicited plasticized card purporting to be a credit card valid for immediate use. The card was still a credit-token within s. 14, notwithstanding that it was not capable of contractually binding the issuer.

> NOTE: Under the CCA the debtor's liability for unauthorized use of a credit card (or other credit token) cannot commence before he either signs it (or a receipt for it), or first uses it: s. 66. Under s. 84, liability for misuse cannot exceed £50 (the new limit imposed by the Consumer Credit (Increase of Monetary Amounts) Order 1983). The debtor is, however, liable without limit for loss arising from misuse of the credit-token by a person who acquired possession of it with the debtor's consent. No liability can arise after the creditor has been given notice of loss or theft. Nor can liability arise if the credit-token agreement does not contain the name, address and telephone number of the person to be contacted on loss of the credit-token. The Consumer Credit (Credit-Token Agreements) Regulations 1983 prescribe that these contact particulars have to be prominent and easily legible.

12. Quotations

Regulations may be made as to the form and content of quotations to customers by a person who carries on a consumer credit or consumer hire business, or a business in the course of which credit is provided to individuals secured on land: s. 52. The Consumer Credit (Quotations) Regulations 1989 have been made under this power. The regulations contain broadly similar provisions to those relating to the form and content of advertisements. The regulations also prescribe that a quotation must be provided in response to a request for written information made in writing, orally on the trader's premises or, in certain circumstances, by telephone.

13. Duty to display information

Regulations may be made requiring a person who carries on a consumer credit or consumer hire business, or a business in the course of which he provides credit to individuals secured on land, to display in the prescribed manner, prescribed information about the business at any premises where the business is carried on and to which the public have access: s. 53. No such regulations have been made.

Progress test 11

1.   How does English law presently deal with the control of advertising generally? Contrast this control with the control proposed by the EEC Directive.   (1, 3)

2.   Describe the self-regulatory system of control over advertising adopted by the UK advertising industry.   (2)

3.   Does the Director General of Fair Trading have a role to play in the control of advertising?   (4)

4.   What advertisements are controlled under Part IV of the CCA?   (5, 6)

5.   What are the Part IV controls over advertising?   (7)

6.   Will (*a*) the advertiser, (*b*) the publisher, (*c*) the deviser, be liable for an advertisement which infringes the Part IV controls? What defence(s) will be available to these respective parties?   (8)

7.   How (if at all) does the commission of an offence against the Part IV controls over advertising affect the legal position of the consumer?   (8)

8.   How does the CCA attempt to curb the doorstep salesman? (9)

9.   A firm distributes from door to door throughout its locality

circulars inviting applications to the firm for advice on borrowing money. A proportion of the circulars fall into the hands of young people under age eighteen. Has the firm committed an offence? **(10)**

10. If the banks promoting the Access credit card were today to send a mass mailing of credit cards to customers, would that be an offence? **(11)**

11. (a) AB Bank plc send C a credit card in renewal of a credit-token agreement. The card is lost in the post. What is C's liability (if any) under the CCA?
(b) D's credit card is stolen by E, who uses it to make purchases totalling £100. what is D's liability (if any) under the CCA?   **(11)**

12. How is the giving of quotations controlled under the CCA? **(12)**

12
Formation of credit or hire agreements

Credit-brokers and credit reference agencies

1. Recovery of credit brokerage fees

The consumer may approach a credit-broker for introduction to a source of credit. By s. 155 of the CCA, a credit-broker is only entitled to a nominal sum of £3 by way of fee or commission for his services, unless a 'relevant agreement' (which includes a regulated agreement) is entered into within six months of the broker introducing the consumer to the prospective source of credit.

> NOTE: The sum of £3 mentioned above, and the sum of £1 mentioned in 2(b) below, are the revised amounts as stipulated in the Consumer Credit (Increase of Monetary Amounts) Order 1983.

2. Credit reference agencies

During the process of negotiating an agreement a creditor or owner is likely to check up on the credit rating of the prospective debtor or hirer with a credit reference agency. The CCA protects consumers in the following ways.

(a) *Disclosure of identity of agency.* A creditor, owner or negotiator, at the request of a debtor or hirer received not more than twenty-eight days after the end of the antecedent negotiations, must disclose the name and address of any credit reference agency consulted about the debtor's or hirer's financial standing: s. 157.

NOTE: The Consumer Credit (Conduct of Business) (Credit References) Regulations 1977 contain additional disclosure requirements as to credit reference agencies consulted, where the negotiations have been conducted through credit-brokers.

(b) *Disclosure of filed information.* A credit reference agency is under a duty to give the consumer a copy of the file relating to him, the particulars being reduced into 'plain English' where necessary. The consumer must pay a fee of £1. The agency must send the consumer a statement in the prescribed form of his rights to have wrong information corrected: s. 158.

NOTE: The prescribed form, *inter alia*, may be found in the Consumer Credit (Credit Reference Agency) Regulations 1977.

(c) *Correction of wrong information.* A consumer given information under s. 158 may, if he thinks it is incorrect and likely to be prejudicial, require it to be removed or corrected. The agency has to inform the consumer within twenty-eight days whether it has removed the entry or amended the file (or taken no action), and if it has amended the file a copy of the amended entry must be supplied to the consumer. Within a further twenty-eight days a dissatisfied consumer may require the agency to add to the entry a notice of correction (not exceeding 200 words) supplied by the consumer. If the matter is then still in dispute, either the consumer or the agency may apply to the Director General of Fair Trading for his determination: s. 159.

3.   Sanctions
Breach by the agency of any of the duties imposed by ss. 157–159 is an offence triable summarily.

Entry into credit or hire agreements

4.   Exemptions
Part V of the CCA is concerned with entry into credit or hire agreements. Certain agreements, however, are exempted (by s. 74) from the Part V requirements, including:

(a) non-commercial agreements (i.e. a consumer credit or consumer hire agreement not made by the creditor or owner in the course of a business carried on by him: s. 189;
(b) debtor-creditor agreements for overdrafts on current accounts, where the Director General of Trading so determines;
(c) small debtor-creditor-supplier agreements for restricted-use credit.

> NOTE: Section 17(1) defines a 'small agreement' as (*i*) a regulated consumer credit not exceeding £50, other than a hire-purchase or conditional sale agreement, *or* (*ii*) a regulated consumer hire agreement which does not require the hirer to make payments exceeding £50, being (in either case) an agreement which is either unsecured or secured by a guarantee or indemnity only (whether or not the guarantee or indemnity is itself secured). The sum of £50 mentioned here is the revised limit set by the Consumer Credit (Increase of Monetary Limits) Order 1983.

But while the above agreements are generally exempt from Part V, note that:

(*i*) the provisions as to antecedent negotiations (s. 56: *see* 13:3) apply to agreements within **(b)** and **(c)** above; *and*

(*ii*) in the case of **(c)** above, the provisions as to disclosure of information (s. 55; *see* **3**) also apply;

(*iii*) in cases **(b)** and **(c)** above, regulations under s. 60 as to form and content of agreements (*see* **6**) apply to any term of the agreement which is expressed in writing: s. 74.

5. Disclosure of information
Regulations may require specified information to be disclosed in the prescribed manner to the debtor or hirer before a regulated agreement is made. If the regulations are not complied with the agreement will be improperly executed: s. 55. No regulations under s. 55 have in fact been made.

(For the legal effects of improper execution of an agreement, *see* **12, 13**.)

6. Form and content
The Secretary of State is required to make regulations as to

the form and content of regulated agreements: s. 60(1). The object of the regulations is to ensure that the debtor or hirer is made aware of his rights, duties, remedies, and the amount and rate of the total charge for credit. The regulations may require specified information to be included in the prescribed manner in documents, and other specified material to be excluded: s. 60(2). (The Director has power to waive any of the requirements in particular cases: s. 60(3).) Legibility is required: s. 61(1)(*c*). Breach of any of the requirements renders the agreement improperly executed: s. 61.

The detailed regulations required by s. 60 have been made. They are the Consumer Credit (Agreements) Regulations 1983 (as amended). The regulations provide that the agreement must be easily legible and must state the following information (*inter alia*):

(a) the amount of credit or credit limit;
(b) the total charge for credit;
(c) the amounts and timing of repayments;
(d) the APR (Annual Percentage Rate);
(e) details of any security provided by the debtor.

The agreement must also contain prescribed statements of the protection and remedies available to the debtor under the CCA, chiefly in relation to cancellation (*see* **14–17**), termination (*see* 14:**4, 6**), and repossession (*see* 15: **10, 11**), in so far as relevant to the type of agreement concerned.

7. Prescribed terms and express terms

The Consumer Credit (Agreements) Regulations 1983 also prescribe certain terms to be contained in the signed document itself (cf. s. 61(*a*) CCA). The prescribed terms relate to the amount of credit or credit limit; the rate of interest; and obligations as to repayments. All other terms (apart from implied terms) must be embodied in the agreement: s. 61(1)(*b*). 'Embodied' means that the agreement either sets out the terms or refers to another document in which they are set out: s. 189(4).

8. Signature

The agreement must be signed by the debtor or hirer *personally*, and it must also be signed by or on behalf of the creditor or owner: s. 61(1)(*a*). (Where the debtor or hirer is a partnership or unincorporated body, the agreement may be signed by or on behalf of such debtor or hirer: s. 61(4).) Improper signature means that the agreement is improperly executed: s 61(1).

The Consumer Credit (Agreements) Regulations 1983 prescribe a form of signature box for the different types of regulated agreements. For example, the prescribed signature box in relation to hire-purchase agreements is as follows:

This is a Hire-Purchase Agreement regulated by the Consumer Credit Act 1974. Sign it only if you want to be legally bound by its terms.

Signature(s)
of Debtor(s)

Date(s) of signature(s)

The goods will not become your property until you have made all the payments. You must not sell them before then.

If the agreement is a cancellable one (*see* **14**), immediately above, below or adjacent to the signature box there must appear a separate box containing prescribed statement of protection (cf. **6**):

YOUR RIGHT TO CANCEL

Once you have signed this agreement, you will have for a short time a right to cancel it. Exact details of how and when you can do this will be sent to you by post by the creditor.

---

9. Copies

Sections 62 and 63 of the CCA contain detailed provisions to ensure that the debtor or hirer receives at least one (and usually two) copies of the agreement (and any document referred to in it). Broadly, the position is as follows. If the unexecuted agreement is personally presented to the debtor or hirer for his signature, he must be given a copy there and then. If the unexecuted agreement is sent to the debtor or hirer for his signature, he must be sent a copy at the same time. If the agreement is not executed on signature by the debtor or hirer, he must be given a second copy within 7 days of the agreement being executed. In the case of a cancellable agreement (*see* **14**), the second copy must be sent by post (*see* **10** for further requirements).

Copies have to comply with regulations as to form and content: s. 180(1). The regulations which prescribe (in detail) the form and content of copies are the Consumer Credit (Cancellation Notices and Copies of Documents) Regulations 1983 (as amended in 1984 and 1989). Copies must be easily legible.

Breach of any of the requirements as to the supply of copies renders a regulated agreement improperly executed: ss. 61–63.

10. Notice of cancellation rights

The Act contains special provisions as to notices where the agreement is cancellable (*see* **14**), with a view to ensuring that the debtor is informed about the right to cancel. If the agreement is cancellable, all copies referred to in **9** above must contain a notice in the prescribed form setting out the rights of cancellation: s. 64(1)(*a*). If only one copy of the agreement is required by the rules, a separate notice of cancellation rights must be sent by post within 7 days following the making of the agreement: s. 64(1)(*b*). (It has already been mentioned that in the case of a cancellable agreement, if a second copy is required it must be sent by post: s. 63(3).

A notice of cancellation rights must indicate:

(a) the right of the debtor or hirer to cancel the agreement; and
(b) how and when to cancel it; *and*
(c) the name and address of a person to whom notice of cancellation may be given: s. 64(1).

The Consumer Credit (Cancellation Notices and Copies of Documents) Regulations 1983 (as amended) prescribe (in detail) the form and content of copies in conformity with s. 64.

A cancellable agreement is improperly executed if the requirement as to notices are not met: s. 64(5).

NOTE: By virtue of the Consumer Credit (Cancellation Notices and Copies of Documents) (Amendment) Regulations

1984, agreements which are not cancellable agreements within the meaning of the CCA but which confer on debtors or hirers similar rights of cancellation are to be treated as cancellable agreements for the purposes of giving copies under ss. 62 and 63 of the Act, and, under the Consumer Credit (Cancellation Notices and Copies of Documents) (Amendment) Regulations 1989, there are certain dispensations granted regarding copies of agreements relating to land.

11. Securities

The Act requires any security provided by a person other than the debtor or hirer in relation to a regulated agreement to be expressed in writing and in the prescribed form: s. 105 (and cf. the Consumer Credit (Guarantees and Indemnities) Regulations 1983). There are also provisions as to copies. Breach of these requirements means that the security is not properly executed.

12. Effect of improper execution of the agreement

The agreement will be enforceable against the debtor or hirer only on an order of the court: s. 65(1). The court must dismiss an application for enforcement if, but only if, it considers it just to do so having regard to the prejudice caused by the contravention and the degree of culpability for it. The court must also have regard:

(a) to its powers on making an order to impose conditions or suspend the operation of the order, and to vary any agreement or security; *and*
(b) to its powers to compensate the debtor or hirer by reducing or discharging any sum payable by him: s. 127.

13. Cases where no enforcement order can be made

In the following cases no enforcement order can be made whatever the other circumstances:

(a) where no agreement containing all the prescribed terms was signed by the debtor or hirer: s. 127(3);
(b) in the case of a cancellable agreement, where the debtor or hirer is not supplied with a (proper) copy of the executed agreement before the commencement of the proceedings: s. 127(4)(*a*);

(c) in the case of a cancellable agreement, where the requirements as to notice of cancellation rights were not complied with: s. 127(4)(*b*).

> NOTE: If the court declines to enforce an agreement (*see* **12**), or cannot make an order for its enforcement, one consequence is that the consumer can retain without further payment any goods in his possession under the agreement, for the reason that a retaking of goods is an 'enforcement' of the agreement: s. 65(2).

The right of cancellation

14. Cancellable agreements

A regulated agreement may be cancelled by the debtor or hirer if:

(a) there were antecedent negotiations;
(b) which included oral representations;
(c) which were made in the presence of the debtor or hirer; *and*
(d) the agreement was signed by the debtor or hirer otherwise than on permanent or temporary business premises of

(*i*) the creditor or owner, *or*

(*ii*) any party to a linked transaction (other than the debtor or hirer or relative of his), *or*

(*iii*) the negotiator in any antecedent negotiations: s. 67.

> NOTE: It appears from Example 4, in Sched. 2 to the Act, that negotiations by telephone are not made 'in the presence of' the debtor or hirer, and so if all the negotiations take place by telephone the agreement will not be cancellable. This is regarded as unfortunate by those who are depressed by the increasing use of telephones as marketing tools.

15. Cooling-off period

Cancellation may be effected by notice given by the debtor or hirer at any time between his signing of the unexecuted agreement and:

(a) the end of the fifth day following the day on which the debtor or hirer received the second statutory copy of the agreement, or, if no second copy was required, the statutory notice of cancellation rights;

(b) alternatively, if the need for the statutory notice has been waived by the Director in the exercise of his powers (cf. s. 64(4)), the cooling-off period will terminate at the end of the fourteenth day following the day on which the debtor or hirer signed the unexecuted agreement: s. 68.

16. Notice of cancellation

By s. 69, the agreement is cancelled by the debtor or hirer serving notice ('however expressed') to that effect within the cooling-off period. Notice may be served on:

(a) the creditor or owner; *or*

(b) the person specified in the notice under s. 64(1) (*see* **10**); *or*

(c) the creditor's or owner's agent (including a credit-broker or supplier who is the negotiator in antecedent negotiations); *or*

(d) any person who, in the course of a business carried on by him, acts on behalf of the debtor or hirer in any negotiations for the agreement.

A notice of cancellation sent by post to a person is deemed to be served on him at the time of posting whether or not it is actually received: s. 69(7).

NOTE: No special form is mandatory for giving notice of cancellation, but the Consumer Credit (Cancellation Notices and Copies of Documents) Regulations 1983 (as amended) do prescribe an optional form of cancellation for use by the debtor or hirer. The creditor or owner must include the form in the second statutory copy of the agreement, or, if no second copy was required, in the statutory notice of cancellation rights.

17. Effects of cancellation

The notice operates to cancel the agreement and any linked transaction, save for those excepted by the Consumer Credit (Linked Transactions) (Exemptions) Regulations 1983 (*see* 10:**13**, NOTE): s. 69(1). The effects are as follows.

(a) All sums paid by the debtor or hirer are repayable, and all sums due cease to be payable: s. 70(1).

(b) The debtor or hirer has a lien over goods in his possession for any sum repayable to him on cancellation: s. 70(2).

(c) Under a restricted-use debtor-creditor-supplier agreement, or a consumer hire agreement, or a linked transaction, a debtor or hirer who is in possession of the goods is under a duty to restore them after cancellation of the agreement (subject to any lien he may have). The consumer may if he wishes send the goods back, but he need only redeliver the goods at his own premises. Meanwhile the consumer must take reasonable care of the goods, though this duty ceases after twenty-one days following the cancellation: s. 72.

(d) Where goods were taken in part-exchange, the negotiator (defined in s. 56(1) to include credit-brokers and suppliers) must return them to the consumer (in substantially as good a condition as when the consumer delivered them to the negotiator) within ten days of cancellation, otherwise a part-exchange allowance must be paid. The consumer has a lien over goods in his possession in respect of this obligation: s. 73.

(e) Except in the case of a debtor-creditor-supplier agreement for restricted-use credit, an agreement which has been cancelled continues in force as far as it relates to payment of credit and interest. But no interest is payable by the debtor on any sum repaid within one month of cancellation or, in the case of credit repayable by instalments, before the date on which the first instalment is due: s. 71. If credit repayable by instalments has not been wholly repaid by this date, the creditor must make a written and signed request in the prescribed form recalculating the remaining instalment: s. 71(3) and Consumer Credit (Repayment of Credit on Cancellation) Regulations 1983.

18. Withdrawal from prospective agreement

If offer and acceptance have not yet taken place according to the normal rules of contract, the prospective debtor or hirer can withdraw by written or oral notice, however expressed: s. 57(1), (2). Withdrawal has the same effect as cancellation, even where the agreement if made would not have been cancellable. A notice to the debtor's or hirer's own negotiating agent will be sufficient:

s. 57(3). An agreement purporting to bind a prospective debtor or hirer to entering into a future regulated agreement is void: s. 59. (There are certain very limited exceptions to s. 59: cf. Consumer Credit (Agreements to enter Prospective Agreements) (Exemptions) Regulations 1983.)

19. Prospective land mortgages

The right to cancel does not apply to prospective land mortgages on account of the technical difficulties which would be involved. Instead, provision is made in certain types of prospective land mortgage for a compulsory seven-day 'consideration period' during which the creditor or owner must not approach the debtor or hirer at all, except in response to a specific request. The consumer is by this means to be afforded opportunity to reflect upon and, if he so decides, to withdraw from the prospective agreement. These provisions are not applicable to bridging loans nor mortgaged land. (Cf. ss. 58 and 61 of the CCA.)

> NOTE: The Consumer Credit (Cancellation Notices and Copies of Documents) Regulations 1983 (as amended) prescribe the form of withdrawal notice which must be included in the copy of the agreement to be given to the debtor or hirer under the CCA at the commencement of the consideration period.

20. Extending the right of cancellation to cash sale

It had long been regarded as extraordinary that a policy consideration extending consumer protection to those who enter into 'doorstep' agreements' on credit should not have been available to those who enter cash agreements as well. The opportunity to extend this protection, indeed the obligation to do so, arose with the adoption by the EC of a Directive which was implemented by the UK by means of the 'Consumer Protection (Cancellation of Agreements Concluded away from Business Premises) Regulations 1987. The effect of these regulations is (broadly) to give the consumer a seven-day cooling off period if he agrees to a 'doorstep' sale for cash after an 'unsolicited' visit by the trader or his representative.

NOTE: The Director General of Fair Trading has expressed concern about some of the methods used to promote the sale of 'timeshare' interests in property ('I find some of the techniques used to sell timeshare wholly unacceptable ... there is a section of the industry that has rejected ethical practice and appears to hold the public in contempt.'). He has proposed, in his 1990 Report on timeshares, a legislative package a key element of which would be a 14-day 'cooling-off' period. Thus, the idea of consumers having the right to cancel, to think again, would be further extended.

Variation of agreements

21. Formal requirements on variation

Where the creditor or owner, in exercise of a power contained in the agreement, varies a regulated agreement, the variation will not take effect before written notice of it is given to the debtor or hirer in the prescribed manner: s. 82(1). The effect of variation is to revoke the earlier agreement, and the modifying agreement is treated as reproducing the combined effect of the two agreements: s. 82(2). If the earlier agreement is a regulated agreement but the modifying agreement is not, the modifying agreement is nevertheless to be treated as a regulated agreement unless it is for running-account credit: s. 82(3). The Consumer Credit (Notice of Variation of Agreements) Regulations 1977 prescribe the manner in which notice of variation must be given: generally seven days' notice must be served on the debtor or hirer.

Progress test 12

1. In what circumstances does the CCA limit the recovery of credit brokerage fees to £3? **(1)**

2. How does the CCA protect the consumer against the filing of incorrect information about him by credit reference agencies? **(2)**

3. What regulated agreements are exempted from the Part V

CCA requirements? How completely are such agreements exempted from the requirements? **(4)**

4. What information must a regulated agreement provide by virtue of the Consumer Credit (Agreements) Regulations 1983? **(6)**

5. Mr A proposes to enter into a regulated hire-purchase agreement in respect of certain hi-fi equipment. The agreement is signed by his wife on his behalf. Mr A obtains possession of the equipment. He then decides that he cannot afford to pay the agreed instalments, but he wishes to have the equipment. What is his legal position? **(8, 13)**

6. At what stage or stages in the formation of a regulated consumer credit or hire agreement should the debtor or hirer receive copies of the agreement? **(9)**

7. When will a regulated agreement be cancellable? If it is cancellable, how does the CCA seek to ensure that the consumer will be aware of his rights and how to exercise them? Describe the ways in which the right to cancel has been extended in recent years. What further extensions are proposed? **(10, 14)**

8. What factors must the court take into account in deciding whether to accede to an application for enforcement of an agreement which has been improperly executed? In what cases can no enforcement order be made whatever the other circumstances? **(12, 13)**

9. If an agreement is cancellable, how much time is the consumer given in which to cancel? To whom may notice of cancellation be given? Is there any prescribed form for cancellation? **(15, 16)**

10. What are the effects of cancellation of an agreement? On cancellation, what is the legal position with regard to:

    (a) goods in the consumer's possession;
    (b) goods given in part-exchange;
    (c) the payment of credit and interest? **(17)**

11. A trader persuades a customer to sign on his premises an immediately binding agreement to enter into future regulated consumer credit agreement. Later, when the customer reads the information contained in the prospective agreement, he does not wish to proceed with the transaction. Can the customer withdraw and get the deposit back?   **(18)**

12. How does the CCA operate to give a 'cooling-off' period in the case of prospective land mortgages?   **(19)**

13. Where a regulated agreement may be varied under a power contained in the agreement, what requirements must the creditor or owner observe in order effectually to exercise the power? What is the legal effect of variation?   **(21)**

13

Consumer credit: liability for defective goods and services

A summary

1. Review of liability

The following may be liable for defective goods or services which the consumer purchases with the aid of some form of financial accommodation.

(a) *The supplier of the goods,* who may be liable for:

(*i*) misrepresentation (*see* Chap. 4);

(*ii*) breach of express term (condition, warranty intermediate stipulation (*see* Chap. 4));

(*iii*) breach of implied term (title, description, quality, fitness, samples (*see* Chap. 5));

(*iv*) breach of duty of care in the tort of negligence (*see* Chap. 9).

(b) *The supplier of the services,* who may be liable under the Supply of Goods and Services Act 1982 (*see* Chap. 5).

(c) *The manufacturer of the goods,* who may be liable for:

(*i*) breach of obligations assumed by him in a guarantee;

(*ii*) breach of duty of care in the tort of negligence (*see* Chap. 9)

NOTE: Exclusion of liability arising in the above cases is prevented or, as the case may be, subjected to a reasonableness test, by the Unfair Contract Terms Act (*see* Chap. 6).

(d) *Persons conducting antecedent negotiations (see* **2**).

(e) *The supplier of the credit (see* **4–6**).

Persons conducting antecedent negotiations

2. Credit-brokers

The category of persons who may conduct antecedent negotiations with the consumer (*see* s. 56) comprehends credit-brokers. 'Credit-brokers' is widely defined in ss. 189 and 145, and includes persons who effect introductions of individuals desiring to obtain credit to persons carrying on a consumer credit business. So dealers who introduce customers to a finance company are credit-brokers, whether the credit provided is a personal loan, or takes the form of hire-purchase, conditional sale or credit-sale.

A dealer may be liable to the consumer in the following ways.

(a) *Breach of a collateral warranty. Andrews* v. *Hopkinson* (1957): a dealer told a consumer that a certain car was 'a good little bus; I'd stake my life on it. You will have no trouble with it.' The consumer entered into a hire-purchase agreement with a finance company, to whom the dealer sold the car. HELD: The dealer was liable to the consumer for breach of collateral warranty (i.e. the dealer's statement was a warranty the consideration for which was the consumer's willingness to enter into the hire-purchase agreement with the third party finance company) when a steering defect caused him injury.

> NOTE: In the typical tripartite hire-purchase situation the consumer will not be able to sue the dealer for breach of the implied terms as to title, description, quality, fitness (*see* 4). This is because of the doctrine of privity of contract. The legal position is that the dealer sells to the finance company and the consumer's contract for the goods lies with them. The consumer is not privy to any contract with the dealer, unless a collateral contract can be construed, and cannot sue the dealer for breach of implied term (*Drury* v. *Victor Buckland Ltd* (1941) CA).

(b) *Breach of duty of care in the tort of negligence.* In *Andrews* v. *Hopkinson* (above) the dealer was also held to be liable in negligence, as the steering defect could have been discovered by the exercise of reasonable care on the dealer's part.

NOTE: The supplier of the goods may be liable to the supplier of the credit under the terms of a contract (e.g. a recourse agreement) between them.

3. Agency under s. 56 of the CCA

Under common law principles a statement by the credit-broker will not bind the creditor unless the relationship of agency exists between them. Thus a dealer's representations will not generally bind the finance company at common law. This normal outcome at common law is altered by s. 56 of the CCA. Section 56(2) provides that in the case of debtor-creditor-supplier agreements, negotiations 'shall be deemed to be conducted by the negotiator in the capacity of agent of the creditor as well as in his actual capacity.' This deemed agency would apply typically in hire-purchase, conditional sale and credit-sale transactions. Antecedent negotiations include any representations made by the negotiator to the consumer and any other dealings between them. It follows from s. 56(2) that the creditor (e.g. a finance company) will be liable for misrepresentations made by a dealer. Notice of rescission may be given to the dealer as agent of the creditor for this purpose: s. 102.

Any attempt to contract out of s. 56, whether by providing that the negotiator is to be treated as agent of the consumer, or by purporting to exclude the creditor's liability for the negotiator's act or omissions, is nullified by s. 56(3).

NOTE: Non-commercial agreements and small agreements are not excluded from the operation of s. 56 (*see* 12:4). Contrast the position with regard to s. 75 CCA (*see* **5**).

Supplier of credit

4. Where the supplier of credit also supplies the goods or services

In these cases the liability of the supplier will be as above (*see* **1, 3**). Typical examples of such 'two-party' credit transactions are hire-purchase, conditional sale and credit-sale agreements. It will be recalled (*see* 5:13) that the Supply of Goods (Implied Terms) Act 1973 (as amended) imposes the same implied terms in hire-purchase agreements as are imposed by the Sale of Goods Act in contracts of sale, namely:

(a) title (s. 8 of 1973 Act);
(b) description (s. 9);
(c) merchantable quality (s. 10(2));
(d) fitness for purpose (s. 10(3));
(e) samples (s. 11).

Further, the restrictions on exclusion clauses in hire-purchase agreements and contracts of sale are identical (s. 6 of the Unfair Contract Terms Act: *see* 6:19).

Liability for breach of the above implied terms lies with the legal supplier of the goods, i.e. the dealer if he finances his own hire-purchase transaction, but otherwise the finance company (cf. *Drury* v. *Victor Buckland Ltd*; *see* **2(a)** note).

NOTE: The implied terms in hire-purchase agreements apply whatever the amount of credit involved and whatever the status of the customer — they are not confined to regulated agreements.

5. Joint liability under s. 75 of the CCA

Section 75 applies to all debtor-creditor-supplier agreements where the creditor and the legal supplier of the goods are *not* one and the same person. This is the so-called 'connected lender' type of transaction, as for instance where the debtor's contract to buy goods from a retailer is financed by a loan agreement with a finance house with whom the retailer has a business connection. In such cases, where the debtor has, in relation to a transaction financed by the agreement, any claim against the supplier in respect of a misrepresentation or breach of contract, he has 'a like claim' against the creditor: s. 75(1). Creditor and supplier are jointly and severally liable (s. 75(1)), though by s. 75(2) the creditor has a statutory right of indemnity against the supplier for loss suffered in satisfying his liability. Section 75 applies notwithstanding that the debtor, in entering into the transaction, exceeded the credit limit or otherwise contravened any term of the agreement: s. 75(4). Contracting out of s. 75 is ineffective by virtue of s. 173(1) (*see* 10:9).

The s. 75(1) liability does not apply to:

(a) a non-commercial agreement (defined in 12:4**(a)**);
(b) a claim in so far as it relates to a single item to which the supplier has attached a *cash* price not exceeding £100 or more than £30,000 (s. 75(3); nor of course would s. 75(1) apply if the *credit* ceiling of £15,000 were exceeded).

In *Porter* v. *General Guarantee Corporation Ltd* (1982), the court wrongly applied s. 75 to a hire-purchase agreement. The truth is that s. 75 can never apply to hire-purchase or to conditional sale or credit-sale, because in these transactions the supplier of the credit also supplies the goods to the consumer. But the consumer is adequately protected in such contracts since both s. 56(2) (*see* **3**) and the statutory rights (*see* **4**) will be applicable. Indeed, a prime consequence of s. 75 is to impose on the connected lender effectively the same liability for defects in respect of a transaction financed by a personal loan as is imposed on the creditor by other means in a transaction financed by hire-purchase, conditional sale or credit-sale. The provisions of s. 56 overlap, however, with those in s. 75 governing connected lender transactions. This could be significant, for instance, in cases of misrepresentation where the supplier of an item has attached a cash price not exceeding £100; here the connected lender would be liable only under the deemed agency provisions of s. 56. The connected lender's liability under s. 75 (where applicable) is, however, potentially more extensive than his liability under s. 56 would be, inasmuch as s. 75 will include liability for breach of the statutory rights by the supplier under the supply contract.

It is a general point of policy behind ss. 56 and 75 that since the creditor has an interest in the transaction financed by him then he should share in any liability which arises under it. Furthermore, an extension of this leads to the creditors, in a sense, 'policing' the traders with whom they are connected.

U.D.T. v. *Taylor* (1980): in this Scottish case the facts were that the consumer (T) bought a motor car from dealers with finance supplied by U.D.T., who had business arrangements with the dealers. The car turned out to be unroadworthy and T rejected it for misrepresentation and breach of contract. U.D.T. nevertheless sued T to enforce the loan agreement. HELD on appeal to the Sheriff Principal: Where the debtor had the right to rescind the supply contract, he could also rescind the credit contract ('a like claim'), and would therefore have a good defence to an action by the creditor.

NOTE: It is questionable whether the 'like claim' does extend to the right to *rescind* the credit contract as well as the supply contract; but the actual result in the above case must be correct because the consumer's claim against the dealer would include his wasted expenditure under the loan agreement and that claim for damages would be 'a like claim' and valid as a counterclaim to the creditor's action.

6.   Credit cards and s. 75

Where the consumer purchases goods with a cash price of over £100 against a credit card, the credit card company is at first sight liable under s. 75 for misrepresentation or breach of contract by the supplier of the goods. But the application of s. 75 to credit cards presents anomalies. First, certain credit cards (e.g. the American Express green card and Diners Club) are exempt from s. 75 altogether because they require payment of the whole amount of the credit provided in each billing period to be made by a single payment (*see* 10:8). These cards (and some others) are often referred to as 'charge' cards, but there is no magic in the name. The distinction is made between cards inside and outside s. 75 by reference to the obligation to repay, not by the naming of the card. Secondly, s. 75 came into operation on 1 July 1977, but only in relation to regulated agreements made on or after that day: Sched. 3, para. 16. The effect of this seems to be that the statutory protection is not available to cardholders who first obtained their cards before 1 July 1977. After discussions with the Office of Fair Trading, however, Barclaycard and Access voluntarily agreed to accept liability to such cardholders in circumstances where s. 75 would otherwise have applied. But this voluntary acceptance of liability is limited to the amount of the transaction charged to the cardholder's account. This limitation could in practice reduce the cardholder's protection, since damages caused by defective goods (e.g. a television set which bursts into flames) could well exceed their purchase price. Even should the cardholder have recourse to s. 56 (in cases involving misrepresentation, for example), there is still the problem that s. 56 itself will probably not apply to cardholders who first obtained their cards before April 1977: cf. Sched. 3, para. 1. There are, therefore, a number of 'classes' of credit card holders, each protected to a different extent. It is anticipated that this situation will be neither addressed nor resolved, rather that, as the years go by, it will recede.

Progress test 13

1. Summarize the ways in which the undermentioned persons may be liable to the consumer for the supply of defective goods or services which the consumer has purchased with the aid of some form of financial accommodation:

    (a) the supplier of the goods;
    (b) the supplier of the services;
    (c) the manufacturer of the goods. **(1)**

2. A dealer introduces a consumer to a finance company, who then let the goods sold to them by the dealer to the consumer under a regulated hire-purchase agreement. Is the dealer a 'credit-broker' within the meaning of the CCA? **(2)**

3. B, a motor-dealer, tells C that a certain second-hand car 'goes like a bomb'. The D Finance Co., pursuant to a pre-existing arrangement with B, then lends money to C under a regulated agreement so that C can buy the car from B. The car's brakes are defective and C is seriously injured.

    (a) Has C any cause of action against B?
    (b) Do the D Finance Co. have any liability towards C?
    (1, 3, 5)

4. E, a motor-dealer, tells F that a certain used car is 'a good runner'. The G Finance Co. subsequently buys the car from E and lets it under a regulated hire-purchase agreement to F. The car's gearbox jams as F is driving the vehicle away from E's premises.

 (a) Has F any cause of action against E?
 (b) Does the G Finance Co. have any liability towards F? (2–4)

   Would it make any difference if the hire-purchase agreement contained a clause stating: 'the credit-broker introducing the prospective debtor to (the Finance Co.) shall be deemed to be the agent of the debtor'? (4)

5. The H Finance Co., which has a pre-existing arrangement with J, a dealer, lends K £14,500 under a regulated agreement to enable K to purchase a yacht from J. K does purchase the yacht, at £31,000. The yacht proves to be unseaworthy and it sinks and is not salvageable. Has K any cause of action against the H Finance Co.? (5)

6. L buys an electric kettle, manufactured by M, from N, a retailer, financing the transaction on L's Access credit card. The purchase price of the kettle is £18. The kettle short-circuits, causing L a severe electric shock. Consider the respective liabilities (if any) of M, N, and Access. (1, 5)

7. P has Diners Club and Barclaycard credit cards, both first obtained in 1976, and American Express and Access credit cards, both first obtained in 1978. P contemplates (*i*) buying a video cassette recorder, and (*ii*) paying for a package holiday against one of the credit cards. Are there any consumer protection reasons why P should use any one credit card in preference to the others? (6)

14

Termination of credit agreement by the debtor

Rebate on early settlement

1. Early settlement

The debtor under a regulated consumer credit agreement is entitled at any time, by written notice to the creditor, to discharge his indebtedness under the agreement by paying all amounts payable to the creditor: s. 94.

2. The statutory rebate

The debtor is entitled, under regulations made pursuant to s. 95, to a statutory rebate of charges for credit if he discharges his indebtedness earlier than the time fixed by the agreement. The Consumer Credit (Rebate on Early Settlement) Regulations 1983 give detailed formulae for calculating the rebate.

3. Duty to give information

In order to bolster up the right to a statutory rebate, the creditor is placed under a duty, on receipt of a written request, to give the debtor a statement indicating the amount of payment required to discharge his indebtedness under the agreement: s. 97. By virtue of the Consumer Credit (Settlement Information) Regulations 1983, the creditor must provide the settlement information in the prescribed form within 12 working days after receiving the written request. The information given must include, in particular, details of any rebate to which the debtor is entitled.

NOTE: Sections 77–79 give the debtor or hirer a general right during the currency of the agreement, on payment of a fee (now 50p), to a copy of the executed agreement and to information from the creditor or owner as to the state of the account between them. Regulations prescribe that the information must be provided within 12 working days after receipt of the written request by the debtor or hirer. (The relevant regulations are the Consumer Credit (Prescribed Periods for Giving Information) Regulations 1983, and the Consumer Credit (Running-Account Credit Information) Regulations 1983.)

Voluntary termination of hire-purchase or conditional sale agreements

4. The right to terminate

At any time before the final payment under a regulated hire-purchase or conditional sale agreement falls due, the debtor is entitled by giving written notice to terminate the agreement: s. 99. This right is quite separate from the right to early settlement under s. 94 (*see* 1).

5. The 50 per cent provision

The liability of the debtor terminating an agreement under s. 99 is to pay the following:

(a) All sums accrued due: s. 99(2).

(b) Any additional sum needed to bring the total paid to one-half of the total price, unless

    (*i*) the agreement provides for a smaller payment, *or*

    (*ii*) the court is satisfied that a lesser sum would be equal to the loss sustained by the creditor: s. 100(1), (3) (and *see Yeoman Credit* v. *Waragowski* (1961), 15:5).

(c) Damages if the debtor has failed to take reasonable care: s. 100(4).

NOTE: Where an installation charge has been specified in the agreement as part of the total price, one-half of the total price means the whole installation charge plus one-half of the remainder of the total price: s. 100(2).

6. Return of goods

It will be appreciated that where the debtor exercises the right to terminate in s. 99, as opposed to the right of early settlement in s. 94 (*see* **1**), then the goods have to be returned to the creditor. If the debtor wrongfully retains them the court, unless satisfied that it would not be just to do so, must order the goods to be delivered to the creditor without giving the debtor an option to pay the value of the goods instead: s. 100(5).

Voluntary termination of hire agreements

7. The right to terminate

The hirer under a regulated hire agreement is entitled by giving written notice to terminate the agreement prematurely. Notice cannot be given to expire earlier than eighteen months after the making of the agreement. The minimum period of notice, unless the agreement provides for a shorter period, is the length of the shortest agreed interval between the making of rental payments by the hirer, or three months, whichever is less. Premature termination of a hire agreement in this way does not affect any liability which has already accrued under the agreement. (Cf. s. 101).

> NOTE: Section 101(7), (8) provides for the exemption from these termination provisions of certain commercial leasing transactions and, more generally, of any agreement where the annual payments exceed the sum of £900 (as now stipulated by the Consumer Credit (Increase of Monetary Amounts) Order 1983).

Progress test 14

1. How can a debtor obtain a rebate of credit charges under a regulated consumer credit agreement? **(1, 2)**

2. How can the debtor, if he is unsure, ascertain the amount that is payable in order to discharge his indebtedness under a regulated consumer credit agreement? **(3)**

3. D, a debtor, does not wish to continue payments under a regulated hire-purchase agreement. Can D return the goods and terminate the agreement? If so, how much must D pay? **(4–6)**

4. Explain how the CCA provides for the premature termination by the hirer of a regulated hire agreement. **(7)**

15
Consumer credit: remedies

1. Jurisdiction
The county court has exclusive jurisdiction to determine all disputes relating to regulated agreements: s. 141.

Creditor's remedies

2. The remedies
Breach of a credit agreement may lead to the creditor or owner pursuing one or more of the following remedies (the list is not exhaustive), depending upon the circumstances:

(a) Action for arrears.
(b) Termination of the contract.
(c) Action for damages.
(d) Action for repossession of goods.

3. Action for arrears
Whatever the type of credit agreement, the creditor may always sue at common law for any arrears in the repayments as they fall due. The following points in the CCA should be noted.

(a) The agreement may provide for the payment of interest on arrears (default interest). The Act provides that the debtor under a regulated consumer credit agreement shall not be obliged to pay any such default interest at a higher rate of interest than that charged in the agreement: s. 93.

(b) The court is given wide powers, on application in appropriate cases by either party to the agreement, to make a 'time order', i.e.

an order giving the debtor or hirer the opportunity to pay arrears by such instalments, payable at such times, as the court considers reasonable having regard to the means of the debtor or hirer: s. 129. In the case of a hire-purchase or conditional sale agreement a time order may also deal with sums which, although not payable by the debtor at the time the order is made, would become payable if the agreement continued in force: s. 130(2).

(c) The agreement may contain an acceleration clause, i.e. a clause providing for immediate payment of the entire outstanding balance on default by the debtor or hirer, or on the occurrence of other stated contingencies (e.g. execution levied by another creditor against the debtor's goods). Such an acceleration clause is a perfectly valid device provided that it is not construed as a penalty clause, a result which can be avoided by the inclusion of provision for an appropriate rebate on early settlement (cf. 14:2). Under the Act at least seven days' notice in writing of the intention to operate any acceleration clause is required: ss. 76(1), 87(1). In default cases the debtor or hirer may then rectify the matter within the specified time, in which case the acceleration clause does not become operative: s. 89. If the default is not rectified within the specified time, it will then be too late for the debtor to exercise his right to terminate under s. 99 (*see* 14:4): *Wadham Stringer Finance Ltd* v. *Meaney* (1980). In this eventuality a time order (*see* 3(b)) could still avail the debtor.

(d) The court may find the credit bargain to be extortionate (*see* 16).

4. Termination

A credit arrangement may expressly provide for its termination by the creditor or owner on default by the debtor or hirer or on the occurrence of other stated contingencies. Further, under the common law the creditor or owner will be entitled to treat the agreement as terminated if the debtor or hirer defaults and the default is sufficiently serious to amount to repudiation of his obligations. Whatever the reason for termination the CCA affords the consumer some protection in the case of a regulated agreement.

(a) *Default cases.* At least seven days' written notice ('default notice') is necessary before the creditor or owner can become entitled to terminate the agreement: s. 87. The default notice must be in the prescribed form and specify:

(*i*) the nature of the breach, *and*

(*ii*) the action required to remedy it, or (if the breach is not capable of remedy) the sum (if any) required as compensation for the breach: s. 88.

The default notice must also contain information in the prescribed terms about the consequences of failure to comply with it: s. 88(4). If the debtor or hirer takes the specified action the breach is treated as not having occurred: s. 89. Or the debtor may apply for a time order.

> NOTE: The prescribed form and content for default notices will be found in the Consumer Credit (Enforcement, Default and Termination Notices) Regulations 1984.

(b) *Non-default cases.* Even in non-default cases at least seven days' written notice, in the form prescribed by the above-mentioned regulations, is necessary before the creditor or owner can become entitled to terminate an agreement of specific duration in exercise of a contractual right to do so: s. 98. Here the debtor's or hirer's only protection (unless the credit bargain is extortionate: *see* **16**) is to apply for a time order under s. 129 (*see* **3(b)**).

5. Action for damages

The creditor may wish to bring an action for damages on breach by the debtor of a hire-purchase or conditional sale agreement. (Breach of a credit-sale or loan agreement normally only allows the creditor to sue for instalments in arrears; an acceleration clause can be invoked if the agreement contains one.) Faced with an action for damages, the debtor's legal position will depend upon whether the agreement has been repudiated or terminated.

(a) *Repudiation.* It has already been noted that if the debtor terminates a regulated hire-purchase or conditional sale agreement pursuant to s. 99 (*see* **14:4**), then his liability is generally limited to payment of arrears plus such additional sum as is needed to bring the total paid up to one-half of the total price (*see* **14:5**). But the debtor may not exercise his statutory right to terminate under s. 99. He may instead simply go into arrears or otherwise be in breach of contract. If the breach is a major one it will amount to repudiation of the debtor's obligations and will entitle the creditor to treat the agreement as terminated and to sue for damages. In such a case the measure of damages is governed by the common law and will be based upon the decision of the Court of Appeal in *Yeoman Credit Ltd* v. *Waragowski* (1961). This case held that the creditor is entitled to be compensated for his loss of profit on the transaction, i.e. to be put in the same position as he would have been in if the contract had been fulfilled. Thus the debtor will have to pay:

(*i*) all sums accrued; plus

(*ii*) the balance of the total price;

but less

(*iii*) the proceeds of resale of the repossessed goods (the creditor must sell at the best price reasonably obtainable);

(*iv*) the sum (usually nominal) payable for the option to purchase;

(*v*) a discount for accelerated receipt (*Overstone Ltd* v. *Shipway* (1962) CA).

(b) *Termination*. In contrast to the heavy measure of damages imposed by the *Waragowski* decision, if the debtor is merely in breach of contract in circumstances not amounting to repudiation, and the creditor is provoked into exercising a contractual right to terminate the contract, then the measure of damages will be much less. Here the debtor will only be liable to pay:

(*i*) instalments in arrear at the date of termination plus interest (*Financings Ltd* v. *Baldock* (1963) CA);

(*ii*) damages if the debtor has failed to take reasonable care of the goods.

The reason given for this lesser liability is that the creditor's loss results not from the debtor's breach but from the creditor's decision to terminate the contract.

It is apparent from the above rulings that a game of cat and mouse is to be played out between creditor and debtor. In order to minimize his liabilities a debtor who has fallen into arrears must not repudiate the contract or even terminate it under s. 99; he must instead provoke the creditor into terminating the contract (or seek a time order). In *Waragowski* the debtor paid the initial deposit but no more. The creditor terminated the agreement six months later. This amounted to repudiation by the debtor. On the other hand, in *Financings Ltd v. Baldock* the debtor failed to pay the first two instalments, and although he expressed a willingness to try and pay, the creditor terminated the agreement. The Court of Appeal held that this did *not* amount to repudiation by the debtor. It may be added that wrongful disposition of the goods by the debtor will always amount to repudiation.

Debtor's protection against snatch back

6. Repossession

Termination of a hire-purchase agreement terminates the bailment of the goods so that the creditor, as legal owner, is entitled to repossession. Likewise under a conditional sale agreement the seller on termination will be entitled to repossession, because the property in the goods will have remained with the seller as the conditions as to instalments or otherwise will not have been fulfilled. This outcome — repossession — could, and frequently did, work injustice to the debtor, who might have paid much of the total price under the contract only to see the legal owner retake ('snatch back') the goods in consequence of termination of the agreement through breach (possibly purely technical) by the debtor. The CCA contains provisions protecting the debtor against snatch back, and this protection is considered in the following paragraphs.

7. The protection

The protection is threefold:

(a) notice is required;
(b) entry on premises to take possession is restricted;
(c) the goods may be 'protected'.

8. Notice

It will be recalled that notice prior to termination is required in both default and non-default cases (*see* **4**). In default cases this affords the debtor the opportunity of remedying the default and so nullifying the threatened termination; or the debtor may apply for a time order (possible too in non-default cases) under s. 129.

> NOTE: By virtue of the Consumer Credit (Enforcement, Default and Termination Notices) Regulations 1983 (as amended in 1984), the default notice must contain a statement in the prescribed form as to the debtor's right under the Act to get back all the money he has paid under the hire-purchase or conditional sale agreement if the creditor retakes protected goods without the debtor's consent or a court order (*see* **10, 11**).

9. Entry on premises

The creditor or owner is not entitled 'to enter any premises' to take possession of goods subject to a regulated hire-purchase, conditional sale or consumer hire agreement, without a court order: s. 92(1). Entry in contravention of this requirement is actionable as a breach of statutory duty: s. 92(3).

> NOTE: The debtor or hirer may always consent at the time of entry to entry without a court order: s. 173(3) (*see* 10:9); the point is that consent cannot validly be given in advance.

10. Protected goods

The creditor is not entitled to recover possession of protected goods without a court order. Goods are 'protected goods' at any time when:

(a) the debtor is in breach of a regulated hire-purchase or conditional sale agreement relating to goods; *and*
(b) the debtor has paid to the creditor one-third or more of the total price of the goods; *and*
(c) the property in the goods remains in the creditor: s. 90(1).

> NOTE: Where an installation charge has been specified in the agreement as part of the total price, one-third of the total price means the whole or the installation charge plus one-third of the remainder of the total price: s. 90(2).

11. Contravention of s. 90

The consequences of contravention are that:

(a) the agreement is terminated;
(b) the debtor is released from all liability;
(c) the debtor is entitled to recover from the creditor all sums paid by the debtor under the agreement: s. 91.

The following points should be noted:

(a) The debtor is not entitled to recover possession of the goods themselves, as the agreement is terminated (*Carr* v. *James Broderick & Co. Ltd* (1942)). Nor can the creditor revive the agreement by returning the goods to the debtor (*Capital Finance Co. Ltd* v. *Bray* (1964) CA).
(b) Section 90 aims at preventing protected goods from being retaken, without a court order, 'from the debtor'. so s. 90 will not be contravened if the debtor has parted with possession of the goods by (say) selling them to a third party (but note that delivery up of the goods by the debtor to a third party for some limited purpose, e.g. repairs, will not be parting with possession of the goods).
(c) Section 90 does not apply where the debtor terminates or has terminated the agreement: s. 90(5).
(d) Section 90 is not contravened if the debtor consents at the time to the creditor retaking possession of the goods: s. 173(3) (*see* 10:9). The consent must be genuinely voluntary: cf. *Mercantile Credit Co. Ltd* v. *Cross* (1965) CA.

> *Bentinck Ltd* v. *Cromwell Engineering Co. Ltd* (1971): the debtor was in possession of a car on hire-purchase terms. After a serious road accident he left the car at a garage and, three months later, disappeared without trace. Nine months after the accident the creditors retook possession of the car with the consent of the garage proprietor and sold it. HELD: As the car had been abandoned the protected goods provisions in the Hire-Purchase Act 1965 had not been contravened. It is thought that the same result would ensue under s. 90 of the CCA, because (*i*) if the goods have been abandoned, the creditor does not repossess 'from the debtor', (*ii*) alternatively, the debtor in abandoning the goods consents to repossession under s. 173(3).

12. Financial relief under consumer hire agreements

Section 90 applies only to goods under regulated hire-purchase and conditional sale agreements. A different form of protection is afforded in the case of consumer hire agreements. Where the owner under a regulated consumer hire agreement recovers possession of goods other than by court action, the hirer may apply to the court under s. 132 for an order that:

(a) the whole or part of any sum paid by the hirer to the owner in respect of the goods shall be repaid; *and*
(b) the obligation to pay the whole or part of any sum owed by the hirer to the owner in respect of the goods shall cease. The court must grant the application in full or in part if it appears to it to be just to do so, having regard to the extent of the enjoyment of the goods by the hirer.

These provisions are strengthened by the further power granted to the court to make an order for financial relief along the above-mentioned lines wherever the court makes an order in proceedings relating to a regulated consumer hire agreement for delivery of the goods to the owner: s. 132(2).

13. Protection orders

The court, on the application of the creditor or owner under a regulated agreement, has power to make such orders as it thinks just for protecting the creditor's or owner's property from damage or depreciation pending the determination of proceedings under the Act: s. 131.

Special orders in relation to hire-purchase or conditional sale agreements

14. Return orders

The court has power to make a 'return order', i.e. an order for the return of the goods to the creditor, in relation to a regulated hire-purchase or conditional sale agreement, where:

(a) an application is made for an enforcement order or a time order; *or*
(b) an action is brought by the creditor to recover possession of the goods: s. 133.

The order, like all orders in relation to regulated agreements, may be conditional or suspended: s. 135. The court will frequently combine a suspended return order with a time order; in other words, the operation of a return order will be suspended for so long as the debtor observes the requirements of a time order by paying the specified instalments at the specified times.

15. Transfer orders

The court also has power in relation to a regulated hire-purchase or conditional sale agreement to make a 'transfer order': s. 133. This is an order for the transfer to the debtor of the creditor's title to certain of the goods included in the agreement, and the return to the creditor of the remainder of the goods.

Extortionate credit bargains

16. Reopening of credit bargains

The Moneylenders Acts of 1910 and 1927 gave the court power to reopen 'harsh and unconscionable' moneylending transactions by money-lenders, there being a rebuttable presumption under the 1927 Act that interest of or above 48 per cent was harsh and unconscionable. The CCA (ss. 137–140) gives the court much wider powers, which apply where a credit bargain is held to be 'extortionate' (*see* **17**). If extortionate, any credit bargain may be reopened where the debtor is an individual, *whatever the amount of credit involved*. The debtor, or a surety, need not wait to be sued by the creditor under the credit agreement before applying to the court for relief (cf. s. 139(1)).

'Credit bargain' is defined to include not only the credit agreement itself, but also other transactions where those other transactions are to be taken into account in computing the total charge for credit: s. 137(2). Hiring agreements, however, cannot be reopened under these provisions (but cf. s. 132: *see* **12**).

17. When bargains are extortionate

A credit bargain is extortionate if it requires the debtor or a relative of his to make payments which are 'grossly exorbitant', or if otherwise 'grossly contravenes ordinary principles of fair dealing': s. 138.

NOTE: 1. There is under the Act no threshold above which a rate of interest is presumed to be exorbitant. Indeed, in *Ketley Ltd* v. *Scott* (1981) a short-term secured loan at an equivalent annual rate of interest of 48 per cent was held on the facts not to be extortionate.

2. During 1991 the Office of Fair Trading conducted an extensive survey of the nature and extent of extortionate credit bargains. Legislative change may well follow if the DGFT is convinced that consumers are being exploited by moneylenders.

18. Guidelines

The Act contains guidelines (in s. 138) relating to both objective and subjective factors which the court is to take into account in determining whether a credit bargain is extortionate. Regard is to be had to 'all relevant considerations' including:

(a) interest rates prevailing when the credit bargain was made;

(b) the age, experience, business capacity and state of health of the debtor, and the nature and degree of financial pressure which he was under when he made the credit bargain;

(c) the degree of risk accepted by the creditor, his relationship to the debtor, and whether or not a colourable cash price was quoted for any goods or services included in the credit bargain.

Wills v. *Wood* (1984): Mr Wills, a retired hotelier, deposited £11,000 with his solicitors to be lent to their clients from time to time. In this way he lent sums totalling £3,000 to Miss Wood, a spinster aged 57. The loans were secured on a second mortgage at 12.5 per cent interest per annum. At the time moneylenders generally were charging 18–24 per cent on second mortgages. HELD by the Court of Appeal: The credit bargain was not extortionate. The word was 'extortionate', not 'unwise'. There must be at the least be a substantial imbalance in bargaining power of which one party had taken advantage before a credit bargain could be considered extortionate. The debtor was of full age and capacity and capable of taking professional advice, which she had done. There was nothing oppressive or objectionable about the loans. (Nor was Mr Wills an unlicensed moneylender under the Moneylenders Acts; he was not carrying on the business of a moneylender, but was merely investing his savings in secured loans. Cf. now s. 21 CCA: *see* 16:**6**.)

19. Onus of proof
Once the debtor has raised the issue by alleging that a credit bargain is extortionate, it is for the creditor to prove the contrary: s. 171(7).

20. Nature of relief available
The court has wide powers under s. 139(2) to make orders 'for the purpose of relieving the debtor or a surety from payment of any sum in excess of that fairly due and reasonable'. For example, the terms of the credit agreement may be altered, or the creditor may be required 'to repay the whole or part of any sum paid under the credit bargain or any related agreement by the debtor or surety, whether paid to the creditor or any other person'.

NOTE: The court's powers outlined above apply to agreements and transactions 'whenever made' (Sched. 3, para. 42). But an order 'shall not alter the effect of any judgment': s. 139(4).

Progress test 15

1. Which courts have jurisdiction to determine disputes relating to regulated agreements? **(1)**
2. If a debtor falls into arrears in the payment of instalments due under a regulated hire-purchase agreement, can the creditor (*a*) claim default interests; and (*b*) invoke an acceleration clause? **(3)**
3. What is a time order? **(3)**
4. How many day's notice must a default give? What must it specify where the agreement is an hire-purchase or conditional sale agreement? **(4, 8)**
5. What steps can a debtor take to protect his interests when he has been served with (*a*) a default notice; or (*b*) a notice of termination in a non default-case? **(4)**

6. What is the measure of damages to which a debtor is liable on (*a*) repudiation of a hire-purchase agreement by the debtor; or (*b*) termination by the creditor of a hire-purchase agreement for breach by the debtor?   **(5)**

7. How does the CCA seek to protect the debtor against 'snatch back'?   **(7–10)**

8. When are goods 'protected'?   **(10)**

9. What are the legal consequences of the creditor retaking protected goods without a court order?   **(11)**

10. The protected goods provisions in the CCA do not apply to consumer hire agreements. What form does the protection take when the owner repossesses for default by the hirer?   **(12)**

11. What is (*a*) a protection order; (*b*) a return order, (*c*) a transfer order? In what circumstances are they available? Explain how the court is likely to combine a return order with a time order.   **(13–15)**

12. What is a 'credit bargain'? When may the court find it to be 'extortionate'? What guidelines are given to aid the court in determining whether a credit bargain is extortionate?   **(16–18)**

13. Is the burden of proof on the debtor to satisfy the court that a credit bargain is extortionate?   **(19)**

14. If the court does find that a credit bargain is extortionate, what is the nature of the relief that it can order? Give examples.   **(20)**

15. A finance company let a car to D under a regulated hire-purchase agreement. D pays a deposit and the first two instalments, but fails to pay the next two instalments. The finance company find the car parked in the road outside D's house and they take it away. D then sees it advertised for sale outside a local garage and, without anyone's consent, retakes the car. The finance company now propose to sue D for damages. What is the legal position between D and the finance company under the CCA?   **(4, 5, 10, 11)**

Part two

Administrative remedies and criminal law sanctions

Introductory note

In Part Two of this book we leave consideration of the consumer's private law rights and turn to administrative remedies and criminal law sanctions. The consumer's private law rights can often be rather illusory: he may be ignorant of his rights; he may lack the initiative or confidence to seek a civil law remedy; he may lack time or money to seek proper legal advice and then to institute civil proceedings, with the attendant delays and risks. So regulation by administrative authority offers better prospects for the protection of consumers at large. The trader's liability to criminal law sanctions will normally reinforce the powers possessed by administrative authorities. Administrative remedies will thus combine with criminal law sanctions to have a preventative effect in consumer protection.

Administrative remedies and civil law remedies will often overlap. For example, a misdescription will be likely to involve the commission of an offence under the Trade Descriptions Act as well as amounting to breach of contract by virtue of the Sale of Goods Act. On the other hand, it must be stressed that the consumer's contractual position will not generally be affected by reason only of the commission of a criminal offence by the trader, as we shall see. Individual consumers who are prejudiced by a trader's default, however, may succeed in obtaining an indirect remedy, in the form of a compensation order (*see* Chap. 21), after a successful prosecution has been brought by the administrative authority. The significance of this is that resort to an administrative authority is frequently the consumer's most practicable remedy.

Part Two concludes with a survey of the institutional framework, largely provided by the state, for the settlement of individual consumer disputes.

16

Functions of the Director General of Fair Trading under the Consumer Credit Act

1. Introduction

The post of Director General of Fair Trading was created by the Fair Trading Act 1973. The Director's consumer protection functions under that Act are dealt with in Chapter 17. It is convenient to deal first in this chapter with the additional duties imposed upon the Director by the Consumer Credit Act.

General functions of Director under the Act

2. Part I Consumer Credit Act

Part I imposes upon the Director the following duties in connection with credit:

(a) to administer the licensing system set up by the CCA (*see* 6);
(b) to superintend the working and enforcement of the CCA;
(c) to keep social and commercial developments relating to the provision of credit or bailment under review, and to advise the Secretary of State: s. 1;
(d) to arrange for the dissemination of information and advice to the public about the operation of the CCA and the availability of credit facilities: s. 4.

3. Enforcement

The Director is responsible for superintending the enforcement of the CCA and regulations made under it, and he can, where necessary or expedient, take enforcement steps himself: s. 1(1). But day-to-day enforcement is the responsibility of the local weights and measures ('trading standards') authority: s. 161. The local weights and measures authority must give notice to the Director of an intended prosecution for an offence under the Act, and they must wait for an acknowledgment from the Director, or for twenty-eight days, before proceeding: s. 161(2). In addition they must, when and as required, report to the Director on the exercise of their functions under the Act: s. 161(3). In these ways is a balance achieved between centralized enforcement of the Act, and efficient local enforcement in cases of only local significance.

Finally, it may be noted that where a person is convicted of an offence, or a judgment given against him, the court may make arrangements to bring the conviction or judgment to the Director's attention: s. 166. Information of this kind may influence the Director in the exercise of his licensing functions under the Act.

Introductory note on licensing

4. Licensing as a means of control

Licensing of business is a flexible yet powerful means of control. A trader or organization persistently infringing the criminal law, or deliberately breaking contracts, in the expectation of showing a profit despite the loss of the odd criminal prosecution or civil suit, may find the threat of withdrawal of a trading licence a stronger stimulus to fairer dealing. A licence revoked, or not renewed, effectively prevents further trading on account of the criminal law sanctions and civil law disabilities which unlicensed trading is likely to incur.

At the end of September 1989 the following 'problem traders' had been either subjected to refusal or revocation of their licences (the first figure) or had received warning notices from the DGFT:

Motor dealers: 487, 127
Finance companies and moneylenders: 171, 382
Retailers and hiring firms: 177, 451
Builders and home improvement firms: 72, 184
Debt collectors: 42, 80
Estate agents, insurance and mortgage business: 122, 236

5. Examples of licensing

Licensing in the field of credit has been previously attempted, namely the licensing of moneylenders. This licensing was ineffective because it was not systematically enforced. There are many examples of licensing intended to protect both consumers and honest traders. Recent developments are the registration of insurance brokers under the Insurance Brokers (Registration) Act 1977; the registration under the Data Protection Act 1984 of data users who hold personal data and of persons carrying on computer bureaux who provide services in respect of personal data; and the proposed licensing of non-solicitor conveyancers. Perhaps of greatest significance for the consumer in the area of licensing is the system for licensing consumer credit business, in operation under the CCA.

> NOTE: An interesting scheme of *negative licensing* was introduced under the Estate Agents Act 1979, which empowers the Director General of Fair Trading to prohibit unfit persons from doing 'estate agency work': s. 3. By May 1990 96 traders had been banned entirely.

In April 1990 it was announced that new legislation is to be introduced to regulate further the activities of estate agents. This would bring an extension of the Trade Descriptions Act and the banning of certain notorious practices such as bidding up prices and tie-in sales.

Licensing functions of director

6. Licensing under Part III

Part III of the CCA sets up a licensing system. A licence is required to carry on a consumer credit or consumer hire business: s. 21(1). Any such business — whether carried on by sole trader, partnership, limited liability company, or other body — requires a licence, but not a local authority, or body corporate empowered by a public general Act to carry on a business: s. 21(2), (3). The scope of the licensing control is therefore extensive (cf. 10:**2**), and by s. 147(1) it includes ancillary credit businesses (credit brokerage, debt-adjusting, debt-counselling, debt-collecting, credit reference agencies, all defined in s. 145). However, a person is not to be treated as carrying on a particular type of business merely because occasionally he enters into transactions belonging to a business of that type: s. 189(2). (Cf. *Willis* v. *Wood* (1984): *see* 15:18.)

> NOTE: The activities which arise in the normal course of a solicitor's practice comprehend credit brokerage, debt-adjusting, debt-counselling, and debt-collecting; a licence is therefore required, and in fact a group licence is in operation (*see* 9).

7. Standard licences

These are issued to a named person, or to a named partnership; or unincorporated body of persons, for a period of five years. Before June 1 1991 the period of validity was 15 years. Welcoming the change, the DGFT said 'in my view, this will help make the consumer credit licensing system an even more effective instrument of consumer protection'. In this statement the DGFT took the opportunity to review the system's 15-year history . . . 'Nobody in 1976 could have foreseen the persistent expansion of credit throughout the period. This has resulted in a total of over 300,000 applications for licences against an original estimate of 50,000.' The licence covers such activities as are described therein. A licence covers the canvassing off trade premises of debtor-creditor-supplier agreements or regulated consumer hire agreements only to the extent that it specifically so provides: s. 23(3). (*See* 11:9).

8. Fitness

A standard licence is to be issued by the Director to an applicant who satisfies the Director that he is a fit person and that a name under which he applies to be licensed is not misleading or otherwise undesirable: s. 25(1). In determining fitness the Director must have regard to any relevant circumstances, in particular to evidence tending to show that the applicant has been involved in fraud or other breach of the law, or in practices which, while not necessarily unlawful, are deceitful, oppressive, unfair or improper: s. 25(2).

NOTE: In his June 1991 statement about licensing the DGFT commented 'Central to licensing is the requirement that traders should be able to demonstrate their fitness. To date I have served notice on nearly 2,900 traders whose fitness has been called into question, that I was minded to refuse a licence or revoke an existing one. There is a significant deterrent in having a licensing system. Traders who are aware that they are unfit are prevented from entering the credit industry and those who have been granted licences and are dealing in credit are less likely to stray from the straight and narrow'.

9. Group licences

A group licence may be issued by the Director if it appears to him that the public interest would be better served by doing so than by obliging the persons concerned to apply separately for standard licences: s. 22(5). The Director must give general notice of the issue of any group licence: s. 22(8). Group licences have been issued in respect of:

(a) solicitors holding a practising certificate;
(b) liquidators and executors appointed to take temporary charge of a business involved in consumer credit activities;
(c) Citizens' Advice Bureaux registered with the National Association of Citizens' Advice Bureaux;
(d) Age Concern and other old people's welfare organizations;
(e) chartered accountants and certified accountants holding a practising certificate.

10. Conduct of business

Further control through licensing may be achieved by regulations made by the Secretary of State as to the conduct by a licensee of his business: s. 26.

11. Register

The Director maintains a register, open to public inspection on payment of a fee, containing, *inter alia*, particulars of licences applied for or in force; revocations, suspensions and variations of licences; and decisions of the Director and appeals therefrom: s. 35.

12. Sanctions

It is a criminal offence to engage in activities requiring a licence when not a licensee, or to carry on a business under a name not specified in the licence, or to fail to notify changes in the registered particulars: s. 39.

The enforcement of regulated agreements by an unlicensed credit or hire trader requires an order of the Director: s. 40. In determining whether to make an order, the Director must have regard to any relevant factors including the prejudice caused to debtors or hirers by the trader's conduct, and the trader's degree of culpability in failing to obtain a licence: s. 40(4). Further, the enforcement of regulated agreements made by a credit or hire trader through the agency of an unlicensed credit-broker likewise requires an order of the Director: s. 149.

13. Appeals

If the Director refuses to issue, renew or vary a licence, or compulsorily varies, suspends or revokes it, or refuses to make an enforcement order under ss. 40 or 149 (*see* **12**), then appeal lies to the Secretary of State (ss. 41 and 150), with further appeal on a point of law to the High Court: s. 42.

Progress test 16

1. Summarize the duties of the Director General of Fair Trading under the Consumer Credit Act. **(2)**

2. (a) How does the CCA seek to ensure that local weights and measures authorities liaise with the Director in the enforcement of the Act? When can the Director take enforcement steps himself?
(b) If a trader is convicted of an offence, or has a judgment given against him, is the matter likely to come to the Director's attention? **(3)**

3. Why is licensing thought to be a good method of controlling business? Give examples of the use of licensing. **(4, 5)**

4.   What businesses require a licence under the CCA? What reforms have been proposed?   **(6, 14)**

5.   What is a standard licence? How long does it last? What activities does it permit?   **(7)**

6.   What factors must the Director take into account in determining the fitness of an applicant for a standard licence? **(8)**

7.   When may the Director issue a group licence? What group licences have been issued?   **(9)**

8.   How may a member of the public ascertain whether a particular trader is duly licensed?   **(11)**

9.   What sanctions does the CCA impose in respect of unlicensed trading?   **(12)**

10. What right of appeal is open to a licensee or applicant for a licence who is dissatisfied with a decision of the Director concerning the licence?   **(13)**

17
Fair trading

Director General of Fair Trading

1. The post of Director General of Fair Trading
This post was created by s. 1 of the Fair Trading Act 1973 (in this chapter referred to as 'the Act' or 'FTA'). Much of the FTA is concerned with competition law, a subject which is outside the scope of this book. Our present concern is with the consumer protection powers of the Director.

2. The Consumer Protection Advisory Committee
This Committee, which as its name suggests is purely advisory in function, was created by s. 3 of the FTA. The Committee had so few references made to it, and took so long about its consideration of them, that it has now been disbanded.

3. Powers and duties of Director
Apart from his powers under Part II and Part III of the FTA (*see* below), the Director has the following powers and duties under the Act.

(a) He must keep under review and collect information relating to the carrying on of commercial activities in the UK which relate to goods or services supplied to consumers in the UK, with a view to his becoming aware of practices which may adversely affect the economic interests of UK consumers: s. 2(1)(*a*) FTA.

(b) The Director must receive and collate evidence of practices which may adversely affect the interests (whether economic interests *or* interests with respect to health, safety or other matters) of UK consumers: s. 2(1)(*b*).

> NOTE: Section 2(1)(*a*) imposes an active duty to collect information; whereas s. 2(1)(*b*) imposes the purely passive duty to receive evidence. On the other hand, the s. 2(1)(*a*) duty relates only to practices which adversely affect the economic interests of consumers, whereas s. 2(1)(*b*) relates to practices which may adversely affect a much wider range of consumer interests.

(c) The Director can arrange for the publication of information and advice for consumers: s. 124(1). Among other publications put out by the Office of Fair Trading ('OFT') are the many free leaflets for the guidance of consumers, obtainable in public libraries, Citizens' Advice Bureaux and elsewhere.

(d) The Director must encourage trade associations to prepare codes of practice: s. 124(3). This aspect of the Director's duties is considered further below (*see* **5**).

(e) The Director can make recommendations to the Secretary of State as to any action which he thinks it would be expedient for the Secretary of State or any other Minister to take: s. 2(3)(*b*). This power is quite separate from the recommendations which the Director can make under Part II of the FTA (*see* **8**). It was under s. 2, following publication in 1975 by the OFT of its Consultative Document entitled *Bargain Offer Claims*, that the Director recommended action against all sorts of bargain offers. In due course the Price Marking (Bargain Offers) Order 1979 was made under the Prices Act 1974, incorporating some of the recommendations. This Order proved unsatisfactory in practice and has now been repealed and replaced by the Consumer Protection Act 1987, Part III (*see* 19: **11**).

(f) Mention may be made here of the Estate Agents Act 1979, which empowers the Director to prohibit unfit persons from doing 'estate agency work' (*see* 16:5).

(g) Finally, it should be noted that the OFT does *not* act on behalf of individual consumers to resolve disputes.

Voluntary codes of practice

4.   Codes of practice as an instrument of consumer protection

A code of practice, provided it is precise and does not merely contain vague generalizations, is a useful and flexible instrument of consumer protection. If voluntary, it may gain added strength by having the support of the industry whose practice it regulates, and it may also contain provisions which it would be impractical to reduce into inflexible legislative requirements. For example, the availability of spare parts and servicing facilities is one problem (*see* 5:10) which can be dealt with by voluntary codes, as in the AMDEA and RETRA (*see* 5:10), which have the approval of the OFT.

There is obviously a fine line between improving consumer protection and pure publicity. There is no doubt that one of the primary purposes of trade associations is to improve the public image of the trade in question. A clear example of this is the implementation of 1 July 1990 of a new code of standards aimed at improving the (sometimes woeful) reputation of second-hand car dealers and garages. The code lays down new conditions for the issue of warranties for used cars and repair work and sets out standards for the facilities available at garages. The trade association took the opportunity to change its name too — from the Motor Agents' Association to the Retail Motor Industry Federation (it has 13,500 member companies). The Federation intends the new code to separate the reputable trade from what it called the 'back street and bombsite boys'. There are to be minimum warranty periods for second-hand cars: ranging from 90 days (or 3,000 miles) for cars with less than 20,000 miles on the clock to 30 days (or 1,000 miles) for cars with between 40,000 and 60,000 miles on them. Furthermore, the mileages should be guaranteed, and if there is any doubt about it, then this should be made clear to customers. There are further provisions regarding estimates and quotations for repair work, and so on. The new code received a guarded welcome from such organisations as the Consumers Association.

Of course, a code of practice need not necessarily be voluntarily produced by industry. It may have a statutory status in giving the guidance which it does, as for example, the code of conduct drawn up under the Insurance Brokers (Registration) Act

1977 by the Insurance Brokers Registration Council and approved by the Insurance Brokers Registration Council (Code of Conduct) Approval Order 1978.

The major problem with a voluntary code of practice is that in the last resort it lacks adequate sanctions for its enforcement, though it may be enforceable as a collateral warranty if a trader has publicly claimed to honour a particular code. Adverse publicity, emanating either from the trade association responsible for the code, or from the OFT, may be a partial deterrent to breaches of the code, and the threat of expulsion from membership of a trade association may also work in the same direction. But expulsion will not necessarily deter the rogue trader, who may not even be a member of the association in the first place.

5. The role of the OFT

The Director is under a duty to encourage trade associations to prepare, and to disseminate to their members, codes of practice for guidance in safeguarding and promoting the interests of consumers in the UK: s. 124(3). FTA. While some voluntary codes of practice owe their existence to other sources of encouragement than the OFT (e.g. the British Code of Advertising Practice: *see* 11:2), the OFT acting under s. 124(3) is proving an active source of encouragement for voluntary codes. Commencing with the AMDEA Code (*see* 4) in 1974, over twenty codes — and the number is growing — had by July 1987 been negotiated and approved by the OFT. These codes cover such matters as electrical goods, servicing of electrical appliances, shoes, sale and repair and servicing of new and used cars and motorcycles, dry cleaning and laundries, mail order catalogues and publishing of mail order advertisements, package holidays, funeral services, photography, leaflets. The Post Office and British Telecom also have codes approved by the OFT, and published leaflets about them.

A feature of the codes is that most of them contain provision for conciliation or independent low-cost arbitration of unresolved disputes. The consumer retains the right, however, to take his case to court instead; indeed, the small claims arbitration procedure in the county court (*see* Chap. 22) may well be cheaper than arbitration under the code where the dispute is not capable of proper resolution on a documents only basis and requires an oral hearing. New or revised codes will incorporate a new model arbitration scheme agreed between the OFT and the Chartered Institute of Arbitrators in 1983. The scheme provides that arbitration shall normally and unless otherwise agreed be on a documents only basis (which places a predetermined limit on costs). The Consumer Arbitration Agreements Act 1988 provides that any contract term which stipulates for arbitration rather than recourse to the courts is unenforceable against anyone 'dealing as a consumer'.

Finally, it should be noted that the OFT monitors the operation of the codes of practice. A code must be properly publicized, and must be observed. If a code is not seen to be working satisfactorily, revision of the code, and reform by the industry concerned in putting it into practice, will be required. If necessary, the OFT's approval of a code would be withdrawn.

6. Statutory general duty to trade fairly

The creation of such a duty has been proposed by the Director General of Fair Trading. The duty would be enforceable through codes of practice, applying to all traders within a particular sector and prepared by the OFT after consultation with appropriate trade associations. Persistent breaches of the statutory duty could lead to proceedings under Part III of the FTA (*see* **16–19**). Consultations on the proposal are continuing, but the DGFT has reported (in July 1990) his desire to create a 'legal safety net' to catch a variety of 'trading malpractices'. It is proposed that the ability to seek 'Part III assurances' (see **15**) be extended to local Trading Standards Officers. This is another aspect of the DGFT's policy of enabling enforcement officers to 'shoot at a moving target' – on the basis that rogue traders are always a half-step ahead of the law.

Reference of consumer trade practices to Advisory Committee under Part II of the Fair Trading Act

7. Reference to Advisory Committee

The Director, or the Secretary of State or other minister, may refer to a formally established Committee (i.e. the FTA provides for reference to the CPAC, although it has been disbanded with a promise of resurrection should the need arise) the question whether a consumer trade practice (defined below: *see* **8**) adversely affects the economic interests of consumers in the UK: s. 14(1) FTA. The Advisory Committee then considers the question and reports on it: s. 14(3).

> NOTE: No reference to the Advisory Committee can be made in the case of certain professions (including law, medicine, architecture and accounting) where a monopoly situation exists or may exist: s. 15; nor (except with the consent of the appropriate minister) in the case of nationalized industries: s. 16.

8. Consumer trade practice

For the purposes of s. 14 (*see* **7**) and the FTA generally, 'consumer trade practice' means any practice which is for the time being carried on in connection with the supply of goods (whether by sale or otherwise) or services to consumers and which relates:

(a) to the terms or conditions (whether as to price or otherwise) on or subject to which goods or services are or are sought to be supplied; *or*

(b) to the manner in which those terms or conditions are communicated to persons to whom goods or services are or are sought to be supplied; *or*

(c) to promotion (by advertising, labelling or marking of goods, canvassing or otherwise) of the supply of goods or services; or

(d) to methods of salesmanship employed in dealing with consumers; *or*

(e) to the way in which goods are packaged for the purpose of being supplied; *or*

(f) to methods of demanding or securing payment for goods or services supplied: s. 13.

> NOTE: 'Consumer' means any person to whom goods or services are or are sought to be supplied in the course of a business carried on by the person supplying or seeking to supply them, and who does not receive or seek to receive the goods or services in the course of a business carried on by him. 'Business' includes a professional practice; and 'goods' includes buildings: s. 137.

9. Proposals for the making of an Order

Under s. 17 of the FTA, a reference by the Director to the Advisory Committee under s. 14 (*see* **7**) may include in certain circumstances proposals for recommending that the Secretary of State should exercise his powers (under s. 22: *see* **11**) to make an order preventing or modifying a consumer trade practice. Proposals of this kind may only accompany the reference if the Director considers that the consumer trade practice has, or is likely to have, the effect:

(a) of misleading consumers as to, or withholding from them adequate information as to, their rights and obligations under a consumer transaction; *or*
(b) of otherwise misleading or confusing consumers with respect to any matter in connection with consumer transactions; *or*
(c) of subjecting consumers to undue pressure to enter into consumer transactions; or
(d) of causing the terms or conditions, on or subject to which consumers enter into consumer transactions, to be so adverse to them as to be inequitable: s. 17.

The proposals may recommend the imposition of prohibitions or requirements, particular examples of which are contained in a non-exhaustive list in Schedule 6 to the Act, namely:

(a) prohibition of the consumer trade practice either generally or in relation to specified consumer transaction;
(b) prohibition of specified consumer transaction unless carried out at specified times or at specified places;
(c) prohibition of terms or conditions purporting to exclude or limit the liability of a party to a specified consumer transaction in respect of specified matters;
(d) a requirement that contracts relating to specified consumer transactions shall include specified terms or conditions;
(e) a requirement that contractual documents relating to specified consumer transactions shall comply with specified provisions as to the size, type, colouring, etc., of lettering;
(f) a requirement that specified information shall be given to parties to specified consumer transactions.

References with proposals for the making of an order must be published in full in the *London, Edinburgh* and *Belfast Gazettes*: s. 17(4).

10. Report of the Advisory Committee

The Committee must report on a reference which includes proposals for the making of an order within three months unless the Secretary of State allows a further period: s. 20. The Committee must take into consideration representations by interested persons: s. 81. The report must be published and laid before parliament: s. 83.

By s. 21, the committee must state in their report whether they find that the consumer trade practice specified in the reference does in fact adversely affect the economic interests of consumers in the UK, and whether it does so wholly or partly by reason of having one or more of the effects specified in s. 17 (*see* 9). If the Committee do so conclude, their report must go on to state whether the Committee:

(a) agree with the proposals set out in the reference; *or*

(b) would agree with those proposals if they were modified in a specified manner; *or*

(c) disagree with the proposals.

11. Orders under s. 22

If the Committee agree with the proposals set out in the reference, or would agree with modified proposals, the Secretary of State may, if he thinks fit, give effect to them (either as set out in the reference, or, at his discretion, as modified in the report) by an order made by statutory instrument. The draft order must be laid before Parliament and approved by resolution of each House: s. 22.

12. Orders made to date

Since 1973 only the following orders have been made under the Part II procedure as described in the preceding paragraphs. (There are unlikely to be any more.)

(a) The Mail Order Transactions (Information) Order 1976. This Order applies to advertisements, circulars, catalogues, etc., in which persons in the course of a business invite orders by post for goods for which a payment is to be made before the goods are dispatched. Such advertisements, etc., must contain a legible statement of the name of the person carrying on the business, and the address at which the business is managed (and not just a box number, for instance). The Order does not apply to advertisements, etc., which are expressly directed at persons who are not consumers. (The government did not adopt the Director's further recommendation that it should be a criminal offence for a mail order company to fail to supply goods ordered or return money paid in advance within a specified period.)

(b) The Consumer Transactions (Restrictions on Statements) Order 1976, and the Consumer Transactions (Restrictions on Statements) (Amendment) Order 1978. For the provisions of these Orders, *see* 6:**24**; 9:**5**.

(c) The Business Advertisements (Disclosure) Order 1977. This Order deals with 'disguised business sales' by providing that a person who is seeking to sell goods that are being sold in the course of a business shall not advertise to consumers that the goods are for sale unless it is reasonably clear from the advertisement that the goods are to be sold in the course of a business.

13. Efficiency of Part II procedure

The object of the Part II procedure was to establish a responsible mechanism for the control as they emerge of consumer trade practices prejudicial to the consumer. Action through Act of Parliament, dependent as it is upon time being found in a crowded timetable, was thought to be too lengthy and unpredictable a process. But in the event much delay has been experienced between the Advisory Committee's several reports and their translation into law by statutory instrument. Both the present Director and his predecessor are on record as expressing their disappointment with the working of Part II of the Act.

14. Sanctions

Contravention of an Order under s. 22 of the FTA is an offence: s. 23. Maximum penalties are:

(a) on summary conviction, a fine of £2,000;
(b) on conviction on indictment, imprisonment for a term not exceeding two years, or a fine, or both: s. 23, as amended.

Enforcement is by the local trading standards authority: s. 27. Duly authorized officers have the necessary enforcement powers, including power to make test purchases, to enter premises, and to inspect and, if needed for testing, etc., seize and detain goods or documents: ss. 28, 29. Wilful obstruction of a duly authorized officer acting in the exercise of his powers is an offence: s. 30.

Contravention of an Order under s. 22 does not of itself render a contract void or unenforceable, nor does it confer a right of action for breach of statutory duty (s. 26), but a compensation order may be available to the consumer at the discretion of the criminal court following conviction of the trader (*see* Chap. 21).

15. Defences

The Act contains a 'due diligence' type of defence for a person charged under s. 23 (*see* 14), i.e. it is defence for a person charged to prove:

'(a) that the commission of the offence was due to a mistake, or to reliance on information supplied to him, or to the act or default of another person, an accident or some other cause beyond his control, *and*
(b) that he took all reasonable precautions and exercised all due diligence to avoid the commission of such an offence by himself or any person under his control': s. 25(1).

If this defence involves the allegation that the commission of the offence was due to the act or default of another person, or to reliance on information supplied by another person, the defendant must, at least seven days before the hearing, serve the prosecutor with written notice giving such information identifying or assisting in the identification of that other person as the defendant possesses: s. 25(2). That other person may then be charged with and convicted of the offence: s. 24.

Publishers, advertising agents and others whose business it is to arrange for the publication of advertisements have a separate defence where contravention of an Order under s. 22 arises by virtue of the publication of an advertisement. The defendant in such a case must prove that he received the advertisement for publication in the ordinary course of business and did not know and had no reason to suspect that its publication would be an offence: s. 25(3).

Action against persistently unfair traders under Part III of the Fair Trading Act

16. Written assurances by traders
Where it appears to the Director that the person carrying on a business has in the course of that business persisted in a course of conduct which:

(a) is detrimental to the interests of consumers in the UK, whether those interests are economic interests or interests in respect of health, safety or other matters; *and*
(b) is unfair to consumers,

the Director must use his best endeavours to obtain from that person a satisfactory written assurance that he will discontinue that course of conduct: s. 34(1).

A course of conduct is 'unfair to consumers' if it consists of:

(a) contravention of duties, prohibitions or restrictions enforceable by criminal proceedings, whether or not the contraventions have led to a conviction: s. 34(2); *or*
(b) breaches of contract or other duty enforceable by civil proceedings, whether or not proceedings have been brought; s. 34(3).

It has been proposed that this activity be extended to local Trading Standards Departments (*see* **6**).

17. Proceedings before the Restrictive Practices Court
The Director may bring proceedings against a person before the Restrictive Practices Court if:

(a) the Director is unable to obtain from the person in question the required assurance to discontinue the unfair course of conduct, *or*
(b) that person has given the required assurance but it appears to the Director that he has failed to observe it: s. 35.

The court may:

(a) make an order prohibiting the course of conduct; *or*
(b) accept an undertaking that the course of conduct will be discontinued: s. 37.

Appeal lies to the Court of Appeal: s. 42. Breach of a court order, or undertaking given to the court, is contempt of court.

NOTE: Up to May 1990 since the introduction of the Part III procedure, 698 assurances, undertakings or court orders have been obtained. Details are published and appear in the Director's Annual Report along with other statistical information.

The first assurance was given in October 1974:

I, Robert James Pickersgill, of Import House, Northallerton Road, Croft on Tees, Nr. Darlington trading as Solaire Electric, hereby give to the Director General of Fair Trading written assurances sought by him pursuant to section 34(1) of the Fair Trading Act 1973:
'That I will use all reasonable precautions and exercise all due diligence to avoid continuing the following course of conduct or any similar course of conduct in the course of my business, namely —

(1) Committing offences under section 1 of the Trade Descriptions Act 1968 by applying false trade descriptions to goods or by supplying or offering to supply goods to which a false trade description is applied.
(2) Committing offences under section 11(2) of the Trade Descriptions Act 1968 by giving indications likely to be taken as indications that goods offered by me are being offered at a price less than that at which they are in fact being offered.
(3) Committing breaches of contract with consumers by supplying goods:

(*a*) which do not correspond with any description by which they are sold as required by subsection (1) of the amended section 13 of the Sale of Goods Act 1893, *or* (*b*) which are not fit for a particular purpose for which they are being bought as required by subsection (3) of the amended section 14 of that Act.

(4) Failing to return to consumers money to which they are legally entitled, that has been received from them in the course of mail order transactions.'

> For the purpose of these assurances the word 'goods' means lamps intended to emit ultra violet rays and/or to emit infra red rays and any accessory supplied or offered for supply with such a lamp.

18. Proceedings in the county court
Where the person against whom the proceedings are brought is not a body corporate having a share capital exceeding £10,000, and the proceedings do not involve a question of law or fact of such general application as to justify it being determined by the Restrictive Practices Court, the Director may, if he thinks fit, bring the proceedings in the county court instead: s. 41.

> NOTE: It was a county court which, in August 1983, gaoled (for 14 days) the first trader to be committed to prison for breach of a Part III undertaking. Each year only a handful of cases in connection with the Part III procedure will reach court, and when they do it is likely in practice to be the county court.

19. Action against an accessory
The Director can proceed against an 'accessory' where the accessory has consented to or connived at the course of conduct in question: s. 38. An 'accessory' is a director, manager, secretary or other similar officer of a company, or a person or body of persons, corporate or unincorporate, holding a controlling interest in a company. Orders by the court may bind both an accessory and an interconnected company: (ss. 39, 40).

Progress test 17

1. Summarize the powers and duties of the Director General of Fair Trading. (3)

2. What are the advantages and disadvantages of voluntary codes of practice as an instrument of consumer protection? **(4)**

3. Explain the role of the Office of Fair Trading in encouraging voluntary codes of practice. What success has the OFT had to date in this regard? What reform has been proposed? **(5, 6)**

4. Define 'consumer trade practice'. **(8)**

5. What is the Consumer Protection Advisory Committee? What is its function in consumer protection? **(2, 7, 9, 10)**

6. In what circumstances may the Director, in making a reference to the Advisory Committee, include proposals for recommending that the Secretary of State should exercise his powers to make an order preventing or modifying a consumer trade practice? **(9)**

7. List the prohibitions and requirements contained in Sched. 6 to the FTA as examples of recommendations which the Director might make in proposals to the Advisory Committee. **(9)**

8. When must the Advisory Committee report on a reference which includes proposals for the making of an order? What must their report state? **(10)**

9. In what circumstances may the Secretary of State make an order under s. 22 of the FTA? What Orders have been made to date? Summarize the respective provisions of these Orders. **(11, 12)**

10. What was the object in setting up the Part II procedure in the FTA? Has this object been achieved in practice? **(13)**

11. What sanctions is a trader liable to incur by contravention of an order under s. 22 of the FTA by virtue of (*a*) the criminal law; and (*b*) the civil law? What particular defence is open to a person charged with contravention of an order? Is it possible to be imprisoned for denying consumers' rights under the Sale of Goods Act 1979? **(14, 15)**

12. In what circumstances must the Director use his best endeavours to obtain from a person a written assurance that a course of conduct will be discontinued? If the assurance sought is not given, or once given is broken, before what court or courts may the Director bring the matter, and what powers and sanctions does the court which hears the matter have?   **(16–18)**

13. When can the Director proceed against an 'accessory' under Part III of the FTA? What is an 'accessory'?   **(19)**

18
Consumer safety

Introduction

1. Safety through criminal sanctions

The legislation governing consumer safety is now to be found in Part II of the Consumer Protection Act 1987, which consolidates with amendments of the previous legislation. The CPA Part II came into force on the 1 October 1987. It is intended that regulations made under the Consumer Safety Act 1978 — and its predecessor the Consumer Protection Act 1961 — shall remain in force (modified as appropriate) until superseded by new regulations made under the CPA 1987 or otherwise revoked: cf. s. 50(4), (5) CPA 1987. The object of the consumer safety legislation, and of the regulations and notices made or served under it, may be encapsulated in the maxim, 'prevention is better than cure'. There are some 7,000 deaths each year in Great Britain arising from home accidents, and the safety legislation is primarily concerned with preventing such accidents through the use of criminal sanctions imposed on manufacturers, retailers, and indeed all those businesses involved in the chain of distribution. These criminal sanctions, detailed in the following paragraphs, complement the consumer's civil remedies, not least the new strict liability regime contained in Part I of the Consumer Protection Act 1987 (*see* 9: **19**).

Statutory general safety requirement

2. General safety requirement

It is an offence to supply, offer or agree to supply, or expose or possess for supply, any consumer goods which fail to comply with the general safety requirement: s. 10(1). This provision implements the general safety requirement foreshadowed in the White Paper, *The Safety of Goods* (Cmnd. 9302) published in July 1984.

> NOTE: 'Supply' (as used here and elsewhere in the CPA) is widely defined and includes (*inter alia*) sale, hire-purchase transactions, and providing the goods under a contract for work and materials: s. 46. The supply must be in the course of a business, though it is immaterial whether the business is a business dealing in the goods: s. 46(5).

Goods fail to comply with the general safety requirement if they are not reasonably safe having regard to all the circumstances including their presentation (e.g. instructions for use), any published safety standards, and the existence of any reasonable means — taking into account the cost, likelihood and extent of any improvement — for making the goods safer: s. 10(2).

'Consumer goods' means 'any goods which are ordinarily intended for private use or consumption' except growing crops, water, food, feeding stuff or fertilizer, gas, aircraft (other than hang-gliders) or motor vehicles, drugs, medicines and tobacco: s. 10(7).

For the purposes of Part II of the CPA, 'safe', in relation to any goods, is defined as meaning that there is no risk, or no risk apart from one reduced to a minimum, that the goods will cause death or personal injury to any person: s. 19(1).

3. Defences

Consumer goods do not fail to comply with the general safety requirement if they comply with any safety regulations, approved safety standards or relevant subordinate legislation: s. 10(3). It is a defence to show that the goods were second-hand or intended for export: s. 10(4). Retailers have a special defence: in proceedings against a retailer it is a defence for him to show that he neither knew nor had reasonable grounds for believing that the goods failed to comply with the general safety requirement: s. 10(4)(*b*). (This defence apart, liability under s. 10 is strict, though there is the usual 'due diligence' type of defence, applicable to all the offences created by the various safety provisions in the CPA (*see* **17** below).

Safety regulations

4. Power to make safety regulations

The Secretary of State may make regulations ('safety regulations') containing such provision as he considers appropriate for the purposes of approving safety standards in relation to the general safety requirement, and of securing that goods are safe, or not made available to persons in whose hands they would be unsafe, and that appropriate information is provided in respect of goods: s. 11(1).

> NOTE: 'Goods' means any goods except growing crops, water, food, feeding stuff or fertilizer, gas, drugs and medicines: s. 11(4).

There are currently in force some thirty sets of regulations made under the broadly similar provisions of the previous consumer safety legislation. These regulations remain in force for the time being — until revoked or replaced by new regulations made under s. 11 of the CPA 1987. The existing regulations govern such matters as aerosol dispensers, asbestos, babies' dummies, bicycles, carry-cot stands, cooking utensils and ceramics, cosmetics, electrical goods, filament lamps for vehicles, fireguards, fireworks, nightwear, certain novelties and ornamental objects, oil heaters and oil lamps, pencils, perambulators, pushchairs, 'Tris'-treated textiles, toys (much revised in 1989), types, upholstered furniture, and child-resistant packaging for certain toxic or corrosive products.

5. Provisions which may be contained in safety regulations

The CPA gives a non-exhaustive list of the matters for which safety regulations may make provision. We may note in particular that s. 11(2) allows safety regulations to contain, *inter alia*, provision:

(a) with respect to the 'composition or contents, design, construction, finish or packing of goods' or with respect to standards and other matters relating to goods;

(b) for requiring goods to be approved or to conform with approved standards;

(c) with respect to the testing or inspection of goods;

(d) for requiring a warning or instruction or other information to be marked on or to accompany goods;

(e) for banning the supply of particular goods or components outright.

6. Consultation

Before making safety regulations the Secretary of State must consult such organizations as appear to him to be representative of interests substantially affected by the proposed regulations and such other persons as he considers appropriate; in the case of proposed regulations relating to goods suitable for use at work he must consult the Health and Safety Commission: s. 11(5). Consultation is not required in urgent cases where the regulations provide that they will not last for more than twelve months (during which period the appropriate consultations can take place before further safety regulations, if necessary, are made in the normal way).

NOTE: Regulations are subject to annulment by resolution of either House of Parliament: s. 11(6).

Prohibition notices, notices to warn and suspension notices

7. Prohibition notices

Where the Secretary of State considers specified goods to be unsafe, he may serve a notice ('prohibition notice') on a particular person prohibiting him from supplying the goods except with the consent, which may be conditional, of the Secretary of State: s. 13(1)(*a*).

8. Notices to warn

Where the Secretary of State considers specified goods which a person supplies or has supplied to be unsafe, the Secretary of State may serve on that person a notice ('notice to warn') requiring him to publish in the specified form and manner and on the specified occasions and at his own expense, a warning about the goods: s. 13(1)(*b*). It will be observed that a notice to warn stops short of giving the Secretary of State power to require those responsible for supplying unsafe goods to *recall* them.

9. Procedure

Schedule 2 to the CPA sets out the respective procedures which the Secretary of State must observe in serving a prohibition notice or notice to warn. These procedural requirements relate to such matters as the giving of notice by the Secretary of State of his proposed action, and the consideration by him of any representations made in respect thereof.

10. Notice requiring information

Where the Secretary of State requires information for the purpose of deciding whether to make, vary or revoke safety regulations, or to serve, vary or revoke a prohibition notice or notice to warn, then the Secretary of State may serve on any person a notice requiring:

(a) the furnishing of specified information; *or*
(b) the production of specified documents: s. 18(1).

Any person who fails, without reasonable cause, to comply with a notice under s. 18(1), or who knowingly or recklessly furnishes false information, commits an offence: s. 18(3). Improper disclosure of information obtained by virtue of these powers is an offence: s. 38(1).

NOTE: In May 1989 the EC Council of Ministers adopted a new 'Decision' — following one which expired in March 1988 — entitled 'Community System for the Rapid Exchange of Information on Dangers Arising from the Use of Consumer Products'. This action requires Member States to tell the Commission all about action taken against products because of the 'serious and immediate risk which that product or product batch presents for the health and safety of consumers when used in normal and foreseeable conditions'. The Commission then relays this information to other Member States.

11. Suspension notices

Where an officer of an enforcement authority (*see* **12** below) has reasonable cause to believe that any safety provision has been contravened, he may serve a notice ('suspension notice') prohibiting the supply (except with consent, which may be conditional) of specified goods: s. 14(1). A suspension notice cannot extend beyond six months. A further notice can only be served in respect of the same goods if proceedings have first been instituted for contravention of a safety provision or for forfeiture (*see* **16** below): s. 14(4). Any person having an interest in suspended goods may appeal to court against the suspension: s. 15. Compensation is payable to any person having an interest in goods in respect of any loss or damage caused by a suspension notice if there has been no contravention of any safety provision and no neglect or default by that person: s. 14(7).

NOTE: 'Safety provision' used here and elsewhere in the CPA means the general safety requirement or any provision of safety regulations, a prohibition notice or a suspension notice: s. 45(1).

Enforcement and sanctions

12. Enforcement

Enforcement of the various safety provisions is the duty of local authority Trading Standards or Consumer Protection departments (technically, the weights and measures authorities): s. 27(1). The Secretary of State, however, may by regulations transfer this duty to another person: s. 27(2).

13. Powers of enforcement authorities

Enforcement authorities may make test purchases: s. 28. A duly authorized officer of an enforcement authority may enter any premises used for business to inspect goods: s. 29(2). If the officer has reasonable grounds for suspecting that any goods are manufactured or imported and have not been subsequently supplied in the UK, he may seize and detain them for the purpose of testing whether there has been any contravention of any safety provision: s. 29(4). Any person having an interest in detained goods may appeal to the court for the goods to be released: s. 33. Compensation is payable to any person having an interest in goods in respect of any loss or damage caused by the exercise of the power to seize and detain them if there has been no contravention of any safety provision and no neglect or default by that person: s. 34. Intentional obstruction of an authorized enforcement officer is an offence: s. 32.

14. Dangerous imported goods

The Commissioners of Customs and Excise may disclose information obtained by them in the exercise of their functions to an enforcement authority: s. 37. Customs officers may seize and detain goods for up to two working days, during which examination can be made by an enforcement authority: s. 31. Thereafter the goods may be seized and detained by the enforcement authority under its normal powers (*see* **13**).

15. Sanctions

Contravention of the general safety requirement, or of any safety regulations, prohibition notice, notice to warn, or suspension notice, is an offence punishable on summary conviction by imprisonment for a term not exceeding six months and/or a fine not exceeding £2,000: s. 10(6), s. 12(5), s. 13(4), s. 14(6). In the case of a corporate offender, conniving officers (e.g. directors) are also guilty and liable to prosecution and punishment: s. 40(2). A court may order reimbursement of the expenditure of the enforcement authority incurred in connection with seizing and detaining goods or in connection with their forfeiture by court order: s. 35.

16. Forfeiture

A court may order the forfeiture and destruction (or other disposal for repair or scrap) of goods where any safety provision has been contravened: s. 16. Forfeiture may extend to the whole batch or consignment on the basis of contravention of any safety provision by a representative sample of the goods: s. 16(4). Appeal may be made against a court order for forfeiture: s. 16(5).

17. Due diligence defence

Contravention of any safety provision is a strict liability

offence. Nevertheless it is a defence for the defendant to show that he took all reasonable steps and exercised all due diligence to avoid committing the offence: s. 39(1). If this defence involves the allegation that the commission of the offence was due to the act or default of another person or to reliance on information supplied by another person, the defendant must at least seven days before the hearing serve the prosecutor with written notice giving such information identifying or assisting in the identification of the other person as the defendant possesses: s. 39(2), (3).

NOTE: The due diligence defence will not be available in cases of reliance on information supplied by a third party unless the defendant can show that he acted reasonably in relying on the information, in particular by taking reasonable steps to verify it: s. 39(4).

Taylor v. *Lawrence Fraser (Bristol) Ltd* (1978): the defendant company was prosecuted for supplying to a shop a toy which contravened the Toys (Safety) Regulations 1974 by having too high a lead content. The company's practice was to require manufacturers to guarantee that the goods supplied complied with the current regulations. Officers of the local Trading Standards department were also invited to take samples at any time for analysis. The toy in question was not covered by guarantee as the regulations had been altered in 1974 and no subsequent steps (such as analysing the paint on some of the toys in the consignment) had been taken to ensure that old stock complied with the new requirements. The company's defence, accepted by the justices, was that it had taken all reasonable precautions to avoid the commission of an offence under the Consumer Protection Act 1961 (which contains a defence corresponding to, but not identical with, that contained in the 1987 Act). On appeal by the prosecutor by way of case stated, a Divisional Court of the QBD held that the justices were bound as a matter of law to convict the defendant company, which could not by maintaining friendly relations with the local Trading Standards department avoid its responsibility for taking precautions. Lord Widgery CJ added that reliance on guarantee of compliance with the regulations was unlikely to be sufficient by itself in the absence of analysis of samples by the company. (Cf. now s. 39(4) CPA, in NOTE above.) (*See* also *Garrett* v. *Boots Chemists Ltd* (1980) where Boots were held similarly to have taken less than reasonable precautions to avoid breaching the Pencil and Graphic instruments (Safety) Regulations 1974 in that they had not sample tested but relied upon compliance clauses in contracts with their suppliers.)

18. The 'by-pass' provision

Where the contravention by any person of a safety provision is due to an act or default committed by some other person in the course of any business of his, that other person is guilty of the offence and may be proceeded against and punished whether or not proceedings are taken against the first-mentioned person: s. 40(1).

Civil liability

19. Validity of contracts

Contravention of a safety provision does not affect the validity of any contract unless otherwise agreed: s. 41(3).

20. Action for breach of statutory duty

Unless otherwise provided in the regulations, contravention of an obligation imposed by safety regulations is actionable, by any person affected by the contravention, as a breach of statutory duty: s. 41(1). Liability for breach of statutory duty is strict. Privity of contract is not a prerequisite of liability.

NOTE: This right of action for breach of statutory duty is unique in criminal statutes involving consumer protection. The corresponding provision in the previous consumer safety legislation, however, has not apparently been tried in the courts. The claimant, of course, will generally have an equally efficacious right of action under the new strict liability regime contained in Part I of the CPA 1987 (*see* 9: **19**).

Towards a European General Safety Duty

21. DTI consultation

In September 1989 the DTI began a consultation process on 'a far reaching European Commission Directive aimed at prohibiting the supply of unsafe products' throughout the European Community. If the Directive is adopted it will cover all products, including food and drink, transport, medicines and medical devices. It would extend beyond consumer goods to those used at work. The minister was quoted as not entirely welcoming all the proposals: 'Some of the detailed requirements in their proposals are unwelcome and unnecessarily burdensome.' In broad outline the suggestion is to extend something very much like the General Safety Duty within Part II of the CPA and add a requirement of constant monitoring by manufacturers and Member States.

Progress test 18

1. Summarize the provisions of the Consumer Protection Acts 1961 and 1971, and name some of the regulations in force thereunder. **(1, 2)**

2. Is there a general prohibition against the supply of unsafe goods? **(2)**

3. For what purpose may the Secretary of State make safety regulations? What is the procedure for making them? **(4, 6)**

4. Indicate some of the provisions which may be contained within safety regulations. **(5)**

5. What is (*a*) a prohibition order; (*b*) a prohibition notice; (*c*) a notice to warn; (*d*) a suspension notice? **(7–12)**

6. What is the extent of the power which is given to the Secretary of State to serve a notice on a person requiring information? Does the power extend to the requiring of

information from lawyers? What criminal law sanctions (*a*) reinforce the use; and (*b*) protect against abuse, of this power? **(10)**

7.   What sanctions is a person who contravenes safety regulations liable to incur under the criminal law? What is the legal position where the commission of an offence by such a person is due to the act or default of some other person?   **(12–17)**

8.   (a) A retailer who sells furniture wishes to ensure that if the goods should contravene the Upholstered Furniture (Safety) Regulations 1980, then he would have a defence to a prosecution brought against him in respect of the contravention. What kind of steps must he take to protect himself against criminal liability for an unwitting contra-vention of the regulations if such should occur?   **(17)**
(b) If an item of upholstered furniture sold by the retailer should, unknown to him, be so manufactured that it would fail the smouldering cigarette test imposed by the current regulations, could the purchaser of the furniture rescind the contract on that account?
(c) If not, would the purchaser have any other right of action in respect of the contravention? If the facts were that the furniture was given by the purchaser to a relative as a gift, would the recipient have any right of action in respect of the contravention?   **(19–20)**

9.   What authority is responsible for the enforcement of safety regulations, prohibition orders, prohibition notices and notices to warn? What is the role of the Secretary of State as regards enforcement?   **(12)**

19
Trade descriptions

The legislation

1. Trade Descriptions Act 1968

The main thrust of the Trade Descriptions Act 1968 (in this chapter referred to as 'the Act' or 'TDA') is to prohibit:

(a) false trade descriptions as to goods; *and*
(b) false or misleading statements about services.

> NOTE: The Act does not apply to misdescriptions of the location, price or physical characteristics of land or houses, although this has been proposed and may see the legislative light of day during the 1990–91 Parliamentary session.

The TDA is designed to protect the public, and does not control purely private transactions, nor a statement made by a private seller to a dealer. The Act does, however, extend to the control of statements made by one trader to another in the course of business.

> *John* v. *Matthews* (1970): a member of a working man's club bought from the club a packet of cigarettes marked '3*d*. off'. He was nevertheless charged the full recommended retail price. HELD: The object of the Act was the protection of the public, and the Act did not apply to domestic situations such as private members' clubs (Divisional Court).

2. Trades Description Act 1972

This Act was held to be in conflict with European Community law so was repealed by the CPA, s. 48(2)(*a*)

False trade descriptions as to goods

3. Prohibition of false trade descriptions as to goods
Section 1 of the TDA 1968 provides: 'Any person who, in the course of a trade or business —

(a) applies a false trade description to any goods; *or*
(b) supplies or offers to supply any goods to which a false trade description is applied,

shall, subject to the provisions of this Act, be guilty of an offence': s. 1(1).
The various elements comprised in the two offences created by s. 1(1) are explored in the following paragraphs (*see* **4–8**). But it may be noted at this point that the courts have glossed s. 1 by adding the requirement that though the false trade description need not induce a contract, it does have to be connected with the supply of goods before an offence under s. 1 can be committed. Not that the supplier is the only person who can commit an offence under s. 1 — it could be the buyer. The following two cases illustrate the position.

> *Wickens Motors (Gloucester) Ltd* v. *Hall* (1972): car dealers sold a car to a consumer, who some forty days later returned to complain about its steering and other matters. The consumer was then told: 'There is nothing wrong with the car'. This was untrue, the car in fact being unroadworthy both then and when sold. HELD: No offence had been committed as the false statement was not connected with the sale of the car (DC).

> *Fletcher* v. *Budgen* (1974): a car dealer told a private seller that there was no possibility of repairing his car and that it was fit only for scrap. The dealer then bought the car for £2, repaired it at a cost of £56, and advertised it for sale at £3̶1̶5̶. HELD: An offence could be committed by a buyer who applied a false trade description to goods on purchasing them in the course of a trade or business (Court of Appeal).

NOTE: Misdescribed motor vehicles and accessories comprise by far the largest category of convictions obtained under the

Act, partly because the motor vehicles consume sufficient cash to provoke dissatisfied purchasers into complaining.

Lewin v. *Fuell* (1990): a stall holder at an open market was convicted of an offence under s. 1 in that he misdescribed cheap watches with expensive brand names. The court was not impressed with his assertion that nobody would take him seriously.

4. Meaning of false trade descriptions

Section 2 of the Act explains that a trade description is an indication, direct or indirect, and by whatever means given, of any of the following matters with respect to any goods or parts of goods, namely:

(a) quantity, size or gauge;
(b) method of manufacture, production, processing or reconditioning;
(c) composition;
(d) fitness for purpose, strength, performance, behaviour or accuracy;
(e) any other physical characteristics;
(f) testing by any person and results thereof;
(g) approval by any person or conformity with a type approved by any person;
(h) place or date of manufacture, production, processing or reconditioning;
(i) person by whom manufactured, produced, processed or reconditioned;
(j) other history, including previous ownership or use: s. 2(1).

NOTE: It will be observed that matters **(a)–(e)** above deal with physical characteristics, while matters **(f)–(j)** deal with the history of the goods.

The Act goes on to provide that a trade description is false if it is false to a material degree (s. 3(1)), or likely to be misleading to a material degree: s. 3(2). Further, anything which, though not a trade description, is likely to be taken as one, is deemed to be a false trade description if false to a material degree: s. 3(3).

Robertson v. *Dicicco* (1972) (DC): the defendant car dealer advertised a car in a newspaper as a 'beautiful car'. The car was pleasing to the eye but unfit for use. HELD: 'beautiful' (and similar adjectives) when applied to a car was likely to be taken as an indication of running quality as well as description of appearance, and so, if inaccurate, was a misleading indication within s. 3(2) of the car's performance within s. 2(1)(*d*).

Kensington and Chelsea (Royal) London Borough Council v. *Riley* (1973) (DC): here the expression used with respect to a car was 'immaculate'. HELD: This was likely to be taken as a description of running quality by the ordinary man and was therefore a trade description as to such quality, even if more experienced buyers would not in fact be taken in by it.

Cadbury Ltd v. *Halliday* (1975): on the abolition of purchase tax and the introduction of VAT the appellants were able to supply more chocolate for the same price. They accordingly supplied chocolate bars with the words 'extra value' printed on the wrappers. In due course these wrappers were discontinued and cheaper bars were introduced. For a period bars were available in both old and new wrappers, but the bars in the old wrappers no longer represented additional value. The appellants appealed against a conviction under s. 1(1) and 23 (*see* **21**). HELD: The words 'extra value' were not a trade description because they were not an indication of any matters within s. 21(1), the truth or falsity of which could be established. 'To say of an article that it is valuable is, of course, to apply a description to it, but in my view such description is not a trade description within the meaning of s. 2. In this case the alleged trade description consists of the words "extra value" and the additional "extra value" only increases the difficulty: inevitably one asks "extra of what"?' (per Ashworth J, who also thought s. 11 of the TDA (*see* **11**) inapplicable to 'worth' and 'value' claims) (Divisional Court).

Horner v. *Kingsley Clothing Co. Ltd* (1989): this case concerned the misdescription of sweatshirts bearing the name 'Marc O'Polo'. The justices dismissed the case on the basis that no buyer would be misled. The prosecutor's appeal was upheld. No reasonable bench could have reached that conclusion.

5. 'In the course of a trade or business'

The goods supplied must form an integral part of the defendant's trade or business.

> *Havering London Borough Council* v. *Stevenson* (1970): the defendant ran a car hire business. His practice was to sell off cars used in the business when they were about two years old. One car so sold had a false trade description as to mileage applied to it. HELD: Although the defendant was not a car dealer, the sale had taken place as an integral part of the business carried on as a car hire firm. The defendant had accordingly contravened s. 1(1) (Divisional Court).

> *Davies* v. *Sumner* (1984): a self-employed courier traded in his one year-old motor car in part-exchange for a new vehicle. The trade-in car had travelled 118,100 miles, but its five-digit odometer read only 18,100. The courier received the appropriate credit against the price of the new car. HELD: The courier had not contravened s. 1(1)(*a*) because the trade-in transaction did not form an integral part of his business as a self-employed courier. The courier had not established a normal practice of buying and disposing of cars, a factor which distinguished the Havering case, where the defendant's business as part of its normal practice bought and disposed of cars (House of Lords).

> *Devlin* v. *Hall* (1990): a taxi-driver who sold a car was not acting in the course of business because he lacked a sufficient 'degree of regularity' in such sales.

6. Applying a false trade description

The Act gives guidance as to when a false trade description is applied to goods. In short, a person applies a false trade description to goods if he uses the trade description in any manner likely to be taken as referring to the goods, for instance by marking the goods or their packaging, or by means of an advertisement: ss. 4(1), 5. An oral statement may amount to the use of a trade description: s. 4(2). Further, where goods are supplied in pursuance of a request which uses a trade description, the supplier is deemed to apply that trade description to the goods if the circumstances are such that it is a reasonable inference that the goods are supplied as corresponding to that trade description: s. 4(3).

> *R.* v. *Ford Motor Co. Ltd* (1974) (CA): in this case Ford were deemed under s. 4(3) to have applied the trade description 'new' to a Cortina even though the order form completed by the dealer did not use the word 'new'; the form clearly contemplated a new car from Ford's stock or production line. (The court went on to hold that although the car had sustained minor damage prior to delivery to the dealer, it was still 'new' as it had been perfectly repaired.)

> *Raynham Farm Co. Ltd* v. *Symbol Motor Corpn Ltd* (1987): this case shows the limit of the court's generosity — a burnt out and refurbished Range Rover was not 'new', or even 'as new'!

7. Offering to supply goods

A person exposing goods for supply or having goods in his possession for supply is deemed to offer to supply them: s. 6. This provision avoids the technical difficulty that use of the phrase 'offers to supply' in s. 1 would otherwise involve. (Cf. *Fisher* v. *Bell* (1961) DC, where flick-knives displayed in a shop window constituted an invitation to treat and not an 'offer for sale' contrary to the Restriction of Offensive Weapons Act 1959; the actual decision was later reversed by statute.) The word 'supply' is wider than 'sale' and would include hire-purchase transactions, etc.

8. Disclaimers

Subject to certain defences (*see* **21, 22**), liability under s. 1 is strict. But such liability can nevertheless be avoided by the appropriate use of a disclaimer. The effect of a disclaimer is to neutralize a trade description; in other words by virtue of the disclaimer no trade description is regarded as having been applied to the goods at all. A disclaimer can therefore be an effective device in avoiding liability under the Act, even though the Act nowhere expressly recognizes disclaimers. Car dealers in particular have used disclaimers to neutralize false odometer readings. However, if it is to be effective a disclaimer must be 'as bold, precise and compelling as the trade description itself' (per Lord Widgery CJ in *Norman* v. *Bennett* (1974) DC). A motor dealer not wanting prospective customers to take any notice of odometer readings must take positive and effective steps to ensure that the customer understands that the reading is meaningless; 'small print' disclaimers will be ineffective to neutralize a trade description (*R.* v. *Hammertons Cars Ltd* (1976) CA). It seems, moreover, that a motor dealer cannot rely on the 'due diligence' defence (*see* **21**) unless he has displayed a prominent disclaimer (*Simmons* v. *Potter* (1975) (Divisional Court)). In *May* v. *Vincent* (1990) it was held that the TDA extends to auctioneers and that a disclaimer in an auction catalogue was ineffectual.

9. Disclosure of information

The Secretary of State for Trade has power to make orders requiring goods to be marked with or accompanied by information or instruction relating to goods: s. 8. Similarly, orders can be made requiring advertisements of goods to contain or refer to information relating to the goods: s. 9. The only order which was made under this power and remains in force is the Trade Descriptions (Sealskin Goods) (Information) Order 1980.

10. False indications of approval by Royalty

It is an offence to give a false indication that any goods or services are of a kind supplied to or approved by the Queen or any member of the Royal Family: s. 12(1). Further, unauthorized use of a device or emblem signifying or deceptively resembling the Queen's Award to Industry is an offence: s. 12(2).

False or misleading indications as to price of goods

11. Misleading indications as to price

The legislation on pricing and bargain offers was reworked in April 1989 with the repeal of TDA s. 11 and the infamous Price Marking (Bargain Offers) Orders 1979. These provisions have been replaced by the Consumer Protection Act (CPA) 1987, Part III. It is now an offence, in the course of any business, to give (by whatever means) to any consumers a misleading indication as to the price of any goods, services, accommodation or facilities: s. 20(1) CPA.

It is similarly an offence to fail to take reasonable steps to correct an indication as to the price of any goods, services, accommodation or facilities, given to consumers in the course of a business, where the indication has subsequently become misleading: s. 20(2).

(a) 'consumer' means, in relation to goods, any person who might wish to be supplied with the goods for his own private use or consumption; and in relation to services or facilities or accommodation, it means any person who might wish to be provided with the services or facilities, or to occupy the accommodation, otherwise than the purposes of any business of his: s. 20(6);

(b) 'services' or 'facilities' include 'any services or facilities whatever', but not services provided to an employer under a contract of employment or services or facilities provided by an authorized person or appointed representative in the course of the carrying on of an investment business: s. 22;

(c) 'accommodation' or 'facilities' do not include accommodation or facilities being made available by means of the creation or disposal of an interest in land (except in the case of the sale, or lease for more than 21 years, of new homes): s. 23.

> NOTE: Subject as above, s. 20 CPA covers services, accommodation or facilities as well as goods, in contrast to the old s. 11 Trade Descriptions Act 1968. Cf. too s. 14 TDA, which does not cover matters of price in relation to services, accommodation or facilities (*see* 17).

12. Meaning of 'misleading' in relation to price

An indication is misleading as to price if what it conveys or implies includes any of the following, namely:

(a) that the price is less than in fact it is;

(b) that the applicability of the price does not depend on facts or circumstances on which its applicability does in fact depend;

(c) that the price covers matters in respect of which an additional charge is in fact made;

(d) that a person expects the price to be increased, reduced or maintained (as the case may be) when in fact he has no such expectation;

(e) that the facts or circumstances by reference to which the validity of a price comparison is to be judged are not what in fact they are: s. 21(1).

13. Meaning of 'misleading' in relation to method of determining a price

An indication is misleading as to a method of determining a price if what it conveys or implies includes any of the following, namely: **(a)** that the method is not what in fact it is;
(b) that the applicability of the method does not depend on facts or circumstances on which its applicability does in fact depend;
(c) that the method takes into account matters in respect of which an additional charge will in fact be made;
(d) that a person expects the method to be altered, or remain unaltered (as the case may be), when in fact he has no such expectation;
(e) that the facts or circumstances by reference to which the validity of a comparison is to be judged are not what in fact they are: s. 21(2).

14. Code of practice

The offences created by s. 20 have been backed up by a Code of Practice, which the Secretary of State approved after consultation: s. 25(1). The object of the Code is to give practical guidance on the requirements of s. 20 and to promote desirable practices as to the circumstances and manner in which price indications are given. The *legal status* of the proposed Code was the subject of some considerable debate. It is now provided that contravention of the Code will not of itself give rise to any criminal or civil liability; but in proceedings for an offence under s. 20 any contravention of the code by the defendant may be relied on — as evidence only — to establish that he committed the offence, and to the same extent the defendant may rely on compliance with the Code as evidence of a defence: s. 25(2).

The Code itself is long and detailed, but it includes:
(a) a general statement that indications which give only the price of the goods are unlikely to be misleading if they are accurate and cover the total charge that is being made;
(b) the general rule that price comparisons must be clear, e.g. higher prices should always be stated ('Sale price £150' alone will not do);
(c) the nature of the higher price should be clear, e.g. 'normal' or

'regular' price, and whose 'normal' or 'regular' price it is! 'Reduced from' should only refer to the seller's own previous price;

(d) initials such as 'ASP' and 'RAP' (i.e. 'after sale price' and 'ready assembled price') should not be used, although 'RRP' is alright (MRP, however, is not! 'Man. Rec. price' is suggested);

(e) when comparing with his own previous price, and unless clearly stated otherwise, the previous price should be (*i*) shown and (*ii*) have been the price at the same outlet within the past six months for at least 28 consecutive days. (This is all that survives of the so-called '28-day rule' which existed under TDA s. 11.)

There are a great number of other details, elaborations and suggestions in the Code, but it must be borne in mind that contravention is not a crime, only evidence of an offence under CPA s. 20. In practice it is highly unlikely that compliance will attract a Trading Standards Officer's attention, whereas contravention might!

15. Power to make regulations

The Secretary of State is empowered to make regulations, after consultation, to regulate the circumstances and manner in which price indications may be given or to facilitate enforcement: s. 26. This regulation-making power is envisaged as a reserve power to be used only if continuing abuses are identified which are not adequately being regulated by the general provisions of s. 20 and the code of practice. The code has not proved popular with TS Departments. It is argued that prosecutions have been made very difficult. The area is currently under detailed review.

> NOTE: CPA Part III requires that where a price indication is given it should not be misleading. It does not, however, require that a price indication be given. In June 1991 the Price Marking Order 1991 was laid before Parliament, to come into effect on September 1. The Order implements EC Directives on the indication of the prices of foodstuffs and non-food products. The Order requires traders to show clearly the selling price of the goods they sell to private consumers. In some cases (e.g. for goods sold from bulk or prepacked in variable quantities) the unit price is also required.

False or misleading statements as to services

16. Services. Section 14 provides that it shall be an offence for any person in the course of any trade or business:

(a) to make any statement which he knows to be false; *or*
(b) recklessly to make a statement which is false;
as to any of the following matters, namely:

(*i*) the nature or provision of any services, accommodation or facilities provided in the course of any trade or business, or the time or manner of their provision, or their evaluation by any person;

(*ii*) the location or amenities of any accommodation provided in the course of any trade or business: s. 14(1).

Anything likely to be taken as a statement as to any of the foregoing matters is deemed to be such a statement: s. 14(2)(*a*).

> NOTE: For the purposes of s. 14, 'false' means false to a material degree, and 'services' does not include anything done under a contract of service: s. 14(4).

There are two offences created by s. 14. Offences under s. 14(1)(*a*) require knowledge by the maker of the statement that it was false. Offences under s. 14(1)(*b*) require recklessness (*see* **19**) in the making of the statement. The knowledge or recklessness must be that of the defendant himself, and not that of an employee. In the case of corporate defendant this means that it must be the knowledge or recklessness of one of the directors or other persons identifiable with the directing mind or will of the company (cf. *Tesco Supermarkets Ltd* v. *Nattrass* (1972) HL: *see* **21**).

The offence under s. 14(1)(*a*) — making a statement knowing it to be false — is, in regard to the actual making of the statement, an absolute offence which is committed merely if a statement is made on a person's behalf in the course of a business and its content is false to the knowledge of the person carrying on the business; it is irrelevant that the defendant does not know that the statement has actually been made (*Wings Ltd* v. *Ellis* (1984) HL), though if the defendant were innocent of fault that might in appropriate circumstances amount to a defence under s. 24 (*see* **21**).

17. Scope of s. 14

Section 14 does not cover a false statement about the price at which services, accommodation or facilities are provided, nor does it cover statements relating to the supply of goods. Section 1, which is concerned with goods, and s. 14, which is concerned with services, are mutually exclusive.

> *Westminster CC* v. *Ray Alan (Manshops) Ltd* (1982): traders displayed a sign at their London branch saying, 'Closing Down Sale'. This was false — the traders continued to trade at the shop. HELD by the Divisional Court: No offence had been committed under s. 14 TDA, which did not deal with the supply of goods. The term 'facilities' in s. 14 meant something akin to services and accommodation, and did not cover 'shopping facilities' such as a closing down sale. (NB: Another point arising in this case is mentioned in **13** above.)

> *Newell* v. *Hicks* (1983): motor dealers advertised that a video cassette recorder would be given 'absolutely free with every X-registration Renault' ordered from them within a specified period. Customers discovered that the recorders were not free because the trade-in allowances on their old vehicles were correspondingly reduced if they sought to take advantage of the offer. HELD by the Divisional Court: No offence had been committed under s. 14, because a false statement offering to supply a free gift related to the supply of *goods* and not to the provision of services or facilities; further, the statement referred to the price of the recorders and for that reason also did not fall within the scope of s. 14, which did not cover a false statement about price. (NB: The traders in this case might have been successfully prosecuted under s. 11(2): *see* **14**.)

> NOTE: Similarly, it has been held that an offer to 'refund the difference if you buy cheaper locally' is not concerned with the provision of services or facilities and does not come within the ambit of s. 14: *Dixons Ltd* v. *Roberts* (1984) DC. In *Kinchin* v. *Ashton Park Scooters* (1984) DC, a helmet, suit, gloves and boots offered free with a motor cycle did not fall within the ambit of s. 14; but it was held that an offer of one year's free insurance was 'facility' within s. 14.

18. Professional services

It seems that misdescriptions made in the course of providing professional services are within the scope of s. 14.

R. v. *Breeze* (1973): an architectural student falsely
represented himself to be fully qualified, and in
consequence his services were employed to draw up plans.
HELD by the Court of Appeal (Criminal Division): A false
statement as to qualifications or experience amounted to a
statement about the provision of services within s. 14, since
it affected the likely quality of the services. Further,
whether or not s. 14 applied to professions, it was not for
the defendant to argue that he was providing professional
services since he was in fact unqualified.

19. Recklessness

The commission of an offence under s. 14(1)(*b*) requires
recklessness. A statement made regardless of whether it is true of
false is deemed to be made recklessly, whether or not the person
making it had reasons for believing that it might be false: s.
14(2)(*b*). Recklessness does not necessarily involve dishonesty or
even deliberate disregard of the truth or falsity of the statement
(*MFI Warehouses Ltd* v. *Nattrass* (1973) DC, *see* below).

If a statement is made without recklessness, subsequent
recklessness (e.g. failure to check that customers are in the event
provided with the promised hotel accommodation, as in *Sunair
Holiday Ltd* v. *Dodd* (1970)), will not involve a criminal offence
under s. 14. Subsequent recklessness in the sense of recklessness
occurring subsequent to the making of a false statement, must
however, be distinguished from the reckless making of a statement
subsequent to the provision of the promised services (*Breed* v. *Cluett*
(1970): *see* below).

MFI Warehouse Ltd v. *Nattrass* (1973): the defendant mail
order form advertised louvre doors on fourteen days' free
approval, thereafter a specified price plus carriage charge
being payable. The same advertisement offered 'Folding
Door Gear (Carriage Free)'. The defendant's intention was
that carriage on the folding door gear would only be free if
the customer also ordered a louvre door. So a customer who
ordered only the folding door gear was charged with the
carriage. The justices found as a fact that a reasonable
interpretation of the advertisement was that it offered
folding door gear for separate purchase carriage free and

on fourteen days' approval. On appeal, a Divisional Court held that the appeal would be dismissed. The word 'recklessly' in s. 14(1) did not require that the advertiser must have deliberately closed his eyes to the truth, or that he was dishonest. It sufficed for the prosecution to show that the advertiser did not have regard to the truth or falsity of his advertisement.

Breed v. *Cluett* (1970): twenty days after making a contract to sell a bungalow the builder falsely stated that the building was covered by the National House-Builders' Registration Council's ten-year guarantee. HELD: This was a recklessly made false statement as to services and was caught by s. 14. It did not matter that the statement did not induce the contract. (Cf. the position relating to the supply of goods — *Wickens Motors (Gloucester) Ltd* v. *Hall*: *see* **3**.)

20. Statements as to the future

Section 14 does not apply to promises as to the future, which cannot be either true or false, even if breach of such a promise involves breach of contract. The problem, familiar enough in civil law, is to determine when a promise as to the future also involves a question of past or present fact. A promise may involve by implication a statement of fact, for example that the promisor has the present intention, or the means, of performing the promise. Brochures and advertisements by package holiday firms often give rise to this problem of determining whether statements involve questions of fact or merely promises about the future.

Beckett v. *Cohen* (1972): a builder agreed to build a garage 'as the existing garage' and 'within ten days'. He fulfilled neither promise. HELD: The Act was never intended 'to make a criminal offence out of what is really a breach of warranty' (per Lord Widgery CJ). A Divisional Court accordingly upheld the magistrates' court's dismissal of the prosecution's case. The decision would have been different if the builder had never had the intention or the means of fulfilling his promises.

British Airways Board v. *Taylor* (1976): this case concerned the overbooking policy considered prudent for major international airlines to operate in order to counteract 'no-shows', i.e. those passengers who fail to turn up having made flight reservations. Occasionally intending passengers have to be off-loaded because of overbooking. The Board were prosecuted in respect of one such off-loading incident by BOAC. The intending passenger's booking of a specific flight had been confirmed by letter from BOAC. At the time of writing the flight had not been overbooked.

A prosecution was brought in respect of the false statement about services contained in the written confirmation. The case eventually reached the House of Lords. HELD: The justices were entitled to find that the confirmatory letter was a statement of fact (i.e. the fact of a certain booking on a specified flight) and not a mere promise as to the future, which statement was false, contrary to s. 14 of the TDA, having regard to the overbooking policy exposing the passenger to the risk that he might not secure a seat on the flight. However, the British Airways Board could not be prosecuted for criminal offences by BOAC (BOAC had been dissolved by Order in April 1974).

Defences

21. Due diligence defence

Despite the fact that the offence created by s. 1 is one of strict liability (that in s. 14 requires *mens rea*) certain defences do exist within the TDA. The main defences are to be found in s. 24, namely: 'In any proceedings for an offence under this Act it shall . . . be a defence for the person charged to prove:

(a) that the commission of the offence was due to a mistake or to reliance on information supplied to him or to the act or default of another person, an accident or some other cause beyond his control; and

(b) that he took all reasonable precautions and exercised all due diligence to avoid the commission of such an offence by himself or any person under his control': s. 24(1).

The defendant has to prove that he comes within the terms of both paragraphs (a) and (b). Moreover, if the defence involves the allegation that the commission of the offence was due to the act or default of another person, or to reliance on information supplied by another person, the defendant must at least seven days before the hearing serve the prosecutor with written notice giving such information identifying or assisting in the identification of that other person as the defendant possesses: s. 24(2). That other person may then be charged with and convicted of the offence: s. 23. Indeed, it has been held that in order to prevent the administration of the Act becoming slipshod, a defendant seeking to rely on s. 24 must do all that can reasonably be expected in the way of inquiry and investigating as to the identity of the defaulting party (*McGuire* v. *Sittingbourne Co-operative Society* (1976) CA).

Finally, in any proceedings for an offence of supplying or offering to supply goods to which a false trade description is applied, it is defence for the defendant to prove that he did not know, and could not with reasonable diligence have ascertained, that the goods did not conform to the description or that the description had been applied to the goods: s. 24(3).

NOTE: Cf. the 'due diligence' defences under the Consumer Credit Act (*see* 11:8); the Fair Trading Act (*see* 17:15); and the CPA Part II (*see* 18:17).

Tesco Supermarkets Ltd v. *Nattrass* (1972): one of Tesco's stores displayed a poster offering a 'flash' offer for Radiant washing powder. When the packets to which the offer related were sold out ordinary packets were sold, but the poster was not removed, the store manager failing to carry out the daily check of special offers as required by his superiors. Tesco were prosecuted for committing an offence under s. 11 of the TDA. The case reached the House of Lords. HELD: The offence was due to the default of 'another person', i.e. the store manager, and the company had taken all reasonable precautions and exercised all due diligence in setting up, as they had, a chain of command which in its detailed operation was an effective system of control to avoid the commission of offences under the Act. The store manager was 'another person' because, unlike the directors and others in top management positions, he could not be identified with the controlling mind and will of the defendant company; nor had the company delegated powers of control to the manager, who was merely one of many store managers directed through the chain of command to take precautions against mispricing. The manager had no delegated powers of independent action in this respect. Tesco accordingly succeeded in their defence under s. 24(1).

NOTE: The TDA does not impose vicarious liability on an employer for the criminal acts or omissions of its employees. But where the commission of an offence under the Act is due to the act or default of some other person, that other person may be charged with and convicted of the offence whether or not proceedings are taken against the first mentioned person: s. 23. It follows that the store manager in the *Tesco* case could have been charged with the offence.

In any proceedings for an offence under s. 20(1) CPA, it is a defence for the defendant to show that he took all reasonable steps and exercised all due diligence to avoid committing the offence: s. 39 CPA.

22. Innocent publication of an advertisement
Where proceedings under s. 20 CPA arise by virtue of the publication of an advertisement, then publishers, advertising agents and others whose business it is to arrange for the publication of advertisements have a similar defence under s. 24(3) CPA to that contained in s. 25 of the Trade Descriptions Act 1968, that is to say the defendant in such a case must prove:

(a) that he received the advertisement for publication in the ordinary course of business; *and*
(b) that at the time of publication he did not know and had no grounds for suspecting that the publication would involve the commission of the offence.

Furthermore, in any processings for an offence under s. 20(1) CPA involving a recommended price, it is a defence for the person giving the misleading indication to show:

(a) that the indication did not relate to the availability from him of any goods, services, accommodation or facilities;

(b) that the price had been recommended to every person from whom the goods etc. were indicated as being available;
(c) that the price indicated was misleading only because of a failure by any person to follow the recommendation; *and*
(d) that it was reasonable for the defendant to assume that the recommendation was for the most part being followed: s. 24(4) CPA.

Sanctions and enforcement

23. The enforcement authority

Enforcement of Part III of the CPA is the duty of the local weights and measures authority: s. 27(1) CPA. A duly authorized officer has powers for enforcing Part III of the CPA similar to those available under the TDA (ss. 26–29). Accordingly, he may make test purchases (s. 28 CPA), enter any premises used for business to inspect goods, and if necessary seize and detain goods or records required as evidence: s. 29 CPA. Intentional obstruction of an enforcement officer is an offence: s. 32 CPA.

24. Sanctions

Contravention of ss. 1 or 14 TDA or s. 20 CPA is triable either summarily or on indictment and punishable by a fine (not exceeding £2,000 if tried summarily, unlimited on indictment where up to two years' imprisonment can also be imposed).

Contravention of any provision made by or under Part III of the CPA does not confer any right of civil action in respect of any loss or damage suffered in consequence of the contravention: s. 41(2) CPA.

The penalties imposed in practice by the courts, even in cases of multiple prosecution, can be of considerable magnitude (cf. *R. v. Thompson Holidays Ltd* (1974), *see* 21:3). They can also be so small as to attract the DGFT's comment, that they are 'laughably inadequate'. He was referring to small fines imposed upon 'car clockers'.

It should be noted that a contract for the supply of goods is not void or unenforceable by reason only of contravention of the Act: s. 35. A compensation order may, however, be available to the consumer at the discretion of the criminal court following conviction of the trader (*see* Chap. 21).

Proposals for reform

25. Dealing in property

The Private Members' ballot for the Parliamentary session 1990–91 provided the opportunity for John Butcher MP to introduce what became during its early stages the Property Misdescriptions Bill.

This measure, if enacted, would have the effect of extending the broad principles contained within the Trade Descriptions Act to those who deal in real property. That is, to estate agents, property developers, builders and even to solicitors, although not for the conveyancing work.

26. DTI Review

The Department of Trade and Industry has recently circulated a consultative document as part of a general review of the Trade Descriptions Act. As long ago as 1976 the then DGFT published a review which suggested certain important changes and extensions for the 1968 Act — but they have (for the most part) been left gathering dust. Nevertheless, it does seem likely that the Act will soon be thoroughly overhauled and we can look forward to increased clarity in this area of consumer criminal law.

Peter Cartwright wrote (141 NLJ at 897): 'The Act was a major step forward, but time has shown how it could be improved. The DTI's consultative document has indicated that reform can be expected soon . . . Only then will the UK's best known consumer protection statute be truly fit for its purpose'.

Furthermore, there are certain other proposals for change which have been rolled up into this process or been shelved until its completion. A noteworthy example is the reform of the law relating to the marketing and sale of timeshare property.

Progress test 19

1. Does the TDA 1968 control statements which are:

    (a) made by a consumer to a dealer;
    (b) made by one dealer to another;
    (c) made by the bartender at a tennis club;
    (d) made by a buyer of goods? **(1, 3)**

2. Why was the TDA 1972 repealed? **(2)**

3. What offences does s. 1 of the TDA 1968 create? **(3)**

4. After carrying out a MOT test for a motorist a garage refuses to give him a MOT certificate, the vehicle tester stating falsely that the car's brakes do not conform to the requirements. Does this statement constitute an offence within s. 1 of the TDA 1968? (Cf. *Wycombe March Garages Ltd* v. *Fowler* (1972).) **(3)**

5. Consider whether the following statements are trade descriptions within the TDA: (*a*) 'hand-made'; (*b*) 'all wool'; (*c*) 'showerproof'; (*d*) 'one-owner'; (*e*) 'extra value'? **(4)**

6. When is a trade description 'false' for the purposes of the TDA? **(4)**

7. A typing agency is selling off some electric typewriters, having replaced them with word processors. The typewriters are described as 'beautiful', but several of them do not function properly. Has the agency committed an offence under s. 1 of the TDA? **(4, 5)**

8. D, a trader, advertises in a newspaper in the following terms: 'drip-dry all cotton shirts, sky blue, £10 each. State collar size . .' The shirts which D had in stock to supply to customers placing orders in response to the advertisement are sky blue and all cotton, but require ironing if they are to be free of creases after washing. Is D guilty of offering to supply goods to which a false trade description is applied. Contrary to s. 1 of the TDA? Would customers have any remedy if D were found guilty? **(3, 4, 6, 7, 24)**

9. E, a second-hand car dealer, does not wish to cover over his vehicles' mileometer readings, but at the same time E does not wish to incur liability under the TDA should the reading in any particular case turn out to be incorrect. What must E do in the circumstances? **(8)**

10. What goods have to be marked with or accompanied by an indication of their country of origin? **(9)**

11. F, a window cleaner, falsely claims that his window cleaning services are patronized by Buckingham Palace. Is this an offence?   **(10)**

12. Can a hotelier be convicted under the CPA Part III of knowingly making a misleading statement as to the price of accommodation?   **(17)**

13. Does the same strict liability basis apply to misdescribed services under s. 14 TDA as to misdescriptions under s. 1?   **(19)**

14. A company publishes a brochure containing a photograph of a named hotel which shows it as having a sandy beach. Someone in the company has made a mistake, however, as the photograph is of a different hotel. The named hotel had a pebble beach. Is the prosecution likely to be able to secure a conviction in relation to this error against the company, assuming that none of the directors was aware of the mistake?   **(16, 19)**

15. K undertook to install a burglar alarm system 'within one week of the customer placing the order'. The job took K one month. Has K committed any offence under the TDA? Would it make any difference to your answer if a strike were causing a shortage of materials at the time that K gave the undertaking, so that K was aware that the job could not be completed within the stipulated time?   **(20)**

16. What are the special defences afforded by the TDA? How 'strict' is the liability of a trader who is charged with applying a false trade description to goods, or (as the case may be) with supplying goods to which a false trade description is applied? Is the position of a publisher who publishes an advertisement which contravenes the Act, without knowing that such is the case, any different?   **(21, 22)**

17. Which authorities are responsible for enforcing the TDA? What sanctions may be imposed on conviction of an offender?   **(23, 24)**

20
Food

1. Introduction

The law relating to the consumer and his food is a complex matter. Of course, the general law of contract and the applied contract law relating to the sale of goods (*see* **1–8**) applies to the sale of food. Furthermore, the general law of product liability, the tort of negligence (*see* **9**), and so on apply too, as does the recent addition to the armoury — CPA Part I (*see* **9**).

Furthermore, there is a body of criminal statute law which is especially designed for food. It is very complicated and detailed, and only the barest of outlines is possible here. The spring of 1990 saw an important step in the development of this law — the Food Safety Act 1990. It seems to show a new approach towards the safety of food.

2. Composition

The contents of some foods are precisely stipulated by the law. This is done by way of regulations made under the Food Act and its predecessors. For example consider the simplicity of the regulations (*see* the Soft Drinks Regulations 1964, as amended) concerning fruit drinks: 'juice' must be pure fruit juice, 'citrus squash' must contain at least 25% fruit juice before it has been diluted, 'comminuted citrus drink' must contain approximately 10% processed fruit if it is to be drunk undiluted, or 2% if it is to be drunk straight from the container, 'citrus crush' which is to be drunk undiluted must contain at least 5% citrus fruit juice, except lime crush, which only needs 3% and 'orangeade', and 'lemonade' need not contain any fruit juice at all!

3.   The Food Safety Act 1990

The name of the statute may appear misleading — the Act covers far more than just the safety of food. The earlier legislation (e.g. the Food Act 1984) has, for all practical purposes, been repealed by this Act. Nevertheless, the many and various Regulations which were made under the previous legislation will remain in force until replaced. This new Act is 'EC compatible' in the sense that it provides the authority for the relevant Ministers to implement EC legislative requirements without further primary legislation.

The Act applies to the 'supply' of food in virtually all circumstances. That is not only restaurants but also canteens, schools, hospitals, clubs and so on. There is no need for the outlet to be profit-orientated. For the first time water is to be classified as food, and unless the contrary is proved, all food ingredients, raw materials and so on that are found upon business premises will be assumed to be intended for human consumption.

4.   Food injurious to health

It is an offence to render food injurious to health by the addition or subtraction or the use of any process or treatment: s. 7.

5.   Nature, substance and quality

It is still an offence to supply to the prejudice of the purchaser food which is not of the nature, substance or quality demanded by the purchaser, s. 14. So cases such as *Smedleys* v. *Breed* (1974) (the caterpillar in the peas) and *Greater Manchester Council* v. *Lockwoods* (1979) (the beetle in the strawberries) will still be instructive.

6.   Food safety requirement

An entirely new concept of a generalised food safety requirement has been introduced by this Act, s. 8. It is an offence to supply food which is unfit for human consumption, which is injurious to health or which is contaminated beyond the extent at which it would be reasonable for use for human consumption. This provision is wider than those which were found in ss. 1 and 8 of the Food Act 1984, but falls short of a general duty to supply safe food. This has been the subject of some criticism, but commentators note that the proposal for a European Directive on

Product Safety — still in the consultation processes — will include food.

7. Powers of 'authorised officers'

The existing powers to inspect, seize, detain and condemn all or part of batches of food have been strengthened and extended: ss. 29–33. 'Improvement notices' (s. 10) can be issued which might require specified steps to be taken to comply with Regulations concerning the condition of premises, equipment, the control of processes and treatments, materials, substances, and so on. Should there be a conviction, a court can issue a 'prohibition order' (s. 11) concerning the use of premises and/or equipment. In extreme cases an authorised officer can issue a notice to the effect that he intends to apply for an emergency prohibition order. This takes effect on one day's notice, but a court must act within three days to confirm it.

8. Emergency control orders

The Minister can make an emergency control order (s. 13) which would have effect beyond a single business enterprise. This is the legislative reaction to recently reported widespread food safety scare stories. There is no provision for compensation should such an order be made in error, although one was proposed in the Lords' debates.

9. Food labelling

Apart from the many and various regulatory requirements about the labelling of foodstuffs, it is an offence to use a label or advertisement or presentation which falsely or misleadingly describes the nature, quality or substance of food: s. 15.

10. Further steps forward

Food premises will either have to be licensed or registered, in accordance with new Regulations: s. 19.

Those who are employed as food handlers will need to be trained: Sch. 1 para 5.

There are to be new Regulations to cope with 'novel foods' s. 18, and special food treatments and processes such as irradiation s. 16, although it is interesting to note that, despite all the fuss that has been made about this process, the word 'irradiation' does not appear in the Act. This term 'novel foods' has caused some puzzlement. It seems that such foods are those which have never been used for human consumption in Great Britain before. So they could include those which have been eaten elsewhere for centuries — such as some bizarre fruit from a jungle. It also includes something like 'state-of-the-art' foods such as the fancy slimming products that we hear so much about.

11. Defences

There is a new 'due diligence' defence s. 21. This is a reflection of other recent developments in criminal consumer law — that it is intended that offences should be strict but that those who have done all that they could reasonably have been expected to have done to avoid the commission of strict liability offences should be able to defend themselves.

Naturally, the extent of the precautions necessary to satisfy the requirement of 'due diligence' will vary depending upon such factors as the size and resources of the business enterprise.

One aspect of the new Act which has caused a little alarm in the food industry is the removal of the 'written warranty' defence. This was available to a defendant who could establish that the food in question was within the law and that he had a written promise to that effect and that he had no reason to believe otherwise, and that the food was in the same state as it had been when he bought it in. This will no longer be good enough.

12. Penalties

While the penalties for offences under the Act such as obstructing an officer in the course of duty and so on remain at a maximum of £2,000, food-related offences will now be subject to a maximum of £20,000: s. 35.

Presumably this massive increase reflects public concern about the safety of food. Nevertheless, it is interesting to ponder upon whether a likely defendant will be tempted to obstruct the officer rather than open himself to the higher penalty — and further whether the Magistrates' Courts are prepared to exercise the full range of their powers in this important area of consumer protection.

Progress test 20

1. Outline the general law which relates to food. **(1)**

2. Describe the compositional requirements which relate to soft drinks. From your own research describe those which relate to another common food product. **(2)**

3. List the various offences which relate to food which are to be found within the 1990 Act. **(3–6)**

4. Describe the defences which are available to those accused of these offences; and the penalties which might induce them to seek the protection of those defences. What was the 'written warranty' defence? What justifications can you think of which might have supported its removal? **(11, 12)**

5. List the powers of authorised officers. Does the Minister have any further powers? **(7, 8)**

6. What are 'novel foods'? **(10)**

21
Compensation orders

The discretionary power

1. Power to make compensation orders

A court on convicting a person of an offence, instead of or in addition to dealing with him in any other way, may make a compensation order requiring that person to pay compensation 'for any personal injury, loss or damage resulting from that offence or any other offence which is taken in to consideration by the court in determining sentence': s. 35 Powers of Criminal Courts Act 1973 (as amended by the Criminal Justice Act 1988, ss. 105–106).

This wide power, introduced by the Criminal Justice Act 1972 and re-enacted in the 1973 Act, while not confined to benefiting consumers, is of great significance in consumer protection. It must be remembered that consumer protection measures imposing criminal law sanctions generally afford no direct remedy to the individual consumer suffering loss, who is left to his civil law remedies (cf., for example, s. 26 of the Fair Trading Act (*see* 17:**14**) and s. 35 of the Trade Descriptions Act (*see* 19:**24**)). Even the Consumer Safety Act only envisages an action for breach of statutory duty in respect of a breach of an obligation imposed by safety regulations (*see* 18: **4, 6**). Accordingly, the discretion given to the court by s. 35 of the Powers of Criminal Courts Act 1973 is an important addition to the consumer's remedies. The courts are prepared to exercise their discretion, particularly in trade descriptions cases.

2. Limitation on the s. 35 power

There are two points to note.

(a) No compensation order may be made for loss to dependants consequent on death; nor for injury, loss or damage due to a road accident (except that in the case of a Theft Act offence a compensation order may, in road accident cases as in other cases, cover damage to the property occurring while the property was out of the owner's possession): s. 35(2), (3).

(b) The compensation ordered by a magistrates' court cannot exceed £2,000 in respect of each offence for which the offender is convicted: Magistrates' Courts Act 1980, s. 40. In the higher courts there is no financial limit.

3. Exercise of the discretion

Section 35 provides that in determining whether to make a compensation order, and the amount of any such order, the court must have regard to the defendant's means: s. 35(4).

The compensation will be such amount as the court considers appropriate, having regard to any evidence and to any representations that are made by or on behalf of the accused or the prosecutor: s. 35(1A). When the court considers that it would be appropriate both to impose a fine and to make a compensation order, but that the offender has insufficient means to pay both, the court must give preference to compensation (though it may impose a fine as well): s. 35(4A).

Decided cases have shown that s. 35 is only intended for simple cases. A compensation order is appropriate only where the legal issues are quite clear. However, with the 1988 CJA an attempt was made to (in the words of the Home Secretary) 'mark the great regard which society now pays to the position of victims of crime'. In 1987 over 103,000 defendants were ordered to pay compensation. Nevertheless, the court will hesitate to embark on any complicated factual investigation. The fact that the loss is not precisely quantifiable is no bar to the making of an order. Finally, it should be noted that compensation orders may be made even in circumstances where the hope of compensation may act to encourage multiple prosecutions.

> *R.* v. *Thompson Holidays Ltd* (1974): the defendants issued two million copies of their 1971 holiday brochure. One of the advertised hotels was falsely described as having certain amenities and on summary conviction under s. 14 of the

Trade Descriptions Act the defendants were fined £450. A subsequent complaint by another member of the public who had been on holiday at the same hotel led to a second prosecution, this time on indictment. The defendants were fined £1,000 and ordered to pay the prosecution costs plus the sum of £50 compensation to the complainant, On appeal against conviction, sentence and compensation order, it was held by the Court of Appeal (Criminal Division) that each communication of the false statement in the brochure was a separate offence; so that the defendants could not plead *autrefois convict*. The present proceedings were not an abuse of process (though the Court did accept that a time might come when further prosecutions would be oppressive and either would have to be stayed or nominal penalties only would be imposed). The compensation order was therefore properly made. The loss could fairly be said to have resulted from the offence of failing to provide the advertised amenities. (The fine of £1,000 was also held not to be too severe in the circumstances.)

NOTE: In *Wings Ltd* v. *Ellis* (1984) HL (*see* 19:**16**), it was pointed out that for the purposes of s. 14 TDA a statement can be 'made' not only on communication to the ultimate recipient but also at earlier stages in the chain of distribution, such as when the brochures are first posted or published in accordance with the original intention of the issuing house.

Procedure

4. Making application for an order
The legislation lays down no express procedure governing an application for a compensation order. In practice if the consumer indicates to the justices' clerk or the prosecutor his wish for a compensation order, the court will consider the matter, whatever the consumer's theoretical lack of *locus standi*. The court may make a compensation order even though no express application for one has been received.

5. Subsequent civil proceedings

If damages are awarded in subsequent civil proceedings, any amount paid by the offender under a compensation order is deducted from the assessed damages: s. 38. The court may discharge or reduce a compensation order if the injury, loss or damage in respect of which the order was made is held in civil proceedings to be a lesser sum, or if lost property in respect of which the order was made is recovered by the victim: s. 37.

NOTE: Under the Civil Evidence Act 1968 a conviction of a criminal offence may be used in evidence in subsequent civil proceedings: s. 11.

Progress test 21

1. What is a compensation order? Why is it significant in consumer protection? (1)

2. What financial limits (if any) are placed on the court's power to make a compensation order? (2)

3. What factors must the court take into account in determining whether to exercise its discretion to make a compensation order? (3)

4. What is the procedure for making application for a compensation order? (4)

5. Can a consumer in whose favour a compensation order has been made acquire compensation twice over by bringing civil proceedings in respect of his loss? (5)

6. In what circumstances may the court discharge or reduce a compensation order? (5)

22
The settlement of consumer disputes

Sources of advice

1. Consumer advice centres

If a direct approach to the trader does not result in a satisfactory solution to a consumer complaint, the consumer may turn to a solicitor for advice and assistance. Alternatively the consumer may turn, at least in the first instance, to other — generally free — sources of help. One such free service is available through consumer advice centres. Initially established and funded with the aid of substantial government grants, consumer advice centres, now funded by the community charge, are run by some fifty local authorities under powers derived from the Local Government Act 1972. Besides giving pre-shopping information and literature, consumer advice centres are often instrumental in helping consumers to resolve disputes with local traders. Sometimes the consumer advice centre will assist the consumer in litigation against a recalcitrant trader.

NOTE: Pre-shopping information is of course also available to subscribers to *Which?* and other publications of the Consumers' Association. Moreover, subscribers to the *Which? Personal Service* have access to a service assisting with individual consumer complaints. The Consumers' Association, a non-profit company limited by guarantee, speaks and campaigns for consumers. In this connection there may also be mentioned the National Consumer Council (successor to the Consumer Council, abolished in 1971), an independent but government-funded body established in 1975. The National Consumer Council does not take up individual consumer complaints, but represents and articulates the interests of consumers to government, commerce and industry, including nationalized industry.

2. Citizens' advice bureaux

The citizens' advice bureau service is a voluntary agency consisting of a network of some 800 autonomous bureaux, which are largely financed by local authority grants. Local bureaux are represented through area committees on the registration and policy-formulating authority of the movement, the Council of the National Association of Citizens' Advice Bureaux.

Up to 20 per cent of all inquiries concern consumer matters. Staff (whose training includes instruction in consumer law) or volunteer lawyers in attendance will advise the consumer and may negotiate with traders on the consumer's behalf. They may refer the consumer to a local solicitor. Many bureaux operate a rota scheme, whereby volunteer solicitors attend at the bureau to give free advice to clients, complex problems being transferred to the solicitor's own office with fees charged to the legal aid fund where appropriate. Some bureaux now have their own salaried solicitors.

3. Neighbourhood law centres

Neighbourhood law centres, which owe their inspiration to experience in the United States, may be characterized as providing in deprived neighbourhoods a comprehensive legal service, including court representation, for groups as well as for individuals. It should be understood that advice on consumer problems forms a relatively low percentage of a law centre workload, problems of more pressing social urgency, such as housing, being given priority. Law centre clients are generally expected to fall within the ambit of the legal aid scheme, and may have to pay a contribution in accordance with the scheme's provisions. Subject to this, the legal service is free to clients. Adequate funding of a law centre often proves difficult, though funds can come from a variety of sources including the local authority.

NOTE: Unlike neighbourhood law centres, *legal advice centres* do not provide a comprehensive legal service but instead give free legal advice, referring anything requiring protracted correspondence or court proceedings to a local solicitor or appropriate social agency. Legal advice centres are typically open for a few hours each week, staffed by volunteers.

4. Consumers' or consultative councils

It should not be overlooked that the consumer with an unresolved complaint against one of the nationalized industries may put the complaint before the appropriate consumers' or consultative council for that industry. The Acts setting up the nationalized industries of closest concern to consumers also set up these consumers' or consultative councils. Apart from considering complaints from the public, the councils act as consumer watchdogs and advise the industry in question on general policy matters. How many teeth the watchdogs have is, however, somewhat problematical. Furthermore, the gradual trend towards privatization of nationalized industries has spawned a number of new agencies (e.g. OFTEL, OFGAS, OFWAT) which are charged with protecting consumer interests and whose efficacy has yet to be established.

Sources of financial assistance

5. Legal aid

Legal aid under the Legal Aid Act 1974 is available in principle for the litigation of consumer disputes as for the litigation of other disputes, provided of course that the applicant falls within the limits of financial eligibility. But legal aid will not be granted for a case which is automatically referred to arbitration under the small claims procedure in the county court (*see* **10**), and in practice legal aid seems rarely to be obtained in consumer cases. Moreover, even if legal aid is obtained there is often a statutory charge in favour of the legal aid fund, whereby money or property recovered or preserved for the client goes first to pay such costs as have not already been recovered from the other party or defrayed by any contribution payable by the client under the financial eligibility requirements of the scheme.

NOTE: The Law Society publishes 28 regional directories

(known as The Solicitors' Regional Directory) which are distributed free to public libraries, citizens' advice bureaux, consumer advice centres and other agencies. The directories indicate the categories of work, including legal aid work, which local solicitors are respectively prepared to undertake. One of the specified categories is consumer problems. Where a solicitor operates the fixed fee interview scheme (*see* 7) this is indicated. Details are also given of legal advice centres. Law centres and citizens' advice bureaux providing legal help.

6. The green form scheme

Of greater utility for consumers is the 'green form' scheme, now to be found in the Legal Aid Act 1974. In relation to consumers the scheme, so called on account of the form to be filled in by an applicant for financial assistance, operates as follows. A solicitor may, without needing authority from the legal aid office, incur up to £50 costs and disbursements exclusive of VAT by way of giving advice, writing letters, negotiating and settling claims, even helping the consumer prepare for a court case. But the solicitor may not himself take steps in court proceedings. Work in excess of the £50 limit requires authorization if it is to be financed under the scheme.

An applicant under the green form scheme has to meet certain financial eligibility requirements. There are limits on the amount of disposable capital and disposable income (i.e. income after deduction of tax, national insurance and allowances for dependants) which an applicant may have. Applicants whose disposable income falls within the limits but exceeds an amount specified by regulations will be liable to pay a contribution towards the solicitor's costs in accordance with a sliding scale. Where the costs exceed the contribution (if any) payable by the client, there is as regards the balance a charge in favour of the solicitor on any money or property recovered for the client (cf. **5**).

NOTE: Consumers ineligible for legal aid or legal advice and assistance might feel inclined to take out an appropriate legal expenses insurance policy against the risk of future problems.

7. The fixed fee interview

This scheme is supplementary to the green form scheme.

Solicitors participating in the fixed fee interview scheme will charge the client not more than £5 including VAT for an initial interview of up to half an hour (where the client's contribution under the green form scheme is nil or less than £5 the lesser amount will apply). The scheme thus enables a prospective client to know for certain before he approaches a solicitor, perhaps on a reference from a citizens' advice bureau or consumer advice centre, what his maximum initial financial commitment will be. Often a brief preliminary interview will not attract a charge from a solicitor anyway.

Small claims

8. Action in the county court

The normal county court procedure is applicable to consumer matters as to other matters within the county court's jurisdiction, which in the case of actions in contract or tort extends to claims of up to £5,000. With the implementation of the Courts and Legal Services Act 1990, the margin between High Court and County Court jurisdiction will be both narrowed and clouded. In general, from July 1 1991 the Small Claims Service will be extended for claims up to £1,000. A description of county court procedure is beyond the scope of this book, but attention is drawn to the booklet, *Small Claims in the County Court,* issued as a general guide for litigants in person and subtitled, *How to sue and defend action without a solicitor.* A revised edition of this clear and informative booklet is available free from county court offices, citizens' advice bureaux and consumer advice centres — if you can get a copy. It is in the process of being replaced by a series of leaflets, the precise contents of which are still being discussed. Meantime the booklet is not being reprinted.

That the ordinary county court procedure was inappropriate for small claims was demonstrated in *Justice out of Reach*, a report published in 1971 by the Consumer Council. The county court was shown to be used largely as a debt-collecting agency by traders and finance houses. The court procedure discouraged private consumers from bringing claims by being too complex, intimidating and expensive. The government responded by rejecting the proposed establishment of a separate system of small claims courts, but it did introduce two significant reforms, namely:

(a) the pre-trial review was instituted;

(b) the small claims arbitration scheme was set up.

9. Pre-trial review

The pre-trial review is designed to be an informal and usually private hearing before the county court registrar. The object is to enable the registrar to elicit the real issues, to ascertain what measure of agreement exists between the parties, and to fix a convenient date for the hearing of the action, if indeed the dispute is not settled by the parties at the pre-trial review itself. Some guidance as to the evidence needed to prove a claim may be given to the litigant in person. Non-appearance by the defendant allows judgment to be entered for the plaintiff on proving his case; non-appearance by the plaintiff may lead to the action being struck out.

10. Arbitration in the county court

Section 7 of the Administration of Justice Act 1973 (now s. 64 County Courts Act 1984) may be regarded as an important piece of consumer law reform because it enabled County Court Rules to provide for the reference of cases to arbitration, thus leading to the introduction of the small claims arbitration scheme in the county court. The arbitrator will usually be the registrar or Deputy Judge, but on the application of any party he may refer the proceedings for arbitration by the judge or an outside arbitrator. The registrar may, on the application of any party, rescind the reference to arbitration if he is satisfied:

(a) that a difficult question of law or a question of fact of exceptional complexity is involved; *or*

(b) that a charge of fraud is in issue; *or*

(c) that the parties are agreed that the dispute should be tried in court; *or*

(d) that it would be unreasonable for the claim to proceed to arbitration having regard to its subject-matter, the circumstances of the parties or the interests of any other person likely to be affected by the award.

The advantage of arbitration is that it is an informal hearing usually held in private. The strict rules of evidence do not apply. The arbitration may be decided on a documents only basis if the parties consent. Whether such arbitration is a satisfactory method for determining small claims depends in large measure upon the readiness of the particular registrar to adopt a more interventionist, inquisitorial approach than the traditional adversarial system characteristic of English law.

There is no right of appeal from the arbitration award but the award may be set aside in very limited circumstances, e.g. error in law on the face of the record or misconduct by the arbitrator. The award is enforceable as a judgment of the county court: s. 64(3) County Courts Act 1984.

11. Safeguarding as to costs

The County Court Rules 1981 provide that where a small claim is automatically referred to arbitration, solicitors' costs as between party and party are not allowed except for the amount stated on the summons, the costs of enforcing the award, and such further costs as the arbitrator may direct where there has been unreasonable conduct by the opposite party in relation to the proceedings or the claim.

In practice, the unsuccessful litigant will rarely be ordered to pay the winner any costs where the claim does not exceed £500. The 'no costs' rule thus makes small claims less hazardous to litigate. Naturally the rule discourages the consumer from being legally represented at the hearing.

NOTE: Court fees (e.g. about 10% of the claim up to £500), witness expenses and out of pocket expenses will be recoverable by the successful party.

12. Voluntary arbitration

It has been noted already that the Office of Fair Trading, besides being a source of information and advice for consumers, approves voluntary codes of practice providing for the arbitration of consumer disputes (*see* 17:5).

Progress test 22

1. Where do consumer advice centres fit in the general structure of consumer advice agencies?   (1–3)

2. Why is legal aid of little practical use to consumers who contemplate taking or defending court proceedings? **(5)**

3. Explain the 'green form scheme' as it operates in relation to consumers. **(6)**

4. Explain the fixed fee interview scheme. **(7)**

5. What is the extent of the county court jurisdiction for actions in contract or tort? Why is the normal county court procedure not thought to be suitable for the determination of small consumer claims? **(8)**

6. What is the object of the pre-trial review? **(9)**

7. When will reference of a county court case to arbitration be automatic? In what circumstances may the arbitrator rescind such a reference? What are thought to be the advantages of arbitration? **(10)**

8. What is the 'no costs' rule and what are the exceptions to it? What effect is the rule likely to have on legal representation of the parties? **(11)**

9. How is an arbitration award enforceable? On what grounds may an appeal against an arbitration award be brought? **(10)**

Appendix 1
Examination technique

1. Preparation

The key to successful preparation is the working of regular but moderate hours. Putting in over-long hours is not an efficient method of study and can be positively counter-productive. So take plenty of time off. On the other hand, be ruthless in working the hours which you set yourself for private study.

Find out what statutory materials (if any) will be provided for you to consult during the examination. Take advantage of this provision by becoming thoroughly familiar with your way around the materials, using the references given in this book as a guide. In the examination room it will be too late.

Get hold of past examination papers, not to indulge in question spotting (always hazardous) but rather to learn the scope of the subject as perceived by your examiners. Plan your studies accordingly. Try to ensure that your tutor sets and marks some past examination questions for you, so that you gain experience at the task and also learn how you are progressing.

2. Revision

When it comes to revision the key is little but often. Repeated short revisions of a topic are a much more efficient way of making the material stick in the memory than is one long session. Most people find memorizing law difficult, and three or four attempts will be necessary before the task is achieved. If you can discipline yourself, as your studies proceed revise something of what you have already learnt. This will greatly facilitate the final revision process.

3. In the examination room

Keep calm when you first read through the examination paper. It may seem impossibly strange at first sight, but as you seek to identify what each question is really all about you will find that you can utilize your knowledge. If you have worked consistently in preparation for the examination you should assume that you have enough knowledge to answer the questions satisfactorily. Jot down the names of relevant cases and statutory authorities as you initially peruse the paper; they may slip your memory later. Decide which questions you will attempt and allocate a roughly equal proportion of the available time to answering each one. Never attempt less than the full quota required. The examiner is more generous with the first 50 per cent of his marks than he is with the second 50 per cent. Five competent answers (say) are likely to gain you more marks than four answers which you think you have done well but at the expense of another question left partially or entirely unattempted.

As you come to each answer, jot down a plan before commencing to write. When you do start to write, write concisely. Remember to score through your plan neatly when it has served its purpose.

In the words of the Consumer Credit Act, your script should be 'readily legible'. If it is illegible the examiner may have to assume that it is incorrect. In any event you can only produce a poor impression by making an examiner struggle with difficult hand-writing.

Do not leave the examination room early, but use any surplus time to correct your script. Marks thus gleaned can be crucial. It is, for instance, amazing how easily a little word like 'not' can creep into the wrong place, with devastating consequences to your intended meaning.

4. Essay questions

There are two types of examination question, the essay question and the problem question. The essay question often takes the form of a statement in quotation marks, followed by the word 'Discuss'. But the technique is the same however the essay question is framed: first identify the subject of the question carefully and then construct an answer. Explain the relevant law and (where appropriate) argue for or against the proposition contained in the question. Finally, draw conclusions. Remember that the purpose of a law examination is to discover whether you know and can apply your law. So take the opportunity to state the law that you do know, provided always that it is pertinent; do not omit relevant material on the grounds that you think it is obvious to the examiner.

5. Problem questions

In many cases it is easier and quicker to pick up marks on this type of question than on the essay question. The technique is as follows. First, identify the areas of law involved in the problem (do not be satisfied until you have identified several areas, because a problem, particularly a consumer law problem, is unlikely to be set on one area alone). Secondly, state the relevant law and cite relevant cases and statutory authorities. Thirdly, apply the law to the problem. Do not neglect to 'follow through' your answer with a consideration of appropriate remedies. Notice that the application of the law comes last, though this procedure does not preclude you from dividing up an answer to a complex problem, identifying, stating and applying the law (in that order) to each part in turn if this would aid clarity. The most serious mistake of technique which candidates make in answering problem questions is jumping straight in with ill-considered conclusions. If you jump straight in you are likely to miss points. You are also liable to make assumptions unconsciously, for the examiner may have deliberately kept back some material information (knowing what information to seek out is part of the lawyer's task). Do not, however, 'duck' difficult legal points by assuming convenient facts — if necessary answer the problem on the basis of alternative assumed facts. You need not be troubled if there is no certain legal answer, for the examiner may well have chosen a moot point for you to deliberate. Provided that you argue your case intelligently you will not lose marks because you arrive at a conclusion which is not the examiner's own preferred solution. But be alert to practical solutions.

6. Use of cases and statutes

Whenever possible give an authority for every legal proposition which you advance. But do not spend time recounting irrelevant factual details of decided cases. The most important point of a case is the legal proposition for which it is an authority, though a short account of the facts can be useful — not least when you have forgotten the case name and so need to identify it by reference to the facts. (Forgetting the name of the odd case is by no means disastrous.)

Finally, if statutory materials have been provided for you in the examination, do not quote them at too great length (there are no marks for being able to read). Quote the exact wording where the legal point at issue turns on the precise phraseology, but otherwise paraphrase, for that demonstrates whether you understand and can handle the material.

Appendix 2
Recent examination questions

The Law Society: Solicitors' Finals

1. Materials Provided:
None

You are consulted by Henry Daily who has acquired a second hand Porsche motor car on hire purchase from Finance Ltd. The price was £19,000 which included both a total charge for credit of £2,000 and a down payment of £5,000 by part exchanging his previous car.

Henry tells you that he is in business as a caterer, and that the agreement was signed on his business premises.

Prior to signing the agreement he had inspected the car at Garage Ltd., which is licensed as a credit broker, and had taken it for a test drive. He was told by the salesman that the price had been specially reduced as the vehicle had been slightly damaged in an accident involving the previous (first) owner. Garage Ltd. introduced Henry to the finance company, Finance Ltd.

Two days after taking delivery Henry felt unhappy with the way in which the car was performing and telephoned the previous owner, who told him that the accident had been quite serious and not just slight damage as the salesman from Garage Ltd. had stated. Henry immediately went to Garage Ltd., who inspected the vehicle and admitted that the company had overlooked certain defects, but claimed that they are capable of speedy and effective remedy. Garage Ltd. are prepared to undertake this free of charge, but Henry is unhappy with the car and wants his money back.

Questions

1. Explain whether the agreement is governed by the Consumer Credit Act 1974, and whether Henry has the right to cancel the agreement under that Act. Assuming he has the right, what should he do and what is the effect? **(15 marks)**

2. (a) Apart from any right of cancellation, does Henry have the right to "get his money back" because the car has been in a serious accident, bearing in mind that he inspected the car before purchasing? Against whom should he make his claim? **(20 marks)**

   (b) What (if any) remedies has he by virtue of the statements made by the salesman from Garage Ltd.? **(10 marks)**

   (c) What steps would you advise Henry to take? **(5 marks)**

   (50 marks)

Part B: Consumer Protection; Consumer Protection and Employment Law, February 1989.

2. **Materials Provided:**
   Extracts from Holiday Booking Conditions
   Letter from Indescribable Ski Holidays Limited

You have been consulted by Ron, who earlier this year took a skiing holiday with his wife Sabrina and their five-year-old son.

He booked the holiday several months beforehand through the tour operator Indescribable Ski Holidays Ltd ("the company").

The holiday was booked at a well-known Swiss resort, at a four star hotel close to the ski lifts and offering creche facilities, a sauna, solarium and indoor swimming pool. Daytime flights were guaranteed. The holiday was booked directly with the company using the booking form appearing in its brochure, which made it quite clear that its standard Holiday Booking Conditions (extracts from which are on p.263) applied to the booking. The total price for the holiday was just over £1,000. Ron paid the deposit for the holiday using his Access Credit Card.

When the invoice for the balance arrived it was duly paid by Ron, again using his Access Credit Card.

Ron and Sabrina received their tickets for the Swiss holiday from the company a week or two before their departure. However, when they arrived at Gatwick Airport for the flight, they were met by the company's representative Tanya, who advised them that because a number of the company's holidays had been underbooked, all its Swiss holidays had been cancelled and were being consolidated with holidays in the Italian Alps. Ron and Sabrina were told they would be departing by night-time flight for Italy, although they were assured by Tanya that they would still have a four star hotel with similar facilities.

They protested, but Tanya told them that the company was permitted to make this change under its Holiday Booking Conditions, and they would get no money back if they refused to go to Italy. Moreover they would get "a substantial refund".

Ron told Tanya that, although this was a totally different holiday from that for which they had booked, they would go under protest and on the understanding that there would be a substantial refund.

When they arrived in Italy, Ron and Sabrina found that, although they had been placed in a four star hotel, it was over two miles from the ski-lifts and had none of the special facilities offered by the Swiss hotel. They protested to the company's Italian representative Gino, who promised he would move them into an acceptable hotel fairly soon, but in fact they never saw him again throughout the holiday. As it happened, they settled well into the hotel and made friends with other families, who assisted with babysitting, and had a generally enjoyable time — so much so that they have promised to go back again to the same resort and hotel next year, although with a different tour operator.

On their return home, Ron immediately wrote to the company's Customer Relations Department, complaining about what had happened and asking for the promised substantial refund. In return he received the letter which is on p.265. He wrote back saying the offer made in their letter was not acceptable, but has so far heard nothing further.

Two weeks ago Ron received notice that his employer had gone into receivership and that he was redundant. He had been with his employer for only about a year, so that he was entitled neither to a redundancy payment nor to more than one week's notice. He and Sabrina have no savings.

He is particularly concerned that most of the cost of the holiday is still owed to Access under its instalment facility, and he has no money to repay this. He wonders if he can legitimately refuse to make the repayment, and indeed if he can get some compensation for the holiday.

Questions
Advise Ron:-

1. What is the basis of Indescribable Ski Holidays Limited's liability (if any) to Ron? In this question ignore the impact of the Conditions set out below.   (10 marks)

2. How would this liability be affected by the Conditions set out below and referred to in the company's letter on p.265?
                                                                (15 marks)

3. What are Ron's rights and obligations as against Access?
                                                                (10 marks)

4. In this question assume that Ron has good grounds to claim compensation. Consider Condition 6 on pp.264–5 and suggest in what alternative ways he may pursue his claims. Advise which you think is best in the circumstances.   (10 marks)

5. What would be your position if Ron admitted to you that in his letter to the Customer Relations Department he lied about some of the detailed complaints, and you suspect he would do the same if the matter came to court?   (5 marks)

                                                                (50 marks)

Extracts from Holiday Booking Conditions

1. If war or terrorist activities, civil unrest, closure of airports, industrial action or any other event outside the control of the company either delays or extends the holiday or compels a change in the holiday destination or travel

arrangements, the company cannot accept liability for any resulting loss, damage or expense.

2. If the events referred to in Condition 1 above occur before the scheduled departure date of your holiday, and consequently the holiday destination or travel arrangements have to be materially modified or cancelled, the company will if possible offer alternative arrangements or, if these are not accepted, a prompt and full refund of all monies paid less any reasonable expenses.

3. The company does not control the day to day management of the hotels used on its holidays, and cannot be held responsible if a hotel does not provide the advertised facilities.

4. However, if the hotel itself is not available, the company will use its best endeavours to provide an alternative hotel in the same area. The policy in such cases is to provide a hotel of similar or higher classification at no extra cost. Where this is unavailable, a lower classification of hotel will be provided and the company will refund the difference in the brochure price plus 5% of the original holiday price.

5. In the event of any dissatisfaction with the hotel or any other service provided by the company in the resort, the matter must be reported immediately to the local representative, agent or hotelier so that action can be taken to remedy the problem. Any complaint made to the company after the holiday must be made in writing to the Consumer Relations Department within one month of return.

6. The customer is entitled to refer any dispute to arbitration under the company's special scheme. Written notice requesting arbitration under the scheme must be made within one year after the scheduled date of return from the holiday. The scheme provides for arbitration on documents alone with restricted customer liability on costs. Provision for a normal attended hearing is also included in the

scheme, but in this case the restricted costs liability on the customer will not apply. Details of the scheme will be supplied on request.

Letter from Indescribable Ski Holidays Limited to Ron

Note: The letter was on Indescribable's company notepaper and was a standard form of printed letter with specific points typed in.

Dear Sir/Madam

Sorry to hear you suffered slight disappointment on your Indescribable holiday, but we are sure that like all our clients you will ski Indescribable again!

Indescribable honours the Holiday Booking Conditions as set out in our brochure in every respect, and the changes made to your holiday were in accordance with those Conditions as listed below:-

1. Switzerland/Italy — Condition 1 and 2.
2. Day/Night flights — Condition 1 and 2.
3. Lack of facilities — Condition 3.
4. Change of hotel — Condition 4.

Although no liability can be admitted, we are happy as a gesture of goodwill to offer £50 in full and final settlement of your claims. This will be forwarded to you if you will sign and return the enclosed acceptance form.

We enclose a priority registration for next year's brochure, and look forward to you skiing Indescribable again!

Yours truly

Note: the acceptance form is **not** reproduced here.

Consumer Protection, July 1989.

The Institute of Legal Executives

3. Explain the main provisions of the Consumer Protection Act 1987.

4. Discuss the rights of action available to Helen under the Sale of Goods Act 1979 in the following unrelated circumstances:

(a) Helen buys a watch advertised in the "For Sale" columns of her local paper as a "gold watch". On arriving home with the watch she discovers that it is in fact only gold coloured.

(b) Helen buys some shirts from a shop. When she takes them out of their packaging she finds a slip of paper stating they are "shop-soiled". The shirts are unfit to wear.

(c) Helen buys a video-recorder after seeing the same model demonstrated in the store. She signs a contract of sale which clearly states that the store will not be liable for any defects in electrical goods. The video-recorder will not work.

Law Paper 2, Part I Examination, May 1989.

5. The area of product liability has been a fruitful source of much debate on the essential nature of the protection that a consumer should have in relation to the original manufacturer. Consider what particular problems have been posed for those who wished to frame a fair and workable piece of legislation in particular in relation to:-

(a) Limitation periods and

(b) The pharmaceutical industry.

6. Zebedee wishes to buy some expensive stereo equipment at Harridges, a large department store. He is concerned as to his legal rights should the equipment prove to be defective. He seeks your advice on how his rights and remedies would differ

depending on whether he chooses to purchase the equipment
by:-

    (*i*)   Using his 'Access' type credit card

    (*ii*) Using Harridge's own budget account card

    (*iii*) Entering into a hire purchase agreement with Ososafe
         Finance Ltd

    (*iv*) Taking a loan from Ososafe Finance Ltd for this and
         other potential transactions.

7.   Tom who is a car dealer buys two second hand cars. He buys
them in good faith and the registration documents seem to be
in order.

    (a) The first car cost £3,000. He is now contacted by a hire
         purchase company which demands the car from him
         because the vehicle is still subject to a hire purchase
         agreement under which £500 is unpaid.

    (b) The second car turns out to have previously been
         acquired by a confidence trickster who had persuaded
         the original owner to sell it to him in return for a
         cheque which was found to have been stolen from the
         true owner and was thus dishonoured.

    Discuss Tom's liabilities and rights in relation to each of the
cars.

Commercial Law, Part 2 Examination, October 1989.

Middlesex Business School, Middlesex Polytechnic

8.   Sharpe is the proprietor of a small car hire firm. From time
to time he sells off vehicles at the prevailing trade price and pays
the proceeds of sale back into the business for the purchase of new
vehicles. Recently he advertised one such vehicle for sale in the
local press, as follows:

'1988 Cavalier 2.0 CDi, one owner from new, absolutely 100 per cent, £8995.'

The car's odometer reads 12,200 miles, whereas the true mileage was 112,200 miles, because the mileage had gone right round the clock on the five digital odometer, such was the extent of the use to which Sharpe's customers had put the vehicle. Unknown to Sharpe, the Cavalier's engine had caught fire at his supplier's before the car had come into his (Sharpe's) possession; but his supplier had fully restored the engine at considerable expense. The form of contract used by Sharpe on sale of vehicles includes this clause in small print, viz.:

'The seller is not answerable for the mileage shown on the vehicle's odometer.'

Sharpe duly sold the Cavalier from his private residence (which was the address given in his advertisement).

What criminal offences (if any) has Sharpe committed?

9. Luke bought a video cassette recorder (VCR) from Easi-View Ltd, electrical retailers. Easi-View had advertised, 'videocassettes, 4 hours recording, absolutely free with every VCR purchased from us'. Easi-View also persuaded Luke to enter into a five-year maintenance guarantee with the Readyservice Guarantee Co. Ltd. Both the VCR and the maintenance guarantee were paid for on one voucher by means of Luke's Barclaycard.

After two weeks' use the recording quality of the VCR deteriorated sharply. Luke telephoned the maintenance guarantee company only to discover that three days earlier it had gone into liquidation. Luke has also discovered that the videocassette records for only two hours instead of the advertised four hours. Easi-View refuse to do anything about the videocassette or the maintenance guarantee contract, but they do offer to correct the faulty VCR by a simple repair carried out under the manufacturers' guarantee. Luke, however, would like to reject the VCR and get all his money back including the sum paid in respect of the maintenance guarantee contract. Luke intends to keep the video cassette.

Advise Luke as to his legal position.

Plymouth Business School, Polytechnic South West

10. It was market day in Perranaworthal . . . .

Denzil had gone to buy a shirt. He stopped at a stall which was advertising '100% cotton shirts — never need ironing — all sizes — £5.99'.

In fact, the shirts were 65% cotton and 35% polyester, they would remain badly creased if unironed, and the stall had no shirt to fit Denzil's ample frame.

Janner, meanwhile, was watching and listening to a fast-talking salesman doing his 'patter' to sell jewellery. After about five minutes of high praise and low price, Janner felt that he would like to buy a pair of cufflinks. The trader had described them as 'rolled gold', and an absolute 'giveaway' at only £4. In fact, the cufflinks were made of a base metal which had been sprayed with a thin layer of gold.

Denzil had moved on to look over the stand which displayed a famous brand of double glazing units. Denzil asked the salesman to describe how the units might look in his old granite cottage. He was shown a picture in a catalogue, and told that the units would make the cottage look just like the one in the picture. Denzil signed up for the work, but when it had been completed, some weeks later, the effect was not as he had been promised.

While Denzil was discussing double glazing, Janner was at the clothes stall. He examined a pair of jeans labelled 'Levis'. Even with his untrained eyes, he could see that the label had been stitched in by a clumsy hand, and that the colour of the thread used differed from that used elsewhere on the jeans. He also examined a jacket from a pile of similar jackets near which was a sign saying 'Wrangler — Style'. Janner read the label inside the jacket. It said 'Wrongler'. He tried it on. It fitted him well. It also seemed to be of good quality

Denzil was now at the jewellery stall. The trader was not demonstrating at that time, so Denzil asked him for a Swiss watch. Without a word, the trader handed him a watch from underneath the counter and pointed to the price tag. It read £10. The trader was talking to another customer so Denzil just placed a £10 note on the counter and put the watch in his pocket. In fact, the watch was not from Switzerland. It was a cheap imitation made in the Far East.

By now Janner was talking to the man on the stand about double glazing. Janner asked how much warmer a room would be if the units were fitted. The trader said that 15% warmer would be a safe estimate. Having seen the manufacturer's advertising campaign on television, Janner also asked about noise reduction. He was promised that the noise in his home from traffic passing by outside would be at least 75% eliminated. The trader was aware that these were exaggerated claims, but he thought that Janner was a likely customer, and he was paid only by means of commission on the sales he arranged.

Discuss the legal position.

11. It was a busy day in the 'Down Home DIY Centre' . . . .

Several people were waiting in a line to see the Manager:

One had been given a 'two speed hammer drill' as a birthday present. The moment he plugged it in to use it there was a flash, and the fuses in his house blew. When he checked the wiring in the plug, which had been supplied attached to the drill, he found that the wires had been put into the wrong places.

Another man waiting there was bandaged heavily. He had been badly cut when using a chain saw that he had purchased from the store only a few days earlier. 'I just started the thing up and it flew out of my hand and cut me, look', he said, waving his bandaged arm for all the customers in the store to see.

A lady was waiting to complain about some paint she had bought. It was described as 'a subtle shade of delicate green'. When she applied it to her bedroom wall it looked blue. She asked some of her neighbours and friends for their opinions. They were split about the matter, but several did agree that the colour was more blue than green. S15 S41Y

Another lady was unhappy about some wallpaper. She had scanned the catalogues and carefully chosen a woodchip paper so that she could redecorate a replastered wall in her old granite cottage. She had employed a local decorator to hang the paper for her. He had charged several hundred pounds for the job. When he had finished, she was disappointed. All the joints between the rolls of paper he had put on the wall showed prominently. She had complained to him, but he had blamed the materials she had supplied. Now she intended to take the matter up with the store manager. SGSR

Towards the end of the line waited an elderly man who had bought, some five years ago, a set of patio furniture. He is complaining today because, as he placed it out for the summer, two of the chairs fell to pieces in his hands. The plastic seems to have become brittle.

At the end of the line stood a man with a brick and a box containing glue in one hand and a piece of iron in the other. He had asked a member of the staff to advise him as to which glue he should use to stick the brick to the metal. He had bought the glue as advised, but it had not worked. Incidentally, he had noticed, whilst waiting in line, that on the box for the glue it listed many of the purposes for which the glue could be used — but sticking bricks to metal was not included on the list.

Discuss the legal position.

Index

acceleration clauses, 172
acceptance/non-acceptance, 84–9,
     99–100
accessory, action against, 204
accidents, 232
accommodation, 224–5, 227–8
advertising, 15, 32–3, 78, 107,
     136–43
     and fair trading, 197, 199–200, 201
     and trade description, 219, 222,
     224, 229–31, 234–5
advice centres and bureaux, 30, 189,
     193, 248–52
Advisory Committee, 198–200
agencies, 22–5, 125, 145–6, 154, 160,
     187–8
agreements, see consumer agreements
antecedent negotiations, 147, 158,
     159–60
Appeal, Court of, 41, 61, 92, 203
approval, goods on, 14–15
arbitration, 60, 74, 195–6, 254–5
arrears, 171–2, 173, 174
ascertained/unascertained goods, 12,
     16, 17–18
Association of Manufacturers of
     Domestic Electrical Appliances
     (AMDEA), 56, 194
auctions, 14, 77
available market, 95, 96, 99, 100

bailment, see hire agreements; hire-
     purchase agreements
banks, 125, 130
bargain offers, 193, 224

bargaining power, inequality of, 65
barter, 4, 6
breach, fundamental, 64, 68–9
breach of terms/obligation and duty,
     summary, 158
British Code of Advertising Practice,
     136–7
broadcast advertising, 137
business liability, definition, 70–1
buyer, definitions of, 4, 11, 133
'by-pass' provision, 215

Cable Authority, 137
cancellable agreements, definition,
     152
cancellation, 98, 131, 149, 150–4
canvassing, 141–3, 188, 197
care, duty of, 58, 71, 109–16, 154,
     168, 174
     and defective goods, 159–60
cash sale agreement, 155
caveat emptor, 36
circulars and catalogues, 141, 199
Citizens' Advice Bureaux, 30, 189,
     193, 249, 251, 252
civil law, aspects of, 1–2, 56, 118,
     183–4, 244
clubs, book and record, 16
codes of practice, 15, 56, 136–7, 193,
     194–6, 226–7
collateral contracts, 6–7, 106
collateral warranty, see warranty
Committee of Advertising Practice,
     137
common law, 3, 4, 27, 87–9, 97, 132

and agency, 24, 160
and creditors' remedies, 171, 172, 174
exemption clause control, 64–9
and services, 60–1, 97, 98
and transfer of ownership and risk, 12
compensation, 91, 201, 213, 244–7
composition, 220
conditional sale agreements, 4, 88–9, 127, 129–31, 160–2
and remedies, 173, 176, 178–9
conditions, 39–41, 57–8, 65, 96, 100–1, 197–8
conduct, 189, 202, 203
consensus ad idem, 64
consumer advice centres, 248–49, 251
consumer agreements, definitions, 126–33, 147, 152
see also conditional sale agreements; credit-sale agreements; hire-purchase agreements
consumer contracts, classification and implied terms, 4–9, 57–61
consumer, definition of, 197, 225
Consumer Protection Advisory Committee, 192
Consumer Protection Departments, 185–6, 200–1, 212
consumer trade practices, definition, 197
Consumers' Association, 194, 248
consumers' and consultative councils, 248–50
contempt of court, 203
contra proferentem rule, 64, 68–9
contracts, classification and implied terms, 4–9, 57–61
contractual terms and intention, 32–3, 39–41
contravention, 125, 176–7, 200–2, 226, 235
of safety requirements, 212, 213–14, 215
contributory negligence, 121
cooling-off and consideration periods, 15, 152–3, 155

copies, 149–50, 151, 152–3, 168
cosmetic defects, 49–50
costs, safeguards for, 254
councils, consumers' or consultative, 248–50
County Court, 170, 204, 252–4
court orders, 129, 145–8, 171–81, 202–3, 213
courts, *see* Appeal; County; Criminal; High; Magistrates'
credit agreements, definition and formation, 126–33, 145–56
credit bargains, extortionate, 125, 171, 172, 178–80
credit brokers, 52, 125, 154, 159–60, 187–8, 190
recovery of fees, 145
credit cards, 128, 129, 131, 142, 163–4
credit facilities, control, 124–5, 138–40
credit with goods or services, supplier of, 160–3
credit notes, 88
credit reference agencies, 125, 145–6, 187–8
credit terms control, 133
credit-sale agreements, 127, 129, 130, 132–3, 160, 162
credit-tokens, unsolicited, 141–2
creditor, definition of, 133
Criminal Court, 15–16, 36, 244
criminal law, 15–16, 78–9, 108–9, 189–90, 206, 244
and food and safety, 118
and overlapping of civil law, 183–4
Crowther Committee Report on Consumer Credit, 124
Customs and Excise, 213

damage and causation, 121
damage, remoteness of, 91–3, 115–16
damages, 35–7, 45, 86, 91–102, 120–1, 246–7
and creditors' remedies, 171, 173–5
and joint liability, 113

dangerous products, 7, 109, 110–12, 213

dealing as consumer, 74–7

death and personal injury, 56, 66, 71, 109–17, 120, 244–5

debt adjusters/collectors/counsellors, 125, 187–8

debtor, definition of, 133

debtor-creditor agreements, definition of, 129–30

debtor-creditor-supplier agreements, definition of, 129–30

debtor's protection, 175–8

deed, transfer by, 5

default/non-default, 172–3, 175–6, 201, 213, 232–3

defect, definition of, 119

defect in title, 25–6, 105

defective products, 75, 86–9, 94–5, 97, 105–21

    knowledge prior to sale, 37, 53–4

    and minor defects, 48–9, 49–50

defences, 119–20, 201, 208–9, 232–5

    development risks/state of the art, 120

    due diligence, 201, 213–15, 224

delays, delivery and payment, 12, 13

deliverable state, 13, 14, 16

delivery/non-delivery, 12, 13–14, 82–4, 86, 94–6, 101

deposits, 101–2, 127, 133

description/misdescription, 45–7, 57, 76, 159, 161, 218–35

disappointment, damages for, 93–4

disclaimers, 48, 223–4

disclosure, 34, 36, 145–7, 213, 224

discretionary power, 244–6

disposition by mercantile agent, 22, 24–5

distress, damages for, 93–4

documents, 24, 65, 149, 196, 210, 253

dual liability, 61

durability, 54, 55

duty and breaches of, 158, 193, 196, 201–2, 215–16, 244

    and business liability, 70–1

care and tort of negligence, 109–16, 158, 159–60

information, 14, 34, 36, 143–7, 167–8, 193

early settlement, 166–8

encumbrance, undisclosed, 44–5

enforcement, 73, 178–9, 185–6, 190, 212–13, 235

    and improper execution of agreement, 151

    no enforcement circumstances, 151–2

    and voluntary codes of practices, 195

entire contracts, 97–8

entry on premises, 175, 176

Environmental Health Officers, 243

estate agents, 32, 193

estoppel, 22–3, 24

European Commission and directives, 117, 120, 216, 244

European Community law, 219

examination of goods, 47–8, 55, 84–5, 112–13

    and Customs and Excise, 213

    reasonable time for, 87

exclusion and exemption, 35–6, 60–1, 64–79, 121, 161

exempt advertisements, 138–9

exempt agreements, 127–9, 146–7

exemption clause, definition, 73–4

expenses, 84, 86, 96, 213

express terms, *see* terms, express

extortionate credit bargains, 125, 172, 173, 179–81

facilities, 136, 224, 225, 227, 228–9

    servicing, 56, 194, 228

Fair Trading, Office and Director General of, 56, 129, 138, 146, 185–90, 192–204

false or misleading descriptions, 136, 140, 218, 219–37

fault, consumer at, 98–102

fault, trader at, 91–8, 117–18, 120, 121

fees, 145, 189, 254

fifty-per-cent provision, 168
finance houses, 28, 125, 130, 132
financial assistance and relief, 178,
  181, 250–2
fitness for conducting business, 187,
  188–9, 193
fitness for purpose, 49, 52–4, 57, 76,
  159, 161
  and false trade description, 203, 218
fixed fee interview, 251–2
fixed-sum credit, 128, 130, 133
food, 56, 116, 216, 239–44
forfeiture, 101, 213
fraud, 24, 27–8, 34, 188, 253
free gifts, 6–7
freedom of contract, 64
frustrated contracts, 17–18
fundamental breach, 64, 68–9
future goods and services, 4, 154–5,
  231–2

good faith, in, 24, 27, 28, 29
goods, definition of, 208
green form scheme, 251
group licences, 188, 189
guarantees, manufacturers', 55, 75,
  87, 88, 95, 105–8

health, 193, 202
High Court, 190
hire agreements, 3, 7, 58, 76, 126,
  145–56
  and financial relief, 178
  and licensing, 187, 188
  voluntary termination, 169
hire-purchase agreements, 3, 5, 7–9,
  88–9, 126–7, 129–33
  creditors' remedies, 173, 176, 178–9
  defective goods and services liability,
    160–2
  and exemption clause control,
    75–6, 77, 78
  and motor vehicles, 29
  signature box, 149
  and terms implied by statute, 56
Hire Purchase Information Ltd, 29,
  30
history of goods, 219

House of Lords, 6, 36–7, 61, 69, 92,
  111, 232

implied terms, *see* terms, implied
imported goods, dangerous, 213
improper execution of agreement,
  151
incorporation, 64, 65–7
indemnity clauses, unreasonable, 74
Independent Broadcasting
  Authority, 137
Independent Television
  Commission, 137
indications, 139, 218, 224
information, 140, 167–8, 201, 211,
  232
  correction of, 146
  and Director General of Fair Trading,
    185, 192, 193
  disclosure of, 145–6, 147, 211, 213,
    224
  display of, 8, 143
infringements, advertising, 140
injury and death, personal, 56, 66,
  71, 109–17, 120
innocent misrepresentation, 35
innominate terms, 41, 59, 158
insolvency, 100–1
installation charges, 167, 175
instalments, delivery by, 84, 86
instalments, payment by, 28, 132,
  154, 171–5
instructions for use, 47–8
insurance, 70, 72, 187, 251
intention, 12–13, 32–4, 171
intentional obstruction of
  enforcement officer, 212
interest, 128–9, 148, 154, 171, 174,
  180
intermediate examination, 112–13
intermediate stipulations, 41, 59, 158

joint and several liability, 113, 118,
  161–3
judicial intervention, 64–5

labelling and marking, 197, 221
land, 70, 120, 127–8, 151, 155, 225

latent defects, 87
Law Centres, Neighbourhood, 249–50
Law Commission, 51–2, 54, 55, 117
law reform proposals, 116–21
law, *see* civil; common; criminal; European Community
legal advice and aid, 249–51
liability, 105–21, 142, 148, 158–64
  and action for damages, 91–102, 173–5
  and exclusion/exemption, 35–6, 60, 65–77
liability, criminal, 36, 78–9
liability, strict, 56, 116, 117–19, 208, 215, 223
licences, 186–90
lien, 44, 101, 154
limitation periods, 121, 133
linked transactions, 131, 153, 154
loss, 13, 75, 91–102, 111–116, 120
  physical, 109–16, 120

Magistrates' Court, 246
mail order, 15–16, 125, 195, 199–200, 204
maintenance contract, 131
manufacturers' guarantees, 55, 75, 87, 88, 95, 105–8
market overt, 22, 23–4
mercantile agents, 22, 24–5
merchantable quality, 47–52, 56, 57
minors, 141
misleading indications and statements, 136, 198, 216–33
mistakes, 17–18, 201, 232
mitigation, 94–5, 99–100
money-lenders, 125, 179, 180, 187
mortgages, 127–8, 155, 180
motor vehicles, 22, 28–30, 194, 223

National Consumer Council, 55, 58, 248–49
negative licensing, 187
negligence, 7, 12, 13, 60–1, 109–21, 159–60
  and exemption clauses, 66–7, 71

negligent misrepresentation, 34, 35, 36–7
Neighbourhood Law Centres, 249–50
nemo dat quod non habet, 21–30
no contracting-out, 129
non-commercial agreements, 147, 160, 162
notice requiring information, 211
notices, prohibition/suspension/ warning, 209–11, 213
notices, termination and default, 153, 172–3, 175–6, 201, 232–3

offering to supply goods, 223
onus of proof, 181
oral agreements and statements, 67, 68, 154, 222
orders, proposals for making, 199–200
overdrafts, 130, 147
ownership, *see* title

packaging, 47–8, 197, 222
part-exchange, 6, 101, 154
performance, 96, 97–8, 101
perishing of goods, 17–18
pre-trial review, 252–3
price, 4–5, 11, 14, 59–60, 127, 243
  and bidding-up, 187
  and measure of damages, 95–102
  misdescription and codes of practice, 193, 218, 224–7
  and termination of agreement, 166–7, 172–80
privity, 66, 105–6, 116, 159
product and producer, definitions, 118
professional services, 229–30
prohibition orders and notices, 210, 218–20
property, *see* title
protected goods, 175, 176, 177, 178
public libraries, 193, 251

quality, 47–52, 55, 57, 76, 96–7, 159
quiet possession of goods, 44–5
quotations, 142

Radio, Electrical and Television Retailers' Association (RETRA), 56, 194
reasonable test, 71–3, 74, 75, 76, 77, 158
rebate on early settlement, 167–8
recall of unsafe goods, 211
receipts, 65
recklessness, 227, 228, 230–31
reform, proposals for, 190
register of licences, 189
regulated agreements, definition, form and content, 126–7, 147–8
regulated agreements, jurisdiction of disputes, 171
regulations, safety, 209–12
rejection of goods, 14, 84, 86–7, 94–6, 98
remedies, 34–5, 91–102, 171–81
creditors', 171–5
remoteness of damage, 91–3, 98, 115–16
repairs, 48, 53–4, 86, 87–8, 95, 97
replacements, 87–8, 95
repossession, 174–5, 176–8
representation/misrepresentation, 33–41, 136, 158, 161–3
and exemption clauses, 35–6, 64, 67–8, 77
repudiation, 173–4
resale, right of, 99–100, 174
rescission, 27, 35, 160
restricted/unrestricted-use credit, 130, 147
Restrictive Practices Court, 202–4
retention, *see* lien
return of goods, 96, 154, 169, 178–9
return of price/money, 96, 204
rights, 44, 99–101, 109–16, 121, 167–9, 173–4
of cancellation and termination, 131, 149–55, 169, 172–6
see also statutory rights
risk, 11–18, 180
rogue, active involvement of, 14, 22–3, 26, 27, 195
Royal Commission on Civil Liability and Compensation for Personal Injury, 117
royalty, false indications of approval by, 224
running-account credit, 130

safe, definition of, 208
safety, 55, 117–19, 193, 202, 206–16
sale by auction, 14, 77
sale by description, 45–7
sale by non-owner, 14, 21–30
sale goods, 50
sale of goods contracts, definitions, 4–5
sale, second or subsequent, 22, 26–7, 86
samples, 6–7, 56, 85, 161
sanctions, 78, 108–9, 125, 189–90, 200–1, 235
and advertising control, 136
and consumer safety, 206, 212–13
and credit reference agencies, 146
satisfactory quality, 55, 57
Secretary of State, 147–8, 185, 189, 193, 209–12
Orders and consumer trade practice, 197–9
securities, 151
seller, definition, 4, 11
services, supply of, 7, 9, 58–61, 98, 101, 225
with credit, 160–1
false or misleading statements, 218, 227–32
severable/non-severable contracts, 86
signatures, 65, 73, 148–50
skill, 9, 53, 58, 71, 116
small agreements, 147, 160
small claims, 252–4
snatch back, debtor's protection against, 175–8
solicitors, 188, 189, 250–2
Solicitors' Regional Directory, 250–1
spare parts and servicing facilities, 55, 194
specific goods, 13–15, 17–18
specific performance, 96
standard licences, 188–9

statements, 78, 108–9, 160, 176, 199–200
  pre-contractual, 32–9
  trade descriptions, 218, 222, 226, 228–32
statutory rights, 44–61, 78–9, 86, 95, 105–9, 116
Strasbourg Convention on Product Liability, 117
strict liability, 56, 116, 117–19, 208, 215, 223
supply, definition, 208
suspension notices, 212

termination of contract, 40, 167–9, 170–8
terms, contractual, 39–41, 197
terms control, credit, 133
terms, express, 11–12, 16, 41, 71, 86, 158
  and prescribed, 148
terms, implied, 3–8, 41, 44–61, 86, 158–9, 161
  and exemption/exclusion, 71, 75–6
  and ownership and risk, 11–12, 16
terms, innominate, 41, 59, 158
tickets, 65, 66, 74
tie-in sales, 187
time orders, 171–9
time, reasonable, 59, 82–7
title, 8, 11–18, 21–30, 101, 105
  and implied terms, 44–5, 57, 76, 159, 160–1
tort, 26, 56, 61, 109–16, 121, 252
  deceit, 34
  negligence, 7, 35–7, 61, 108, 109, 116
  personal injury and death, 117
  and privity of contract, 102, 116

remoteness of contract, 92
total price, definition, 127
trade descriptions legislation, 217–18, 244
trader's puff, 32–3
trading stamps, 5, 6, 7–8, 78
Trading Standards Department, 185–6, 200–1, 212, 214–15
transfer of goods contracts, definition and implied terms, 5–7, 57–8
transfer of risk and title, 11–18, 27, 179

undisclosed encumbrance, 44–5
unfair traders, action against, 202–4
unsolicited goods and credit tokens, 15–16, 141–2

validity of contracts, safety and, 215
void exemption clauses, 78
voidable title, sale under, 25–6, 27
voluntary codes of practice, 56, 136–7, 193, 194–6
voluntary termination, 168–9

warn, notices to, 210–11
warranty, 37–40, 44–5, 67, 78, 194–5
  breach of, 57–8, 86, 96–7, 158, 159
warranty as term for manufacturer's guarantee, 107
Weights and Measures Departments, 185–6, 200–1, 212, 214–15
Which? magazine, 248
withdrawal from prospective agreement, 154–5
work and materials supply, contracts for, 3, 5–6, 57, 60
written assurances, 202